Frog
under a
Coconut
Shell

Published by Times Books International
An imprint of Times Media Private Limited
A member of the Times Publishing Group
Times Centre, 1 New Industrial Road
Singapore 536196
Tel: (65) 2139288
Fax: (65) 6 2854871
E-mail: te@tpl.com.sg
Online Book Store:
http://www.timesone.com.sg/te

Times Subang
Lot 46, Subang Hi-Tech Industrial Park
Batu Tiga, 40000 Shah Alam
Selangor Darul Ehsan, Malaysia
Fax & Tel: (603) 56363517
E-mail: cchong@tpg.com.my

National Library Board (Singapore) Cataloguing in Publication Data
Chia, Josephine.
Frog under a coconut shell / Josephine Chia. – Singapore : Times Books
International, 2002.
     p. cm.
     ISBN : 981-232-398-8
1. Mothers – Singapore – Biography. 2. Mothers and daughters – Singapore. I. Title.
HQ759   306.8743 — dc21   SLS2002023796

Printed in Singapore

Frog under a Coconut Shell

Josephine Chia

For
My new friend, Harry,
with warmest wishes,
Phine
—— (Josephine Chia)
February 2006

TIMES BOOKS INTERNATIONAL
Singapore • Kuala Lumpur

A Tribute to My Mother

For my brothers and sisters —
so that they will remember the way our mother was
before Alzheimer's disease changed her. And also
for all those whose loved ones have Alzheimer's.

"Macham Katak Bawah Tempurong"
(*Like A Frog Under A Coconut Shell*)

~ *A Malay Idiom* ~
The frog believes that the coconut shell under
which he lives is his entire world.
In the same way, a person who is limited in his thinking
believes that what he knows is all the knowledge there is,
so he is like the frog under the coconut shell.

Except for mine and my parents' names,
all other family members' names have been changed.

"Truth becomes fiction when the fiction's true
Real becomes not real when the unreal's real"

~ Cao Xue Qin, *The Dream of the Red Chamber*

This is a story I have to tell.

One

*Y*our mother is beautiful, people say when they see her photograph on the dedication page of my cookbook. Each remark squeezes my heart. Can they see what I see, beyond Mak's old skin, her body shrinking from her *sarong kebaya*, her eyes opaque with cataract, her hips rudely angled from arthritis and having borne several children. Why do I feel that when people are praising her, they are praising me? Have we both swayed to the cosmic dance together, sometimes child, sometimes mother, sometimes brother or sister, spouse to each other in different incarnations?

What I do know is that I am not just my mother's daughter. I am her hope and dreams. When I separated from her at birth, she passed her baton for me to complete *her* race. The handing over of the baton didn't happen in one quick changeover, it has taken years, years of subtle learning through which she feeds me her desires, her hopes, her dreams, her life which has *not* been. I can re-capture her the way she was, tall and slender in her *sarong kebaya*, her face a delicate shape, her full head of hair, the way she moved, fluid and elegant, everything about her so fine. As though I have the Beast's magic mirror, I can conjure up her face in every chosen moment to see the way she tilts her head or the way her lips form crescents of smiles. It is, therefore, ironic that of all her children, it is I who wrought the distance between us, going to a place where she cannot follow.

"How's Mak?" I ask, over the telephone. Mak is short for *emak*, the Malay word for *mother*. *Peranakans* like us speak more Malay than Chinese.

"She's resting," says my sister, Bernadette, in an accent that is part Australian and part American. One half was because she used to work as a secretary in an American firm in town and the other was due to an Australian boyfriend. She has a propensity to glean other manners of speech, unlike myself, who is strait-laced by my cultural tongue. When I return back to Singapore, people often ask, "How come you don't have a British accent, huh?" Five years my junior, Bernadette, who is 45, sometimes feels the burden of having Mother in her home. I do not blame her, she has to put up with a great deal on an everyday basis. I am privileged to be spared the nasty bits. Besides, she was too little to know the quiet heroine I know. The youngest since Robert died, Bernadette mostly gripes about the irascible old woman who refuses to let the Filipino maid do her work, who insists on cooking although she forgets whether she has salted the soup or not. It means that Bernadette's family gets meals that are either over-salted or not salted at all. She sees a stubborn old woman struggling with her rattan basket walking feebly to the wet market, courting danger on the slippery floor when squeaky clean supermarkets are now the norm. She has to tolerate a woman who can't remember the right bus home but is too thrifty to take a taxi, a woman who mixes past events with the present. And worse, she has to deal with the hysteria of a woman who fights phantoms in her waking moments.

"It's all right for you," she often says, "You're so far away."

She doesn't know that I cannot be separated from Mak even though we are ten thousand miles apart. She and I share the same soul space.

"What did the doctor say?"

"Heart attack. Dolores found her in the morning, gasping, clutching her chest, whites of eyes showing. Scared the life out of me."

I get the details in brutal graphics in true Singaporean fashion. Unsparing. Bernadette cannot know how much it pains me. Like when I ask her if Mak knows who has written the cookbook for her. "Ya, she recognises her photo and knows that you sent it. Then five minutes later, she has forgotten. No use at all, *lah!*"

"Shall I come out?"

"Not at the moment I'll keep you posted."

I had wondered earlier if I should go out there for Christmas, which is in five weeks. It is hard to speculate when it might be Mak's last. She's 85 and definitely on the wane. But when you've got family in two different countries, it's not easy to decide how to split yourself; or decide which takes first priority. It's been my dilemma the last 15 years.

"I've put her in a private room. Costs a lot of money, you know. And I've got Dolores staying with her twenty-four hours so that Mak won't be confused when she wakes up."

Bernadette isn't fishing for financial assistance, she's seeking empathy — to be recognised as the one taking responsibility for our mother although she is the youngest. She does have a right. There are so many of us, but the burden has fallen on her. But it's not as if she had been forced. In the beginning, it was our mother who had taken care of her, taking her under her wing when Bernadette was unmarried. Whilst she carved a career for herself, Mak kept Bernadette's flat clean, did all the washing and had meals ready when Bernadette came home. It was natural that when Bernadette got married, Mak would stay on, still keeping house and cooking for Bernadette and her husband. When Andy came along, he had a ready grandmother at home which suited everybody. Our mother was already 76 then, but still able. When she started to find things unmanageable, Bernadette employed Dolores. It was not until Mak was 80 that her forgetfulness became a concern — she got lost a couple of times on her way back from the wet market. Then she started getting disorientated, saying that she wanted to go home when she was already at home. We thought it was a bad case of senile dementia, but the doctor said something worse, "Alzheimer's". It sounded like a sentence. Sadly, we are learning that it *is* a sentence — her spirit imprisoned by a debilitating mind.

So now, the cared has become the carer, daughter mothering the mother. I am grateful that Mak is in Bernadette's main care, because my sister is usually patient, has a heart of gold and is not the type to answer back an elder. Our mother had been hospitalised before for goitre and cataracts removal but not a heart attack — it's her first. It's times like this that I wish she's only a bus hop away. Her progress report dribbles in via emails and, occasionally, the telephone. The days stretch precariously like hardened elastic, as though they might snap. Will she see in the new millennium? And even if she did, will she even understand what it means to be in the new millennium? Her body and mind are both teetering on the point of a sword.

She could have had a different life. Mak was born to play music, embroider and look pretty for her husband. Up until the time when *the* disaster occurred, that was all she was trained for. A school education wasn't even considered. For her brother, it was seen as a necessity, but certainly not for her sisters and herself. Like them, she believed that her good fortune would last forever. Fortunately, *unlike* her sisters, she took advantage of those times of plenty to teach herself many useful things. That luxuriant warm glow of her skin comes from good food and mixed ancestry, an untraced Chinese great great-grandparent with an indigenous Malay wife. *Peranakans*, our people are called. Or Straits Chinese. To differentiate us from the overseas Chinese who stick to their own kind, clinging to their own beliefs and customs. *Peranakans* incorporate Malay customs, language, cuisine and mode of dressing into our culture though we retain Chinese names, religion and New Year. I believe we are the true Singaporeans, a people who have absorbed and integrated with the locals, not just remaining an immigrant race. In many cases, we have also inherited the Malays' large brown eyes, delicate noses and coppertone complexion. And, if we are lucky, their nature — laid back and gentle, more interested in creating a beautiful home, making cakes, music, a craft or a piece of art than in amassing wealth. Fortunately, though, Grandfather had a stronger Chinese streak. He inherited his entrepreneurial skill from our Chinese ancestors and had fruit estates which spanned the breastbone of what used to be called Peninsular Malaya — *durian*, rambutan, mango, *chikku* and other fruits. Before the Second World War, like many wealthy Peranakans who were pro-British, Grandfather wore English suits on special occasions. When he inspected his fruit estates, he wore a safari-type khaki outfit with a pith helmet. Mak often said with a delightful laugh that the helmet was an insurance against the thorny *durian* falling on his head. During his most affluent years, he employed hundreds of workers, mostly Malays and South Indian immigrants. He sold the fruits to market traders in the country and wholesalers in Singapore. If only he had not inherited that other strong Chinese propensity — the love of gambling.

"Every, every morning, we had fresh fruit-fruit for breakfast." Mak told me when I was a child. She had been divorced from her previous life for years but would extract bits of it to recount to me as though they were fresh in her mind. "The servants cut and slice many fruit-fruit, arrange slices on beautiful wooden platter. Look like colorful rainbow. But not *durian, lah*. We never have *durian* for breakfast, otherwise eat too full for anything else."

My mother's words conjured up images in my mind. I could picture the delicious mouth-watering fruits, their different colours layered in a spectrum. At the time she was telling me about them, we had only one sad papaya tree in our sandy backyard in the *kampong* and some banana trees, nothing as exotic as the ones she talked about. The history of our family and people came through her mouth to me, from her grandmother to her, from great-grandmother to grandmother. Nothing was ever written down because women of her ilk could not write, and our history is, therefore, easily warped by memory, fragile as soap bubbles.

Peranakans settled mostly in Malacca or Penang, and later in Singapore, the three places the British named the Straits Settlements. My English husband, David, sometimes tease me about aspiring to royalty when I tell him of the origins of our race. The Straits of Malacca which ran between the Western hip of Peninsular Malaya and the flank of Indonesia was an important shipping lane between the East and the West. Ships from the West who wanted to trade with China had to use this narrow strip of water to reach the South China Sea. In the early 13th or 14th century, the Emperor of China felt that he could exert a measure of control over this important stretch of water by establishing a good relationship with the sultan of Malacca. So he gave his daughter Princess Hang Li Po in marriage to the then-ruler, Sultan Mansur Shah. When the Chinese princess went over to Malaya, she took with her her retinue of servants and courtiers. Chinese merchants also took the opportunity to trade there and they married local Malay girls. These intermarriages resulted in a new racje. *Our* Peranakan race. As Grandfather was an astute businessman, it is more than likely that our family descended from the merchants or even one of the labourers. But when David jokes about how the British colonised Singapore, I get on my high horse to serve back a ball about my possible royal connections. Malacca was first conquered by the Portugese and then the Dutch. The British had a small stronghold, Batavia, in an otherwise Dutch Indonesia. The two powers traded, the British gave up Batavia for Malacca, so that Malaya became wholly British and Indonesia wholly Dutch.

Before the catastrophe, my maternal grandparents had a beautiful bungalow on concrete supports by the shores of Malacca, a house carved out of local wood, the designs on the lintel intricate with mythological tales, an open verandah surrounding the house, the back stairs leading into the sea. The bungalow sat on a private golden sand beach, fringed by palm trees which arched towards the Straits of Malacca. Like much of our family history, my mother's birth year is edged in mystery because there is no birth certificate. She was born sometime between 1914 and 1916, with a given name of Soon Neo, later christened Catherine, though she never used the English name. Soon Neo used to sit on the steps of her parents' bungalow to let the salt waves lap gently over her feet as she watched the sun throw off its mantle of orange as it slipped over the horizon. The child, Soon Neo, elbows propped on knees would breathe in the sea air and the colours of the sky into her memory. Even after her life changed so drastically, she would recall those moments, painting a verbal picture for me as though the scene was ever present in front of her eyes.

"I love to swim, *what*. But not easy in old days. Only *ang mos* (Europeans) wore swimsuits. Show legs, show arm-pit! White flesh on thighs. Our sarongs, if too much above ankles, we got scolding, *lah*! Not like modern young people now. Your grandmother made Great Aunt, Second Aunt, Fourth Aunt and I wear our sarongs, draped around our breasts when we swam. *Susah sekali!* Really cumbersome! The water caused sarong to plume around us when we plunged in. Like balloons. Grandmother made our amahs watch over us, scolding us if we splash-splash and show much-much leg or if we went too far out to sea. One day, I got real thrashing. Grandfather, he really angry. He never used *rotan* on me before but oh, that occasion! Want to hear or not?"

"Want, want," I said.

I must have been about six or seven, still unschooled. When she told me her story, we were both squatting on the threshold of our *attap* hut, my back to her. She was picking the lice from my head, squashing each between thumb and finger. Lice crawled about on many heads in our shanty village — it was a mark of our deprivation. No one had running water at home, rats and cockroaches scuttled about like members of the family. When the population of lice became too dense and therefore too arduous to pick, the ultimate remedy was kerosene, poured generously onto heads. I hated it. It stung my scalp, its fumes made me want to puke. It would have been dangerous to go near anyone with a lighted match. After the dousing, Mak would scrub my scalp with vigour using black carbolic soap. We had no shampoos then. That day when she was telling me her story, the lice were only beginning to birth in my forest of hair.

"It was hot-hot night. I just couldn't sleep, *lah*. I thought how wonderful to swim like fish in cool-cool water. I was about 13 or 14. I slipped out of bed, making sure that my amah, Ah Moi, did not hear me. She was snore-snore, her jaw loose. I quickly, quickly drape sarong around me, then tip-toed out of room, creeping along floor-boards on my bare feet. Can see quite clearly because moon splash-splash light into room, make stand out statues of Goddess Kwan Yin and Grandfather's jade Good Luck Dragon. At top step of stairs leading into sea, I stopped to listen if anybody was about. Only hear tide shush-shush underneath house, like rough tongue scraping sandy shore. Very nice sound. So peaceful. Always make me think safe. Outside, coconut trees toss their heads shy-shy, shaking heads like women just wash long hair, trying to dry in wind. Also, I hear branches scratching attap roof. Sure-sure that I was only one awake, I dropped sarong on verandah and tested my foot in the water. It was little bit cool, *lah*, so flesh go suddenly goose-pimpling. Some people scared of dark sea, but I did not mind it because its crests were made silver by moon. Sure very good, what, dark-dark, no one can see me. I walk down steps slowly and then let waves take me so that I did not make many noise. Water met my skin, silky, sensuous. *Aiiyah*, soooooo nice, *lah*. Very soon, I felt warm, as if I belonged there and was always creature of sea. Sea-waves lick-lick my body, my long hair floating around me like black seaweed. I sliced through water, turned this way and that to face Lady Moon. So heaven, *lah*! I didn't realise how long I lay like that. Then suddenly, cutting through salty sea air, I smelled it — Grandfather's cheroot. Coconut trees were fanning pungent smell to me. Grandfather must be strolling on other side of verandah, unable to sleep, too. Either he was hot as well or he was tensed and worried. I felt a little sad for him, wondering what business problems were keeping him awake. He never discussed business with Grandmother. I knew that on hot night like this, he would only be in his sarong, his chest bare. He was definitely around corner, smell of his cheroot coming to me in puffs like train racing to Singapura. My heart started to beat hard-hard, if he walked this way, he sure to see my sarong. *Mati, lah*! Die, *lah*! Sure get killed, *one*. To be half-dressed was bad enough. To be completely without clothes was very big wrong. But if I was quick-quick, I would escape his eye."

"Pity we don't have picture of Grandfather, *lah*. We ran away from

Malacca with bundle of clothes, some jewellery that Grandmother had saved and our money belts. Grandfather usually has nice, smiling face. So handsome. But when angry, like someone else take over. On that night, I saw very angry-look, *lah*, but never again. So sad, because, after-after at end, I only remember face with broken look, like face is mirror, smashed by hurt. Very sorrowful his eyes when he lost everything."

I was only a child when my mother divulged her sorrow. I was insensitive.

"What happened after that?" I asked.

I pictured a slim young girl, black hair loose, dropping her sarong then stepping gingerly into the water and turning into a mermaid. It was where she was most comfortable. On land, her legs often gave way under her. Weak knees, she said. Mak's voice always seemed like an arrangement of beautiful musical notes. That day when she described the house and the life she led, the music snagged as it missed a few beats. But being a self-centred child, I slid over her emotion, only interested in finding out the consequence of her act.

Even before I could understand it, I felt that there was something special about my mother — she wasn't like the other women in the village, she carried herself differently, spoke in a quietly refined voice, her movements too graceful for her to have been brought up in a village such as ours. And yet, she was never haughty, never behaved to others as if she was from a different class, she took to the low life in the same way she did the high, always with dignity and a gentle smile on her face. Being so young, I didn't pay much notice to the way her voice tripped as she told me of her father's last days. Only when I was grown up and had time to reflect did the telling come back to me with the knowing of an adult mind, only then could I have guessed at her anguish. By then it was too late to ask her, she could no longer sort out the facts. How many occasions in our lives do we say, "If only ..."? But we can't drag those times back from the past, so we ought to let them stay there, instead of trying to feed on them, fill ourselves with regret.

"What did you do?" I tried to find out again as I ignored her soft sigh.

"What to do? I quick-quick swim towards stairs, *lah*. But I can hear Grandfather's footsteps on floor boards, first like he is walking-meditating, then like water-buffalo chasing him. Maybe he heard splashes I made, *lah*. I try to be quiet but more worse sound I make because heart toom-toom like drum. Okay, I think. If I become like duck, looking for fish, I can put head underwater and come up near stairs. Only need to reach out and grab sarong. But you guess it right? Grandfather already there, his foot was on it, tapping-tapping, like saying, oh, so daring that girl! She's going to taste my hand tonight! *Aiiyah*! I knew I was in big trouble. Oh, his face! Like monsoon-clouds over sun. One hand on hip, eyes looking to garden, he handed me my sarong. Then he turned to walk away. No word he said. But I know I must follow. He went to his sitting room, take *rotan* off hook on wall. What to do? I know I do big wrong. So I bite my tongue when he caned me. No good let everybody, especially servants know, *what*."

We have a tendency to see old people as if they have always been old, as though they did not possess a youth before they aged. It is hard to scrape off wrinkles from one's parent's face to visualise them as a child or teenager with taut unblemished skin. And it's harder still to think that your parent who was a flag of authority and discipline could have dared to be defiant and was punished for childish misdemeanours. You would not dream that your parent could have been like you at your age.

Grandmother told my mother something which she in turn repeated to me, "Must know how to cook or run household, *huh*, if not, cannot handle your servants, you know." When Mak told me that, I thought, what chance had I of ever having servants? We were so far removed from that kind of world that she was just mouthing empty dreams. But my mother never stopped dreaming. She carried them in her thoughts and in her being. That was why she fought my father for the education of my siblings and particularly for me so that we could make her dreams a reality, return her to a world she knew. As I was the eldest female who lived, I was her hope and dreams, so she passed her baton for me to finish *her* race. But now, she doesn't know how far we've come — cannot know.

In the one sepiaed photo I have seen of Grandmother, she wore the long version of the *sarong kebaya* — the *kebaya panjang*. The *kebaya panjang* was favoured by the older women as the material for the *kebaya* top was either made from pure cotton or raw silk and not the see-through voile worn by younger women. Because of its length that swept well below the knees, it was more flattering to the broader hips and wider waists of older women. The top was held together by a twenty-four carat gold *kerosang* set, which comprised of three separate brooches, the first one called the *ibu kerosang*, the mother *kerosang* distinguished from the other two by a more elaborate and sometimes flamboyant design, often studded with diamonds. Younger women tended to use the *kerosang rantay*, where a gold chain linked the three brooches which in this instance would match each other identically.

Grandmother had an elaborate gold pin in her bun. The red kerchief which she used to dab the *sireh* juice from her lips was slung over one shoulder. I can see her wagging her finger at my aunts to tell them it was for their good that they learnt to cook. Soon Mei was still at an age where she was playing *masak-masak*, a pretend game of cooking and keeping house. Soon Hua and Soon Chew were not convinced that they themselves had to do housework in order to give instructions. They maintained that servants were paid to work, so why should they have to learn anything except how to enjoy life and make their husbands happy? Grandmother had shaken her head indulgently, confident in the knowledge that they will always have servants. Except, of course, her confidence turned out to be misjudged. When the tragedy occurred, she simply slapped her forehead repeatedly like someone crazed, lamenting, "*Mati, lah! Mati, lah!*/Die, *lah*! Die, *lah*!"

Of the four daughters, only the third youngest took Grandmother's advice and learnt to cook. It was my mother, Soon Neo. Perhaps she liked pleasing Grandmother. Or perhaps, she had a foresight about what the future held for her. Or perhaps it was just in her nature not to be idle and she was really hungry to acquire skills. She was twelve when she invaded the kitchen, following around Grandmother's heels. Grandmother was the typical matriarch in control of her household, giving orders, waving her red kerchief about to indicate something, direction or haste. In the kitchen, Che Asmah, a Malay Muslim lady from the nearby *kampong* with twelve children and a fisherman husband came in to help Grandmother prepare and serve meals. Because of the necessity of earning something to feed her children especially in the monsoon season which affected fishing adversely, Che Asmah waived aside her religious mandate about handling pork. Soon Neo learnt from Che Asmah the correct way to slice an onion for a soup or *sambal*. Ingredients in Peranakan cooking were used in precise ways, an onion sliced lengthwise was not suitable for a dish which required it to be cut across. Even though she was small like a mousedeer, Soon Neo managed to turn the *batu gilling* deftly, so that the granite rolling pin ground the spices nicely against the granite slab. There was an art to the task, tilting the pin to crush the chillies, onions or whole spices before rolling them into smooth paste. When in full rhythm, the body sang with the movement and was a delight to watch. To make smaller amounts of chilli and onion paste, she made use of the *batu lesong* or granite mortar and pestle set instead of the *batu gilling*. Even before I was nine, she tutored to me to these tasks so that preparing spices properly for cooking became ingrained in me. It took me years to wean myself from these labouring devices to make use of modern blenders and choppers because I, like my mother, believed that the intrinsic taste of a dish was in its manual preparation and technique. My mother never cut corners and there was a kind of religiosity in which she engaged with whatever she was doing so that an everyday chore would become a fulfilling creative process. She taught me what she learnt from Grandmother and Che Asmah, showing me how to arrange the food so that their colour and their tastes did not clash and what to serve on different plates and dishes.

As far as she was concerned, it was a sacrilege to serve food in the wrong receptacle, in a dish instead of a bowl or plate or whatever the occasion demanded or to use the wrong utensil.

"It's finer things that matters, you know," Mak often said to me. "Money alone doesn't buy refinement."

From the other amahs, dressed in white *samfoo* tops and black trousers, she learnt how a household was run. From Grandmother, she learnt her manners and customs, how not to walk tall past an adult, that one had to bend at the knees in a show of humility; one must not sweep the floor in front of guests nor on the first day of the New Year. One has to address an elder and invite her or him to eat before one could begin a meal. Many a times, Grandmother would find Soon Neo in the kitchen, forelock damp and curling onto her forehead, frying, stirring and tasting, scaling the fish, cutting, chopping. She didn't mind any work, even drawing water from the well, scrubbing the clothes on the wooden washboard. But she minded having to slaughter the chickens and having to wring their necks. She particularly hated to seeing them writhing on the sandy ground, heads lolling, their wings still fluttering. As if it was a legacy she had handed me, I too hated the sight of the slaughtered chickens writhing on the ground or running around in a frenzy until they realised that they were supposed to be dead. The vision bothered me so much that I eventually gave up eating chicken or anything that had legs to run around with. Has this something to do with my mother or was this my own uninfluenced choice? Sometimes, I wonder where the *Me* who is my mother's daughter ends and the *Me* who is entirely myself begins.

"Try, try," Grandmother said to Grandfather with pride, waving her hand expansively at the array of food, the gold bangles on her arm jangling, "Ah Neo cooked today, *what*."

Tasting the food, Grandfather said, "She'll make some man a good wife."

"Not enough salt, *lah*," Soon Hua made a face.

"Too much chilli," said Soon Chew.

"It's very nice, Third Sister," Kanchil and Soon Mei said.

In a family of females, Kanchil was the only boy, the last child becoming heir apparent. When he was born, he had gangly arms and legs, very much like the Malayan mousedeer and so was nicknamed after it, *Kanchil*. My mother always referred to her brother as Kanchil so that I don't even know his given name. There was five years between Soon Neo and Kanchil. They started the best of friends, then she mothered him for a while until he flew the coop when he was seventeen. Soon Neo liked to challenge herself each day, making her hand fly with the tatting shuttle as she made the lace, edgings for handkerchieves. For less fine lace as in tablecloths and runners, backs of chairs, doilies and bedspreads, she crocheted them, her hand a blur as her fingers moved with lightning speed. Her smooth brow crinkled when she sewed the colourful *manek-manek* onto the piece of hessian fabric, shaping flowers, birds and animals with the glass beads. These pieces of artistry were then made into the front of Peranakan slippers. She beaded purses and handbags, sewed beads and sequins onto clothing. These were some of the things a young woman had to make for her trousseau in preparation for her wedding. Like a magician, Soon Neo could bloom a floral bouquet from crepe paper, cat-gut and silk. She passed all of these skills from her fingers to mine. Once she did her embroideries out of sheer pleasure but later, when I was a child, she did them out of necessity — to earn money to buy the school uniforms, clothes for the New Year, the occasional treat. Her earlier life was like the bright sight of the moon, her later life was its dark side.

Grandmother loved to teach my mother because Soon Neo was ever so keen. She warned her, "Remember, *huh*. Never look directly at man, always lower your eyes. Speak sweetly, like bird singing, not cocks fighting. Only express opinions which he expresses. Always be clean and smell beautiful so that when he wants you, your body is desirable. Feel with your fingers. You eat with them and you love with them. Fingers on a man's body, fingers across the strings of a viola, violin or piano. It's same art. Making joyous music. Pleasing, entertaining. So that your man never errs."

Always be clean and smell beautiful so that when he wants you, your body is desirable. Feel with your fingers. You eat with them and you make love with them. My mother echoes her mother before her, a lesson passed from mouth to mouth. But I have no daughters to pass it to. So I wait for a granddaughter to hand my legacy. By then, the sentiment would probably age into an heirloom, something to treasure because it's associated with the past but has no relevance today. *Only express opinions which he expresses.* How simple and straight-forward it was in my grandmother's and mother's time, their roles so clearly defined. I should have been satisfied as they had been, learnt to be pliable, moulded myself into the opinions of my first husband, swallowed the stones of my words. Then I wouldn't risk being burned in hell for what I had done. But I have only myself to blame. My father was probably right, "Education ruins a woman," he had said.

Two

In her halcyon youth, Soon Neo had expected to marry into a fine *Peranakan* family, a man clothed in rich silks, used to being waited on. Her elder sister, Soon Hua was already contracted to marry the son of a wealthy merchant who lived in a mansion in the Portuguese sector of town. As nothing had been written down and nobody talked about it, I reckon that all these took place around 1931, when Soon Neo had just turned sixteen — just before the disaster. No one had an inkling of what was to happen, of course. Grandfather went about his business and then he came home; sometimes early, sometimes late, predictable in his unpredictability. As in the old days, his outside world did not collide with the one of family — until that fateful day. Grandmother was totally unprepared and because of that, turned inward, unwilling and unable to wrestle with the demons. Her pain and Grandfather's pain were possessed instead by their third youngest daughter, my mother. If you had seen my mother's eyes when she was younger, you would have known how beautiful and clear they were, huge and dark classically shaped with a slight tilt at the corners. For an illiterate person, her eyes expressed profound intelligence and a penchant for gaiety. But if you looked closer, you would have seen a lurking shade of her parents' pain and the misfortune that had befallen her family. A pain that her brother, Kanchil, tried to write out of his history, one which the sisters never discussed.

For years, I did not understand why Mak was not smiling in her sepia-coloured wedding picture. Instead, her dainty face wears a wounded look, her eyes bewildered. But now, I realise that she must have still been suffering the aftermath of shock. She was only 17 but already carrying the burden of adulthood, unceremoniously heaped onto her young shoulders. She had been destined for an arranged marriage anyway, so the fact that love did not enter into the equation was not unexpected. She was just grateful that in the situation she found herself in, my father was simply suitable. It must have been an added bonus that he was handsome, had an athletic body. She was better off than most: some of her friends were forced into marriage with hare-lipped men or hunchbacks or men who were old enough to be their fathers. It was not uncommon in those days for a widower to seek a young bride to help look after the children his late wife had left behind. My best childhood friend, Parvathi, nearly suffered this fate but she took drastic steps to avert it. Therefore, Soon Neo, like many young girls of her time saw marriage as a necessary social contract — it was what they were bred for. Generally, they would not see their husbands until the wedding day. If they were lucky, they were allowed to put their eyes to the peep-hole on the upper floor of their *Peranakan* townhouse where their fathers usually interviewed the potential groom.

"*Aiiyah!* So ugly!" The girls might exclaim softly behind their kerchieves. Or they might say, "*Aiiyah!* So fat one, *lah.*" Or, "He looks as if he smells!" But whatever their comments, they still had to marry the man of their father's choice. It was a measure of their breeding. My own father had always threatened to arrange a marriage for me. Had he been alive, he would have no gumption to choose a husband for me. Perhaps things would have turned out better then.

Although my mother escaped an arranged marriage, her marriage to my father was not totally without its constraints. She had little choice and was only too glad that someone wanted to marry and house her. Despite her fall from the grand heights of luxury to a meagre existence, Soon Neo had the capacity to live her new life with dignity and she had a delightful way of seeing jewels amongst the dirt.

"Believe in goodness," she often told me. "Don't focus on bad things, *one*. What you focus on become more strong-strong."

Her wisdom did not come from books. It was what her heart taught her. Thanks to my other sister, Agatha's diligence and penchant for organising, there is one surviving copy of our parents' sepiaed wedding photo, which I had copied onto photographic paper to produce another. Surely, it must have been our mother's lips which had attracted our father, full and unmistakably sensuous, for even in her sorrow, they called to be bruised with kisses. Her hands are tucked into the folds of the billowing sleeves of her *Peranakan* wedding dress, a bright red outfit, whose colour is believed to ward away evil. (The white in western wedding dresses which represent purity or the virginal status of the bride is a funereal colour for the Chinese. Sikh and Indian widows wear white to indicate their colourless lives after their husbands have died.) My mother's wedding dress really should have been exceptionally elegant and richly embroidered in gold threads, specially tailored for the occasion with an intricate head-dress. The *Peranakan* wedding dress was red silk shaped into a tunic with long, wide sleeves and matching silk sarong. Grandmother would have supervised its design and creation with elaborate motifs and beadwork to show off the family's wealth. Funerals and weddings were the two times to boast and show off the family's ability to finance such occasions, or an opportunity to show the family's respect and concern for the deceased or the bride/groom. But since their circumstances had changed, Grandmother could not afford the luxury of showing off nor such a gracious wedding outfit. But worse still, she could not even rouse herself to show any interest about the pending marriage. My mother, already conscious that she was going to my father like a slave-girl from a poor family, bringing no dowry, was trying hard to hold her head up high. She felt that the least she could do was dress reasonably for the occasion so she searched for someone to lend her an outfit. Being in a foreign country without many friends made this a daunting task, but she was diligent, asking round and meeting new people. At last she found a *bibik*, a nonya woman who too had fallen into bad times herself and who was willing to let Mak borrow her wedding dress for a fee. Aunty Mary's wedding outfit was nowhere near the value of what her parents would initially have bought her but it was not too far below it either that she would have been ashamed. In fact, it was this transaction that gave Mary the brainwave to start *Mary's Wedding Dress Rental Agency*, which pulled her out of her poverty. Since my mother hired an outfit for her wedding, when my own time came, I did not have hers to wear — and so there was no continuity of custom. Besides, we had become modern, the beliefs and mores of our own culture pushed aside by other stronger influences and the western wedding dress became the fashion instead.

My mother had a recurring nightmare. She would have nightmares anyway, waking up in a small attap hut with its leaky roof, wedged amongst other huts, instead of the huge bungalow in its own grounds by the sea. Instead of the sound of the servants' bare feet pitter-pattering on the floor boards as they scuttled about to get the family bath-water and breakfast ready, my mother had to wake up to the sound of rats scuttling below their platform bed, cockcroaches crawling all over their counterpane. It was she who had to rise early to empty the chamber pot, draw water from the well and prepare the family breakfast. But if she had nightmares about this new existence, she did not voice them. But there was one nightmare which she could not stitch close. Snatches of memory mingled with old phantoms and invented ones. She had them as far as I could remember, waking us up in the nights with her shrieks; my father, whom we addressed as Ah Tetia, tried to rouse her, to free her from her old demons.

"The fire, the fire," she cried. "Somebody put the fire out, *lah*."

"There's no fire, Dek-Dek." My father tried to pacify her. "There is no fire."

Ah Tetia used the same dimunitive for my mother as my aunts did, *dek* being the contraction of the Malay word *adek*, meaning younger sister or brother.

"Put it out. Put it out!" She flailed at flames leaping onto her sarong. Slapping them down with her bare hands then examining them as if they have been truly burned. And then the anguish.

"Ah Tio!" She cried for her father. Seeing the flames devour him. Over and over again, she would see him burn in the fire that destroyed their lives.

Her emotions were so strong, her spirit so linked with mine, that sometimes I shudder as if I could see him too, soaked in kerosene, the flames licking him, his arms in front of his face as though trying to shield his eyes. Was this Grandfather's final act of power? An exertion of his will to end his erroneous ways? Had he thought that his debts would burn with him in the fire? Or perhaps he was so far gone that he didn't care anymore, couldn't care. What must it be like for a daughter to watch her father burn? Sometimes, her fear was so palpable that I hear the fire crackling and the ceiling of the wooden bungalow collapsing, flaming wood which clattered downward to crash onto his head, the beautiful house which he designed and built and loved becoming his funeral pyre.

"Rubbish," Agatha said, always forthright with her opinions. "Pure invention. Like she said she had 16 children. Some days it's 12, some days 13. She makes it up as she goes along. Her brain has never been the same since Robert died."

Agatha spoke of our mother in the distant third person even in her presence because Mak's understanding of English was limited. These days, she talks as if Mak's ability to feel has gone the same way as her mind. She is three years younger than me, though she behaves and looks the elder sister, taller, larger; in control. She has a face treasured by the Chinese, full and white, with tattooed eyebrows, permanently seared like flat blue-black worms unchangeable even when her expressions change. A face that speaks of wealth and thereby its implication of sophistication; a face unblemished by the sun, not like mine. Agatha is an exceedingly generous person and, like Bernadette, would let me use her private club's facilities and her car when I am visiting. I am sure she has a very kind heart. It's just that she doesn't modulate her tone of voice nor shift from her own view-point, which gives people the wrong impression about her. She prides herself as being a sensitive, successful business woman. Rich. Has a stable marriage and a stable family. Not like me. A failure. A broken marriage. Wounded children. Rescued only by an *ang mo*, a foreigner.

"How can you know what she says is true?" She challenged.

"How can you know it's not?"

Since it is difficult to separate the Singaporean inclination towards melodrama from straight facts, I cannot arrive at a true picture of Mak's condition from Bernadette's telling. My suspense-filled mind begins to procreate from loose words flung, building up its own scenario that has me quivering with dark anticipation. The eight-hour time difference in autumn means that when the phone rings at 7am, I sit up in bed in extreme anxiety clutching my duvet, forcing David to go and answer the call. But it's only his 37-year-old daughter inquiring about the sleeping arrangements for her two young sons for the coming weekend. Sadie has an infallible belief that because she is up, the rest of the world should be, too. This is not the first of her lark rise calls. She is quick to make known her needs, but has a casual disregard for anyone else's. Especially mine. Recently, she and her husband invited David and I for dinner. Knowing that I have been a vegetarian for 15 years, she served a Pork Roast and Roast Chicken. But when it comes to her needs or her family's, she has a blinding dedication. In the summer, I had invited my in-laws down for the weekend, the only weekend I have available from my other commitments. My stepchildren live in Buckinghamshire, so our seven-bedroom house with an outdoor swimming pool becomes their country retreat, particularly in summer. The house guests that weekend consisted of my mother-in-law and her live-in companion, who is also her sister-in-law, my two stepsons with their girlfriends and their two friends who were visiting from Holland. I allocated the best room to Sadie and her family, an ensuite room converted from Victorian servants quarters of old, a suite wallpapered with pastel magnolias and light green leaves, a colour scheme carried through into the bed clothes, two piece suite and giant Chinese vase. I made up a bed for her eight-year-old on the settee in the room and dragged up garden cushions which I put on the lush pink carpet by the king-size bed, lay them over with sheets, duvet and pillow for the two-year-old. The purpose of my stepdaughter's early morning call is to say that the previous sleeping arrangements were inadequate.

"My sons didn't get any sleep last time," she whines down the telephone line. "They need proper beds."

Sadie obviously thinks we need this kind of wake-up call.

Eventually, when life's constraints permit, I decide to make a dash to Singapore to sort out the situation for myself. My elder son is at Bristol University and he would break up for Christmas. So he would have to manage with David. My younger son is about to go into National Service in Singapore, so if I see Mak, I can have *him* for Christmas, too. If I didn't go out there, I'll fly the younger one out here. David is supremely efficient in organising the ticket, he'd rather have something practical to do than to tackle the complexities of emotions. His is a life of action with little space in-between his multitude of thoughts. He has prospered by his single-mindedness and his super-human zeal and those of us who live by his sweat have to learn to accept this.

The twelve and a half hour flight is interminable when you don't know what news might await you at the other end. I have this gnawing fear that wakes me up in terror some nights, that I might be too late. Unable to keep my mind still enough to read, I watch a new version of *Dr. Doolittle* two times and *Notting Hill* thrice, thankful that Singapore Airlines provides personal video screens even in economy class. So when I see Bernadette through the glass wall at the arrival lounge in Terminal Two at Changi International, waving and smiling brightly, with her eight-year-old son Andy who is hopping up and down with energetic glee beside her, my heart slips into a more restful gear. Bernadette is the prettiest of us three sisters. Like Agatha, she belongs to the half of the family who are fair in complexion, a hereditary trait from my father's Chinese side. She is petite and has a very generous smile and an outgoing personality. Like Agatha, she's always properly made-up and well dressed, every strand of hair in place. Beside them, with my brown face unmade-up, I always look like a poor relation, and worse, am sometimes mistaken for their maid. It is interesting how I can be both beautiful and ugly at the same time. In the West, people admire my tanned complexion; in the East, the colour of my skin makes me out as a peasant. I remember a saying of the Dalai Lama: "Just because you are perceived in a certain way by others, it does not mean that their perception reflects your true character. What your true nature is depends entirely on what motivates you. Nobody outside can see that."

"How's Mak?" I ask.

"Okay, *lah*. She's back home now. But she's really bad-tempered these days. Complains about everything. *Aiiyah*! Her brain is definitely gone! Yesterday, she thought I was her cousin! Every night this week, she has insisted on paying rent for her room."

When our mother is talked about in this manner, I fold inwardly, as though in being referred to in such a way, she is being violated. Perhaps Bernadette talks like that to ease the unspoken sorrow and fear inside her. So I have to consciously suppress the urge to react. After all, Bernadette is a well-meaning person with no cruel intent. Throughout our journey to her house, Andy bounces on my lap and asks questions about England. He is only a week older than my step-grandchild, but is streets ahead in intelligence. He owns a deck of cards with pictures of aeroplanes and their specifications, type of engine, wing span, etc, the kind of detailed knowledge that would normally interest an older child. In great enthusiasm, he points them out to me and reads out the name of each aircraft. His reading skills surpass most children his age and his vocabulary is enormous. Sadie's little boy hasn't even mastered *Postman Pat*'s. In between Andy's continual prattle, Bernadette talks in her interesting mix of American and Australian accent spiced with Singaporean colloquialisms. She talks about her house, her role in her business and her staff. On and on without pause. It's a Singaporean trait, people shooting with words that sail like undirected arrows through the air. I am definitely home.

Returning to Singapore is also a return to heat and noise. For the monsoon season, it's pretty humid, with temperatures that wrap around your body like the stuffings between walls in temperate climates. I can hardly breathe. My blood must have thinned considerably. Newly plucked from the quiet English countryside, the city's white-noise assaults my senses the moment I step off the plane: people talking loudly, the constant drone of machinery, the traffic. What used to be part of the sea is now the new airport with two plush terminals, the reclamation a feat which is highly prized in the nation. Just minutes away via East Coast Parkway is the city with buildings so tall that the Malays called them *sapu awan*, meaning cloud sweepers. The Malay language which the *Peranakans* have incorporated into our own patois is very poetic and is often spoken with the hands. My English mother-in-law has remarked to me on several occasions with a slight note of disdain, "I think if we tie your hands, you won't be able to talk!"

The Singapore skyline is blotted by multi-storied apartment blocks, shopping centres and hotels, one of which is the *Westin*, one of the world's tallest hotels. They elbow each other for space like giant headstones in a cemetery. I found that having lived in the English countryside for so long, I crave a view of open fields and blue sky. If I stay in places like Bangkok and Singapore for some time, I have to run somewhere where I can see ahead without buildings to obscure my vista. Streams of traffic are now flowing alongside Bernadette's vehicle as they speed towards the town centre along the expressways. For a nation with discipline in almost every facet of life, there is little discipline on the expressway: slow drivers hog the outside lane and others overtake on the inside, cars zip in and out of lanes as the fancy takes the driver. Nobody likes to give way. It's the manifestation of the Singaporean *kia su* (afraid to lose) mentality. It is amazing that there are not more accidents. The motorists project a frenzied sense of busy-ness. My heart quickens at this induced pace and I can feel the adrenaline pulsing through my veins. In a need to seek respite, my eyes search the rows of bright bougainvillea and ferns grown in tubs on the central dividers on the expressway and trailing down from the concrete flyovers. There are nice things about Singapore, like the considerable efforts made to beautify the concrete flyovers, unlike their ugly, drab sisters in London and New York. Yet, I am seized with a kind of panic and almost want to get back on the plane. I have not realised how much I have changed.

Bernadette and her husband run their own computer firm, he creating software tailor-made to local and international businesses and she running teaching programmes and selling the hardware. They are obviously successful, having moved from a government subsidised HDB flat into a three-storey house which sits on prime land in an area once renowned for its sea-view, except that the sea has now moved. The local joke is that Lee Kuan Yew, Singapore's Senior Minister and previous Prime Minister, is such a powerful man that he can even move the sea. Some even whisper that he has been seen standing on the seashore attempting to command the waves. Now that Goh Chok Tong has taken over as Prime Minister, Mr Lee has taken a backseat, although he still advises and casts an opinion or two. There is talk that perhaps his son Lee Hsien Loong is destined to walk in his famous father's footsteps. Bedok and Katong still have bungalows on concrete supports where the seawater used to run underneath. These replaced the wooden huts on stilts that had been part of the fishing community eons ago. Disowned by the sea, these houses look orphaned, white elephants in a bustling metropolis where high rise flats in condominiums with tennis and squash courts, swimming pools and huge car-parks stare down at them. Not far from Bernadette's home is a hotel called Sea View Hotel that used to have direct frontage to the sea. Now the view is of a big supermarket and chain store, other houses and other condominiums, BMWs and Mercedezes parked in the concrete driveways. In the colonial days, it was a custom on Sundays for the white populace to have morning coffee at Sea View Hotel, served by Chinese *boys* dressed in starched whites. (Though they were called *boys* by the whites, the waiters were really middle-aged or older.) When folks in England tell me that they "*love Singapore the way it was*", and the "*good, old days*", I know they are talking about their poly-wrapped expatriate lives in beautiful air-conditioned houses ran by local *amahs*, *kebuns*, and *amats*, who looked after their children, ran the households, took care of the gardens and drove them everywhere to their rounds of tennis and afternoon teas. Very few of them have seen the type of *kampong* I was brought up in, let alone ventured into one. Having been raised in such extreme poverty, it is now good to return to a prosperous country where every citizen lives well and in comfort. That is the reason why people of my generation respect Lee Kuan Yew so much. It was he and his Party who moved us out of derelict housing, where there was no electricity and water into apartment blocks with amenities. So I guess a bit of city noise is a small price to pay for such luxuries.

"Welcome to Eastwood," Bernadette says with pride about her new home.

The cast iron gate is opened electronically and Bernadette edges the seven series BMW slowly into the narrow driveway that flanks the neighbour's wall on one side and a patch of lawn which they call their garden on the other. From their boxed HDB flat on the eighth floor where you can hear the neighbours' television and quarrels or someone flushing the toilet, this is upward mobility. (Eighty percent of the population still live in HDB flats or condominium apartments.) Even though the house is one in a row of terraces, in land-starved Singapore it means they have indeed arrived. Certainly, from where we have come from, it is success with a capital "S". The *kampong* or village where we grew up, shanty *attap* houses and outhouses are long gone now, razed to the ground by bulldozers and the village replaced by concrete blocks. To think that once I thought a flat in a concrete block was paradise! I was 25 when I left rural village life and was easily beguiled by the fact that when I turned on a tap, water ran out, that when I touched a switch, the light came on, that when I completed my ablutions and pulled a long chain, water rushed out to clear my mess. It was pure magic.

"Hello, Marm. How are you?" Dolores, the Filipino maid, rushes up to wrest my cases from me. Like many of the imported maids, she is extremely diligent and is a science graduate in her own country and aspiring to be a teacher.

"Hot," I say. "How are your children?"

"Growing up very fast. Imelda is eight now, Carlos five."

She has left behind husband and children in the care of her mother to find more lucrative work here. Four months after she arrived, she had received a letter from her sister to say that her husband had run off with another woman. Wherever you turn, you see people worse off than yourself. It keeps you in perspective. Though she is paid a month what we pay our part-time house help in England a week, Dolores works days and evenings without complaint. She never goes to bed unless the whole family has gone to bed and is up before anyone else. She never takes a single day off (though Bernadette has persuaded her) because she is saving up every cent to send home to her family. There are many maids like her in Singapore, some from her country, others from Sri Lanka and

Indonesia. They are creating a sub-culture in Singapore, meeting at churches and shopping centers, but Dolores thinks that to join them is a waste of hard-earned money. Employers have to pay a bond to the government to allow the maids into the country on a two-year permit with the understanding that they can't work elsewhere and will never become citizens. If by any mishap they should get pregnant whilst being employed, they will be deported immediately and the employer will lose the bond. Dolores is small and thin, a heritage of her life in Manila. Unlike Agatha's maid who is put into a black uniform with a white apron, Dolores wears a loose T-shirt and shorts. She is a jewel with Mak because she is patient and genuinely caring. I am particularly indebted to her because she accords my mother the dignity she deserves. On my last visit, I discovered that she loved to read so I bought her stacks and stacks of popular novels. This time I came with Helen Fielding's *Edge of Reason* and Jilly Cooper's *Score* and two nine carat gold studs for her dainty ears. Like other maids in this country, her spoken English is stilted and she addresses me as Marm and David as Sir David.

"I didn't realise I was knighted," David said when he first encountered her, embarrassed at such a quaint practice.

I step barefoot onto the cool marbled floor of the living room and Mak rises from the settee to greet me. She has been watching our arrival through the French windows that open onto a handkerchief size tiled patio that has a plastic table and two chairs. A wind chime hangs above the table and when there is a breeze from the nearby canal, it tinkles a delightful tune. Both the presence of the canal which carries water or *shui* and the wind chimes that sound the wind or *feng* were Agatha's influence on Bernadette. Agatha is a devout *feng shui* believer who will not move house or office or change jobs until she has consulted a *feng shui* expert. Once she even changed the angle of the door to her house because the *feng shui* expert said that the positioning of the door was letting out all the good luck. That was what was said about the Hyatt Hotel on Scotts Road where I was working in the early 1980s. The ailing hotel was an American hotel run by a French-American general manager at the time. On the advice of the *feng shui* expert, all the glass doors fronting the street were ripped out and new doors put in their places, individually angled to deflect the bad luck and to bring in the good. To augment that, a row of water-fountains were set between the doors and each fountain had to spew water that rose to a specific height and volume. *Feng shui* is an exact science. The placement of the furniture in the general manager's office was most extraordinary, with the desk slanted in the middle of the floor. After the makeover, a team of saffron-robed Chinese monks filed through the hotel chanting *Om* and dispensing incense. I can testify to the fact that after the effort, the hotel did indeed prosper, although I cannot vouch for its cause.

I'm taken aback by my mother's shrunken appearance, although it's only been six months since I last saw her. An accelerated deterioration. Her head is a skull under translucent rumpled flesh, strands of white hair spread thinly over her scalp, her bun a pathetic knot. What used to be bright inquiring eyes are now dulled with cataracts.

"Mak, how are you?" I say to her in our *Peranakan* creole.

"Ah Phine, ah, you've arrived. Have you eaten or not? I couldn't come to airport. My head is always spinning-spinning. No, don't hug me, *lah*. I don't feel well enough."

I am deprived of the comfort of her touch.

"At least she remembers you," Bernadette says sotto-voce.

A sense of loss shoots through me. Mak has changed, both in body and mind. She looks weak and fragile as though rough handling would break her. When I start talking to her, I realise that although she tries to appear normal, her mind has loosened its connection, sometimes here and other times, not. I sit with her and try to make conversation but I get the feeling that I am talking through her, like a breeze passing through a sieve. It disconcerts and unsettles me. Is this somebody I used to know? When I was a child, I had spent evenings with her folding crepe paper into rose buds and flowers. We used coloured cat-gut to wind round thin wires for the stems. Or we would sit chatting while making lace or crocheting blouses. Before the days of television, families spend evenings doing things together, talking, telling folk-tales or reciting *pantun*. We sold the finished products for cash to buy us the exercise books we needed in school, the uniforms or the occasional treat. So whenever I attend craft fairs in England, I look for these things so that I can see the corners of her mouth lift when I give them to her. This time, I had found a decorative straw hat with silk flowers sewn into its wide brim. I explain to Mak that this is for hanging in her room. She enthuses about the yellow and peach flowers, her eyes widening. The next instant when Dolores walks into the room, she acts as if she doesn't understand why I have brought her the gift. She speaks to the maid in English in the syntax of the Malay and Chinese languages.

"Look what my daughter bring. Very pretty hat, *huh*? Pity this face old-old. And my hair all nearly gone. So white, my hair. What for have hat, *one*?"

She puts the hat on, tilts her head this way and that, preening like some supermodel, except that she cuts such a tragic figure. She seems unaware of what she's doing. I am staggered and have to leave her to compose myself. I make an excuse that I need a shower. Not that I needed an excuse. Indeed, my blood has thinned to adjust to the English weather, so the sweat is now pouring from me, making my blouse stick in clammy patches to my body. I can climb up the Chilkoot Trail in Alaska with 50 pounds on my back without getting out of breath but in this humidity, climbing up the stairs to the second floor where Bernadette has allocated me a room is an effort, my breath coming out in spurts. Bernadette has a heart of gold. She has said many times that there will always be a room for me in her house. She doesn't like to think of me being old and alone in England, if my sons decide to live in Singapore or elsewhere. In the room, she has placed framed photos of David and my boys by the bedside chest of drawers and on the dressing table. She's that sort of person. She has certainly inherited our mother's caring ways. I run a cold shower and stand naked under the delicate spray. Cooled and freshened, my heart armoured, I go down the stairs to see what might await me.

Mak sees me and she exclaims with tremendous enthusiasm, her words fresh as if she is saying them the first time, "Eh! Ah Phine, *ah!* When did you arrive, *huh?*"

My good friend Sharon, who lives in Surrey like myself, often talks about her mother to me because we share the same sentiments about our mothers. She expresses the fear that she would not know what to do when her mother's time is up. Her mother, like Mak, is already in her 80s. Sharon knows I tried to channel the energy of my worries into writing a cookery book for Mak. Unschooled, Mak cannot read anything I write. When she was much more coherent, she used to show off my books to anyone who visited. She pointed proudly to the author's photo at the back of a collection of short stories, though she hadn't a clue what the words said. When I took her to the local bookshops in Singapore to show her the display of my books, she smiled from ear to ear, ran her hand over and over again across them. Catching a customer going past without picking up my book, she would tug at their arm, point to my book saying in either Teochew or Malay, "My daughter write this *one*, my daughter write this *one*."

It occurred to me that writing a cookery book with the recipes she taught me would be to honour her. Also, she can look at the coloured photos and have more pleasure from the book than seeing meaningless squiggles. David had the marvellous idea of having her picture on the dedication page. I took two years to work on the book, testing every single recipe several times. It was going to be a book of Singaporean recipes for Western kitchens, using ingredients that were easily available in the West. A special feature of the book is that each of the recipe can be converted to a vegetarian one. I wanted to show that you needn't eat boring, colourless food when you're a vegetarian. Also, there are so many vegetarians these days that many families have one or know someone who is one. Therefore, it seemed sensible to write the recipes in such a way that it can be worked for both the carnivore and vegetarian, simply by changing the main ingredient whilst using the same sauce. Since I acquired a stepson who is a coeliac, I also made sure that the recipes can be used for all those who are allergic to wheat. I wasn't going to compete with eminent cookery writers in Singapore. I hawked the book from publisher to publisher and had substantial interest from a private TV company who subsequently turned me down. They all said that the book should either be a non-vegetarian one or a vegetarian one, but not dual-purpose like mine. Some publishers said that Singaporean cooking was not popular enough, unlike Indian or Thai. Therefore, the process to get the book published took so long that I could not risk Mak not ever seeing her book, so I set up a company and published it myself in time for her 84th birthday in March of the previous year. I worked through my angst by writing the book. It is my way of coping.

"This curry puff is delicious," I say.

Dolores has prepared some local coffee to go with the curry puffs that Bernadette bought. The coffee is commonly known as Malaysian coffee, though I'm not sure why, after all Malaysia as an amalgamated nation didn't exist till 1963 and the coffee blend has always been around, 50% coffee and 50% roasted maize. It is inevitable that when you are in Singapore, you will have plenty to eat. Instead of commenting on the weather, people ask, "Have you eaten?", when they meet. One of the first things people do in this country is to offer food. A visit without your guest having something to eat is inhospitable. That is why my stepdaughter had seemed doubly rude to me on the occasion she denied me any vegetarian food.

"Ahh, I used to make such good curry puffs," Mak says wistfully.

She was indeed renowned for her cooking in our village. When times were hard, she made *nasi lemak* which she packaged and sold. It was laborious work, de-husking the coconut, then shelling it, removing the kernel then grating it by hand, before she could squeeze out its milk to boil the rice in. Coconut-grating machines were not available then. Nor blenders. So the onions and chillies for the sambal had to be ground either in the mortar-and-pestle or on the *batu gilling*.

"Oh, I do remember that. And you make *sesagun* like nobody can. In fact, I don't know that anybody makes it anymore, do you, Dette?"

"No. Perhaps we can go to *Geylang Serai* sometime and look for it."

Talking about food and seeing me must have triggered off something in Mak's mind and she gets up from the settee and shuffles across the gleaming marble floor towards her room, one hand pressed against the small of her back. She doesn't walk upright like before, her spine is a soft curve, her torso, a sloping "C". We hear drawers being open then shut as she searches for something. "Mama, what are you looking for?" Dolores asks, addressing her in the same way as all the grandchildren do.

"Got something I want. Can't find, *lah. Aiiyah*! So troublesome."

Then a little later, we hear her say, "Okay, okay. Got already." She comes out of her room looking pleased with herself. She has the cookery book that I wrote in her hand.

"Ah Phine," she says. "Have you seen this *one*? So beautiful, *lah*."

"Yes, Mak. I have seen it."

She opens the book to the dedication page which has a photo of her in a green *kebaya*. She is sitting on the bottom stairs right here in Bernadette's house, when they first moved in.

"Look at this. There's even picture of me! Old-old already. Do you know what my picture is doing here? Do you know who wrote this?"

Three

Much as I love my mother, reality is a shock to the system. I've wanted to be with her, wanted to hear her voice and here I am and I find the minutes ticking by so slowly when I'm sitting with her. How can you love someone so much and yet find that being with them is a strain? What trick of nature is this? I am riddled with guilt for feeling this way. I had expected that the love I have for my mother will be so much greater than the illness that it would teach me patience. Alas, I am a poor pupil. The doctors say that people with Alzheimer's repeat themselves because they cannot create new memory. This is because the disease starts in the hippocampus, a small area of the brain, no larger than a thimble, which is believed to be the main recorder of new memories. Because an action or word has not been recorded in the sufferer's brain, she will repeat the same thing again because to her, it's as if she doing the action or asking the question for the first time. But it's one thing to know this medical fact but quite another to have to deal with it. Doctors don't teach you how *not* to get irked by the repetitions. In one instance, my mother might say, "Is David here or not?", "No, he's working," I say. "How's his mother, *huh*?" "She's having trouble with her legs." "Oh, that's bad, *what*," she says. In less than five minutes she starts all over again, "Is David here or not? How's his mother, *huh?*" Or she'll say, "Eh? When did you arrive?" Her short term memory is like soap bubbles, it take seconds to blow them, then they float away and burst into the air, then she has to start again. There is absolutely no respite. After answering the same questions about a dozen times, I have to force myself to keep irritation out of my voice. I can see why Bernadette and her husband or Agatha find it trying; they have to live with her. On better days, she goes into long monologues, her most creative phase, she picks a thread from the past and sews it onto something from the present, the images, dates, times and places getting muddled in her mind.

"I'm glad I bought this house, *lah*," she says. "Ah Tetia's retirement money, I've put it to good use, *what*. Now when I die, there's something to be left for children and grandchildren. But, oh, so many trouble I had finding this place! Flood water was high-high. I had to hitch up my sarong. I waded through muddy bottom. There was gibbet next to this house and it looked like someone might have been hung there. That would have been bad *feng shui*. But I went to church to offer novena and I was told that this house is protected from evil spirits. Don't you think there is so much light in this place? How airy it is. Look at this marble on the floor, I thought how easy it is to clean, not like our cement floor in *Potong Pasir* where you have to scrub and scrub. That's why I put the down payment straightaway."

There are variations to the theme, but mostly the flood waters remain an integral part of her story, the flood waters which rose in our village, *Kampong Potong Pasir* back in the early 1950s from the Kallang River which fed vegetable farms. It was during the monsoons and it had been raining for days and days. The fat droplets forced their way through old attap, splitting the dry leaves, to land on our heads. Sometimes centipedes, lizards and insects living amongst the folds of attap lost their foothold and came tumbling down with the rain. Once a lizard landed on three-year-old Bernadette's head and she leapt around screaming, a child crazed. Filled with fear myself, with no adults around, I forced her to keep still and plucked the wriggly thing from her head. Its coldness to the touch disgusted me and it stayed on Bernadette's head fiercely, unwilling to be removed. Eventually it came off with a loud sucking sound, then it leapt out, leaving me to hold its vacant tail. The majority of the *kampong* folks could not afford new sheavings of the entire attap roof, so they had to be repaired by inserting slats of tin to seal off the gaping holes, but these got easily dislodged by the heavy rains and monsoonal winds. When it rained through our house, we all raced around to find containers, alluminium pails and decapitated kerosene tins to catch the indoor waterfalls. The volume of these deluges depended on how large the hole in the attap was: it could be a thin dribble or a raging torrent. When the first large drops hit the empty kerosene tins, they drummed a most unique tune, a sound that is ever present in my own memory, reminding me of home. The drainage system implemented by the colonial government was insufficient to cope with the heavy rainfall and the subsequent rising water. We were not the only village that was affected. The heavy rains pushed water out from the rivers and monsoon drains onto fields and streets. The boundaries to the main canal in Bukit Timah Road were so hidden by the swirling, muddy water that bicycles, trishaws and cars missed their mark and became capsized boats instead, floating on the swell. I don't remember exactly how old I was when the floods occurred. All I remember was seeing the muddy water rise and filling up the attap huts, then lifting furniture out of the huts. And the one image that had stayed stuck in my mind's eyes was that of an ugly Chinese coffin, bobbing up and down on the flood waters. I often wondered whether it held a corpse. But as we were half-a-mile away from *Lai Par*, where the river broke its banks, our row of huts were left intact and so I wonder why the flood had impinged itself on my mother's mind. It is also interesting that Mak even deemed it viable for her to have bought Bernadette's house. My father had been an impoverished store clerk in an English firm and later in his career, just before he died, was a bill collector. We had lived in an *attap* house that had neither bathroom, toilet, electricity nor running water. The pension that my mother inherited from my father upon his death in 1968 was less than five thousand Singapore dollars (a little over £2,000); the house that Bernadette and her husband bought cost more than two and a half million dollars! So it is not even remotely possible for Mak to provided the down payment. So why is there a need in her to feel that she has bought the place? Is it because she feels that providing a place for us to live is part of her nurturing responsibility?

Her inventiveness is a genuine aberration. I can tell from the manner she talks that she believes entirely in what she is telling us. My brother, Matthew, four years older than myself, and I, can see this, but my other elder brothers, Agatha and, sometimes, Bernadette herself despair of Mak's deviation from the truth. They seemed to think that she's being difficult or a purposeful liar. Agatha, in particular, cannot tolerate a rendition which does not comply with her own; she feels it a duty to point out to Mak how wrong she is.

"*Aiiyah!* Mak!" Agatha voices exasperation. "You are talking nonsense. It didn't happen like that, *lah!* Why do you insist on making things up?"

Her words shoot into Mak's eyes like arrows, shattering Mak's confidence in herself and her eyes look confused then pained, as though behind her own fascade, Mak has a vague awareness that there is something going terribly wrong with her own mind. Every time I see her injured, I am injured.

"Why don't you just nod and accept what she says," I say to Agatha. "You know the real facts. Just go along and pretend she's talking sense."

"Of course it's all right for you," Agatha thunders in reply. When Agatha speaks, it's as if everyone else must hear what she says, as though an audience confirms her righteousness. "You don't have to take this all the time. It's very hurtful when she tells anyone who visits that none of the children care for her except Ah Phine. She says nobody gives her money except you and David. Who do you think has been taking care of her whilst you're galloping around the world, huh? Who do you think pays her medical bills?"

Bernadette bursts into tears and say, "Yes, you don't know what it's like. She tells everyone I never give her anything to eat. She says to people that if Ah Phine was here, she wouldn't have to starve."

I didn't ask to be the goody nor the saint in Mak's eyes. I shall be the first to say that I am neither, but what Mak and I share is something beyond this space and this time. We have been soul-partners for many life-times and have participated in each other's nurturing and caring. That is the reason for her instinctive faith and reliance on me. It is true that I don't have to deal with Mak on an everyday basis, my siblings are not having it easy I know. And yet, I feel that if they understand Mak's affliction better, they wouldn't be taking everything so personally and so hard. I feel weary and ineffective. I do know that the more they react, the more they would be hurt for our mother is already inhabiting a world of her own making now and nothing anybody says or does will make a difference. In some way, I feel that it's probably healthier for Mak to continue to assert her world, at least she has something to identify with. What will happen when that no longer happens? Would she retreat into a world of silence? But I cannot find the words nor the heart to take my sisters to this different threshold of understanding. When I had married and went to England, I had proposed to Mak that she come to live with me but she declined, she had found England too cold, it hadn't got the kind of hawker food she craved and she could not speak the language. Since I do not take care of her, who am I to judge what is right or wrong for our mother? So I have to swallow the stone of rebuttal and acknowledge to my sisters that they are indeed right. It is inevitable that the disease will take further toll. Then what would become more important than disagreements would be that our mother receives proper care. And my sisters here in Singapore are the ones who will be giving it, not me so far away. I know that they will try their best to keep her at home until it becomes truly necessary to send her to a nursing home. For their concern and their effort, I will always be in their debt.

Alzheimer's corrodes the mind day by day, a mental rusting. It's a true death of the brain cells, never to be reversed. The disease is progressive. As more and more cells die, they affect the function that the cells are engaged in: recent memory, language, judgement, spatial relations, personality traits and others. It can't get better, only worse. It's a terrible future. I bleed for my mother. Coming down from my bedroom which is air-conditioned to descend the stairs into the non-airconditioned part of the house feels like I'm descending into a furnace. The rooms are separately air-conditioned and the main hall is kept at temperate air because Mother's arthritis is made worse by the cold. One morning, as I come down the stairs, I hear a commotion: Dolores trying to pacify Mak. I quicken my steps to find Mak in extreme agitation and in tears, her grey hair loose and not in its usual pathetic knot. There is hysteria in her voice. The calm mother I knew who has always been in prefect control is thrown asunder by her emotions. I have never seen her like that and for a few minutes is rooted in sadness. Dolores is trying to calm her but Mak is fending her off as though even Dolores had suddenly become the enemy.

"We can't let them in, *lah*! We can't let them in. They're going to take everything away from us. They're going to steal everything."

Apparently, Bernadette had organised someone to come to fix a faulty air-conditioner and had informed Mak, who has quite forgotten what the visit is about and won't let the technician in. My nursing training reminds me to distance myself from my own confusion and act responsibly. This woman, my mother, is no longer in charge of her rationality. She is obviously frightened. As far as she is concerned, the stranger who has come to the house is a threat. This irrationality is symptomatic of Alzheimer's patients, they suffer from delusions; simple situations take on fearful gargantuan proportions, shatters their sense of security.

"Okay Mak," I say. "I'm sending the man away. Right this minute. You have nothing to worry. Dolores, can you get her some coffee?"

It seems the best decision to make at the time. It's hard to see an old woman cry, let alone my own mother. That is when I realise that my role of child is over, a chapter that is from a different book. It is a signifcant realisation and not without regret, for the only time when one can safely slip back to being a child is with one's parent. The childhood years are nurturing years and memories with one's parents provide the foundation of one's character. (When I am reminded of these things, my heart aches with regret for what I have lost with my own children.) My brothers and sisters have probably learnt that our mother have passed the role of mothering, and that like them, I too have to learn to be mother to my own mother. It is not an easy role to play. I sit her down and talk softly to her, help her to comb her hair, knotting it. In less that five minutes, the creases on her forehead smooth out, normality returning back to her eyes. As swiftly as her disquietude has arisen, it evaporates just as quickly.

Until you deal with such lightning changes, you cannot fathom how unsettling it all feels. Now that the fear is gone, her body loses its rigidity, her spine giving in to the soft cushions of the settee, her face returning to the face I know and love so well. Dolores brings her coffee which is well sugared and after sipping it, Mak starts telling me about the time she came to buy this house as if the drama of a few minutes ago hadn't even occurred, as if she has not told me before about her buying of the house. My mind drifts but I offer her a look of attention. In some ways, it is a blessing that Alzheimer's sufferers have no new memory, it means that she cannot remember how she had acted only a few moments before. Later, Bernadette calls from her office, the technician had been in touch with her to let her know that he wasn't given access to the house.

"Do you know how much trouble I had in making that appointment?"

"Mak was really agitated and was in tears," I offer an explanation. "I had to decide. Perhaps next time it would be a good idea to get Dolores to keep on reminding Mak if a stranger was coming into the house."

The molten lava of Bernadette's frustrations must have been building up and building up within her. I am only beginning to recognise it in her voice and mannerisms. Unable to express them, the emotional pressure is starting to peak. So the incident is the trigger she needs for she suddenly erupts in volcanic proportions.

"*Aiiyah!* It's so easy for you to talk. You come here and you make all sorts of decisions involving us and when you go away again, I have to face the consequences. You really don't understand what it's like! I have to deal with this every five minutes, every day, Dolores calling about this or that. If it's not Dolores, it's Mak, calling every few minutes to see if I'm coming home for dinner. It's not easy for me, you know. No matter what I do, you are supposed to do it better. Every single day, I have to deal with

Mother's tantrums. No matter how I handle it, there are scenes and scenes. I have a business to run you know!"

She bangs the phone down. I stand and stare at the receiver in my hand.

I go out and buy Mak a *durian*. It's her favourite fruit but she doesn't get to eat it much because Bernadette and her family cannot stand its smell. Occasionally, Agatha or Matthew would buy *durians* and invite Mak to their homes. A *durian* is called the King of the Malayan fruit and has its own distinctive smell and taste. It's the most expensive fruit around. Most westerners are repulsed by its smell, complaining that it smells of sweaty feet. I prefer to say that it smells of ripe Camembert. Yet most Asians (except the likes of Bernadette) awaits its short season in June. During the season, it is usual to throw *durian* parties where nothing is eaten except *durians* because the fruits are very filling. It has a hard thorny exterior, *duri* means thorn in Malay and *durian* means made up of many thorns. Inside, it is segmented and each segment cradles the custardy fruit wrapped around a stone. At David's first *durian* party, thrown by my second brother, Jeremiah, nearly 20 years ago, he had to pinch his nose as he took his first taste. He was glad he did because he genuinely thought it tasted wonderful though he still couldn't stand the smell. But he has got used to it now. Mak is all smiles as we sit on the patio to eat our *durian* with our fingers. (I daren't take the *durian* indoors because the smell tends to linger and Bernadette might get a whiff of it when she comes home.)

"You know, *huh*. Grandfather had *durian* estate. Our *durians* tasted so good. Very high quality," she says, and for a moment slips back into her own past. "Have I ever told you or not that Grandfather used to wear helmet when he went to inspect his *durian* estates? He said it was an insurance against fruit-fruit dropping on his head."

She laughs her delightful laugh and hearing it, I am reminded of how young and stately she once was, so full of joie-de-vivre. But now the uninhibited laugh seems somehow incongruous with her old skin, her dull eyes, her thinning hair. But still, I love listening to her talk about her parents and the life they used to lead and I would prompt her with further questions. It is amazing how long-term memory is much easier for her to recall than the things that happened to her minutes ago. She describes her past with the same accuracy that she had described them to me all the years I was growing up. Her face literally rejuvenates when she recalls her childhood. She must have loved that bungalow by the sea because she can tell me about it time and time again. Thoughts of one home lead to the other causing her to skip the years and end her reminiscence by saying, "Don't you think I make a good choice in buying this house?"

I agree and she proceeds to tell me again how she came to buy this house. She never seems to tire from a repetitive subject, an organ grinder grinding out the same old tune again and again. And again. It must be the 50th time I've heard it since I came back, although for her it's a new subject each time. I realise with a sadness that it's no longer possible to carry on a sensible conversation with my mother now. Firstly, her memory is short-lived — in the span of five minutes, she can ask you the same question at least ten times. Secondly, she talks without listening. It's as if she has a ravenous need to talk — or to be listened to.

I pack the *durian* shells in plastic bags and put them away in the rubbish bins outside the house. We go in the house to wash our hands. The phone rings and it's David. When I am in England and working upstairs from his office, he hardly remembers that I am there. He spends hours on the telephone to everybody else, at meetings and on his computer. We see each other only for meals. Yet, whenever I go away, he would call me on the phone regularly, sometimes twice in a day and for an hour each time. He was doing this so much when he was courting me that my mother said, "You'd better marry him, *lah*! Less expensive than his calling-calling." But I am always glad that he calls. I love the sound of his voice. Particularly today. In the turmoil of my mother's worsening condition, it is reassuring to talk to someone who is dependable, steady and loving. I take the opportunity to spill my heart to him about Mak, how she gets upset because she's forgetting things.

"Oh, tell her not to worry, tell her that I always forget where I put my keys and my glasses, that every time we are to go abroad, I spent half the night looking for my passport and driving licence. That should cheer her up."

Indeed, his forgetfulness colours our family saga. He leaves spectacles in fridges and house-keys in shoes. To circumvent his problem, he makes duplicate keys and spectacles by the dozen. He has misplaced anything that can be misplaced. If he parks the car in a multi-storey carpark, he forgets which floor it's on. So far, he has not managed to lose me yet, but he has forgotten to meet me at the right places before, which keep our lives peppered with surprises. If we go out and then part with a time and place to meet, I always carry a book so that I won't get irritated if I had to wait for him and he's at the wrong place. At least these days, with mobiles, we can contact each other. But his is a forgetting of non-connection, a distancing of his mind from his body. Usually, his mind is flooded with thoughts, mostly about business and he is unaware of what his hands and body are doing, the only person I know who has such complete separation between mind and body. He can collect cuts and bruises on his body and won't even know how or when they had happened. So of course, he can't *remember* where he had left his keys or his passport. But really, it's not so much the fact that he can't remember, it's more that he doesn't know, since his mind wasn't taking note of where he had placed the object of search. But my mother's forgetting is one of non-adherence, her doing slides away from her mind like paper on poor quality glue, whatever she says or do a few minutes ago cannot adhere to her brain. Nothing sticks so there are no new memories, only old ones which have rubbed into the tissues of her mind, stuck when the glue in her brain was strong. But even then she's getting them mixed up, her circuits getting crossed, events spliced and joined with other strands of memories, nothing makes sense to other people. Does it make sense to her? It must do, in some way because she speaks them with animation, her eyes lighting up.

Half an hour later, I join Mak on the settee.

"You know what," she says. "I've this *nafsu* (yearning), to eat *durians*. It's been a long time since I had them because Dette can't stand the smell, you see."

"Mak! We just had some. Only minutes ago!" I am a little cross. Ashamed as I am to admit it, my voice rises a decibel. I want her to remember, am *willing* her to remember. I am terrified of her slipping so quickly into the dark corridors of her mind. I take her hands and put them to her nose. "Smell your fingers, *lah*. You've just been eating *durians*."

"*Ya, juga,*" she affirms that her fingers still smell of the fruit. "But I don't remember eating them. Ahh, I am so useless now."

Her tone tears me apart and I am sorry that I forced her into remembering. And the second realisation hits me, a very sad one, that it seems almost pointless to say or do anything for Mak anymore because she is going to forget it anyway, in a matter of minutes. It appears that there is no future for her, every instant is a *now*, everything that happens is happening for the first time in her mind, as though she is frozen in Simple Present Tense, all her 24 hours crammed into one single moment. Part of the pleasure of doing something for someone is when they recall you doing so. So if Mak can't remember if you have done something nice for her, is there any point in doing it? It is then that I learn that when I am doing something for someone, I am really doing it for *me*, because my action gives *me* pleasure.

"Mama is very happy when you're here," Dolores tells me. "Not one day pass when she doesn't mention your name or Sir David. She always says you're so good to her. When you're not here, there is trouble every day, she will lose her temper, and scream and cry. And she will scold everybody."

"It's her way of getting attention," Agatha says of these episodes.

It's as if she's talking about someone else, a person I don't know.

Bernadette invites me out to dinner the next day, apologises for putting the phone down so abruptly, "Must be my period," she says. She is not the type to bear grudges. She and her family take me to a food centre where I pig myself on local hawker fare. For me, the most wonderful thing about Singapore is its local food, which is so varied and colourful. I can eat three or fours times a day and in multi-racial Singapore, never have to eat the same dish twice in a month! It makes eating an exciting adventure. Often when David grumbles and say, "I don't know how you can eat so often." I reply, "Because we have such variety in our food." There is just nowhere in the world like Singapore for its hawker food, with its high standard of hygiene. Hawker food is the one thing I get really nostalgic about when I'm on distant shores. Hawker food is so called because they were peddled by itinerant hawkers in the old days. Before bicycles and tricycles became available to common folk, hawkers used to carry their goods slung in wicker baskets attached to a pole that they carry on their shoulders. When they progressed to using push-carts, they congregated in open spaces, thus giving birth to the first hawker centre. One of the most famous one was called "The Carpark", literally the carpark in Orchard Road, just in front of what used to be called Cold

Storage, the first air-conditioned supermarket in Singapore, catering mainly to the English and expatriate community. About 20 years ago, the distinctive building was ripped apart to make way for a new shopping mall named *Centrepoint*. In the old days, the carpark space in front of Cold Storage was cleared of cars by 6pm to make way for the hawkers. It was quite a sight to see the hawkers dribble in at intervals, arriving with their push-carts, tricycles and on foot to set up their stalls, yelling greetings to one another or instructions to their helpers. Each stall was lighted up by a hurricane, kerosene or carbide lamp, each spluttering its own characteristic sound. It was a special treat for our family to go to "The Carpark", where one could select from a myriad of dishes: Malay, Chinese, Indian, Western, hence the place was also called "Glutton Square". After setting up their stalls, the hawkers put out some tables and chairs. Then the cooking began and the lovely aroma of different foods would rise and fill the air, making mouths water and even those who had not wanted to eat would begin to get a craving. The stallholders squatted by huge pails of water to do their washing-up, china bowls, spoons and chopsticks sitting patiently in metal buckets waiting to be washed. Stray dogs and cats, and even rats would turn up to scavenge for leftovers, running round the feet of customers and hawkers alike. Yet nobody minded then, the atmosphere was festive and unbeatable. Today, hawkers are no longer itinerant and are given stalls in sanitised food centres with running water, and electricity or gas. If so much as a cockroach is seen on their premises, the food inspector who does a regular round would pounce on them and their licence would be in jeopardy. There is still a festive, jolly air about most of the present-day food centers, but it's not quite the same as the atmosphere at the "The Carpark".

There are food centres completely under shade but I favour the outdoor type, particularly in the evenings when they open to the sky and stars. So Bernadette and her family take me to my favourite one, which serves the best *Chye Tow Kuay*. Generally translated as *carrot cake*, it is a savoury dish made with freshly grated moolie, which is called a white radish/carrot in Chinese. It is absolutely delicious when fried properly with crispy eggs, chilli and fresh coriander. Coupled with a bowl of ice-cold *chendol*, a dessert made with fresh coconut milk, I'm in my heaven. One of my dreams is to go on a luxurious cruise ship where I can eat all I want and gamble all night. I certainly have inherited one of my grandfather's characteristics. *Chomp Chomp* is in Serangoon Gardens, which used to have the best fish and chips wrapped in newspaper. The area was home to British soldiers and their families, houses which I thought were palatial compared to our leaky attap huts in the *kampong*. When either of my parents struck the 4-D lottery or when my father had a bonus at Christmas, we could afford one packet of fish and chips, which was shared amongst the whole family. So it was wonderful to sit in the food centre and be in a position to order whatever we wanted to eat. I am continually grateful for such things because I can never forget my beginnings. Bernadette always means well and I am rather fond of her although we are miles apart in interests. We have a lovely evening and she buys a packet of *Chye Tow Kway* as well to take home to Mak. We get home late, the main chandelier lights have been switched off. When we walk in, Mak is pacing the floor, torchlight in hand, looking frantic. Dolores is already in bed, which suggests that Mak had gone to bed and then re-awakened.

"Where have you been, *huh*? Why doesn't anybody tell me where they're going? I've been so worried. There's no one here to give me my food, *one*. I've been so hungry. Nobody cares for me."

There is no way that Dolores would have neglected to give Mak her meal.

"We did tell you we were going out for dinner, Mak," Bernadette explains softly. "We even asked you along. Look, here's some *Chye Tow Kway* for you."

"Nobody tells me anything, *lah*. I am left here on my own. *Hati saya hanchur sekali.* (My heart is in smithereens.)"

My own is sliced by her words. I am pained by her anguish, her sense of being abandoned. It's her old wound weeping again. A small incident can prise it open, but I can see it and understand. Not because I am either observant or wise but because I *am* her twin soul. I settle her and take her a hot Milo. Her mood has influenced mine and I cannot sleep, so I take my Laptop downstairs next to her bedroom to work, to somehow be closer to her. Her bedroom is her first ever ensuite bedroom. When Bernadette moved in and allocated her the room, she was overjoyed. So used was she in sharing a room, she could not imagine an entire bedroom to herself. She thought she was sharing it with Dolores. She extolled the ease in which she could go to the bathroom and was happy that she needn't climb two flights of stairs to the bedrooms upstairs.

"So big-big this room," she had said. "Like my old room in Grandfather's bungalow."

At last, we have returned her to the kind of grandeur she was used to. At least Bernadette has. After about half an hour, I hear Mak shuffling about in her slippers. The light comes on in her room and she walks out, her scanty, white hair in tendrils around her face. I expect more loose emotion, fractured words and girt myself for them. Instead she smiles broadly and says, "Ah! Working late again, *huh*? You've always been like that, *one*. Do you remember many-many nights you kept me awake reading by candle? I was worried that you might fall asleep and set *attap* on light. Oh, did I hear Dette say we have some *Chye Tow Kway*? Shall we have supper?"

Four

There was a Pathe News clip in original black and white film which, for some reason, stays etched in my memory. It was one which featured Mahamat Gandhi who was becoming known for his philosophy of gentle persuasion and *ahimsa* or non-harming. During that colonial era, Pathe News always preceded a film screening of the cartoons and main feature. The film would crackle and the cock would crow before a very English voice started to give us news of the world and especially of Britain. It was a great day when we got to go to the pictures when I was a child. It wasn't until I was much older that I actually visited a proper cinema auditorium, like the Alambara, Lido or Cathay; and especially one which had air-conditioning. The first cinema auditorium that my father took me and my siblings was somewhere in Geylang whose name escapes me, but it was an like an amphitheatre with a half-roof that covered the more expensive seats. But it was a step-up from the village film screening so we loved it. My father loved the cinema and it was he who instilled that same love in me. But before that, we could only afford the freebie films screened outdoors. We would all wait anxiously by the wooden shack which served as the village club-house. When the film van arrived, we would shout and hail it like it was some messiah. We must have seemed like street urchins to the projectionist, our feet bare, many of us half-dressed; the boys clad only in shorts, and us little girls in cotton panties, our torsos deeply brown and naked. I wore a dress only when we had visitors or were going out or when the weather was really cool. How I sulked when Mak told me to wear dresses *all* the time when I turned eleven. I resented the loss of freedom in feeling the breeze lick my bare skin and the rain trailing its delicious fingers down my back and chest. Clothes are such encumbrances, they fence you against nature. In England, I feel imprisoned by winter clothes, which stop the sun from finding my skin. I particularly detest the rough scratch of wool and its suffocating warmth. But there was no need for wool or leather in my days in the hot sunny *kampong*. We wore mostly cotton, put together by our diligent mothers proficient on the Singer sewing peddling machines. There was a lovely camaraderie living in the *kampong*; our front and back doors were hardly ever closed till bedtime and people talked to neighbours and looked out for one another. There was a genuine sharing. The film van only came round once a month and those who witnessed its arrival would spread the news so that no one would miss the treat.

"Uncle is here! Uncle is here!"

Adults and children alike waited patiently, watching the projectionist anxiously as he unloaded the reels of films and screen. One full length feature film would probably take up to two or three of the huge reels. Often in the screening, the film crackled and groaned, and sometimes, it would even snap, raising moans amongst the audience eager to know what was going to happen next. The audience also grumbled when each reel ran out and the projectionist had to unload one reel to replace it with another. If we were in an auditorium, the lights would come on, raising still more protests as this replacement was taking place. Couples smooching with each other would leap apart as if the bright lights burned them.

At our *kampong*, the film man hoisted the screen onto a stand which had been set up on the cemented outdoor badminton court. Around him was a buzz of activity and excitement, people arranging their seats, from low stools to straw mats. Like all the other children, we were allowed to sit on wooden benches fashioned from a single plank crossing the tops of two kerosene tins. We had to be careful not to fidget too much, otherwise the plank would slide off the kerosene tins and we would land on our bottoms on the hard cement floor.

"Oi!" Inche Samad, a well-respected elder of the village called out. "Taller children behind please."

We got off our places on the planks reluctantly and scuttled to change seats, the little ones went to the front with smirks on their faces. In the *kampong,* I was considered quite tall.

"Please don't rain, please don't rain," we chanted in Malay. Those of us who knew some English sang, *"Rain, rain go away, come again another day."* Usually immigrant Indians, the baker, the ice-ball man and the *kachang putih* man plied their trade near the badminton court. Sometimes, the lady selling *muah chee* set her stall close by so that we got a whiff of sesame oil and seeds. The baker and the *kachang putih* man carried their wares on their cloth-bound heads in a square wooden tray. There was something enticing about the aroma of freshly baked bread. The baker sold tin loaves, French loaves and slices of bread which he slapped thinly with home-made *kaya,* an amber-coloured egg-jam. Sometimes he had *nonya kaya,* a delicious Peranakan version which was made with the addition of coconut milk and *pandan* juice. The *kachang putih* man set his wooden tray down to display the variety of freshly roasted or steamed nuts which sat in small separate sacks. Both children and adults would crowd round him, even when they could not afford to make any purchase.

When I had five cents, I would buy my favourite, the *kachang kudah*, steamed chick peas: golden nuts with their translucent loose skins.

"*Banyak, banyak chilli*," I would say, asking for more of his special chilli sauce to go with it.

The seller made a paper cone out of squares of newsprint, filled it up with the nuts, then shook his bottle of chilli sauce over them.

"Can I have some or not?" Parvathi asked.

She was my best friend in the *kampong* and lived next door but one to us. Although she was three years older than I was, she seemed to act as if she was younger. Her eyes were like round black marbles and her long hair was always sleeked with coconut oil. My earliest memory of Parvathi was when I was six and she was nine. But her dark brown fingers plunged into my paper cone as if she was only five. How could I have known the fate that was to befall her?

"What about me? What about me?" Agatha rushed at my paper cone.

We sat there in delight eating the nuts and watching the film. When the nuts ran out, we sat there sucking each of our fingers until they were clean of the chilli sauce. We split open the paper cone to make sure that we hadn't missed any nuts, picking small bits of nuts or their loosened skin that might be stuck on the inside of the cone. "There's some more! There's some more!" We shouted with glee if we found even a fragment of a nut.

On evenings when the first drop of rain started to fall, people looked round in trepidation. If it drizzled, waxed umbrellas mushroomed upwards to block our view of the screen. If the rain got heavier still, the film man would pack up the screen and we could not see the end of our movie which was always a disappointment. There was a kind of suspense generated as we never know if we were to see the end of a film or not, and so we were much more appreciative when we did get to see the entire feature.

The news clip that is etched in my memory showed Mahamat Gandhi walking in leather-thonged sandals through feathery rain on the hard streets of Liverpool. He smiled for the workers at the mills for spinning their cloths, something he advocated in his own home-country. Even in the cold, he was shrouded only in his dhoti, a length of white cotton draped around his thin shoulders, his chest bare. I'm not sure why that clip made such an impression on me, I hardly understood what his beliefs were then, though I do now. I didn't know that he was an eminent lawyer, I thought he was some kind of peasant-saint. The way he was clothed and the colour of his skin and the manner of him made him so incongruous in that environment — as if he did not belong there, even on so short a visit. Like the other village children, I did not know where Liverpool was, except that it was somewhere in England where we believed everybody to be rich. We knew there were white people there and, of course, from our history, we knew that the *Mat Sallehs* were lords and masters, queens and kings. We knew they all lived in brick houses, where there was running water and electricity. Obviously, everybody had lots of food to eat because they could afford to feed their dogs with huge chunks of meat that our families didn't see for weeks.

Years later, when my mother came to England to attend our garden party to celebrate my new life with my English husband, she looked to me as Gandhi had looked in the Pathe News clip, somewhat lost, somewhat displaced. In her embroidered voile *kebaya* and her batik sarong, with open-toed sandals on her feet, she was shot to the bone by the chill of an English summer. That was in 1986 when she was 70, eight months after David and I were actually married. We had waited for kinder weather to accommodate my family coming over from Singapore. Mak came with

Bernadette and my two elder brothers. My ex-husband didn't allow my children to attend, whilst David's showed their disapproval by not attending. I know the fact that I was not accepted by David's children grieved my mother, but we didn't discuss it. Her visit was a lovely occasion. Prior to the party, I had sent a petition out with the invitation. I said that we would prefer not to have wedding presents, but if people felt generous, they could donate to an orphanage that David and I supported in Pattaya, Thailand, which was run by Father Brennen, an old Irish priest. I enlarged a photograph of the orphans and pinned it to the main marquee. Mak pointed to the picture and asked me what it was about. When I explained, she said, "I've raised you right, *lah*." The response to my petition was phenomenal and the local bank manager took charge of all the cheques and provided his bank's services for free to send the cheques on to the orphanage.

I was pleased that Mak was pleased. It was not just a case of seeking or needing her approval but it was a larger thing, as if in doing things right, I am somehow feeding her spirit, our spirit. She who has fed and clothed me must now be fed by me, even if it is through her spirit. Our relationship is one that has spanned millenniums and I feel this truth in my bones, our sinews forged by the shared high notes and pitfalls of our mortal lives. It is a shame that she was not suited for England. Hugging the cardigan tightly round her, she looked tiny in the vast landscape. The English summer was Singapore's worst winter weather. Mak's lips and heels cracked, weeping blood. Her digestive tract quarreled with English food. She could not understand the language, nor why the sun rose so early and set so late. She was so used to getting up with the sun that it took a while to persuade her that she didn't have to fix breakfast the moment the sun rises, especially when the sun rises at 5am.

"You've done well to cope," she said. "No neighbours, no hawker centres. This biting cold-cold. You must have been English in one of your incarnations, *lah*."

She was still able then, so she cooked for me everyday, cutting, chopping, frying, steaming — all the food she thought I had missed, so that by the time she left, my freezer was crammed with jars and tupperware containers. In feeding my body, she was feeding my spirit, the preparation of food an expression of her love.

I had already been in the country for eight months by the time my family arrived. I was proud to be able to drive them everywhere to show them the various interesting places. I was striving to give my family and particularly my mother the impression that I was settled and happy in my adopted country, in my chosen destiny. I did not voice the utter feeling of loneliness and desolation when you marry into a stepfamily who didn't welcome you, didn't want you there. Having being raised in a family of nine where there's always someone about, someone to talk to or argue with, it was a shock to the system to find myself alone with my new husband in a 30-acre property with no family members dropping in or visiting. I did not mention the discomfort that arose when people looked at me because I spoke differently, looked different. The loss of my children, the price that I had paid for a second chance at marriage was so high that I had to make it a success. I radiated newly-found happiness, exceptional confidence. My mother must never know the truth. It would hurt her.

"Isn't Phine clever, *huh*?" Mak said to Bernadette and my brothers. "Look at her driving round all these twisty and narrow roads."

Because she loved flowers, we went to as many garden centres as her legs could manage. She oohed and ahhed over the brilliant mauve and lilac petals, and flowers which were rare in the tropics. She marvelled at the size of roses and bought seeds to take home to Singapore to plant.

But of course, the humidity and strong temperature cut their life before they had a chance to grow. Her disappointment permeated through the telephone when she told me they had died. But while we were at the garden centres, she gathered flowers by the armful to take back to our guest cottage so that she could fill vases of all shapes and sizes with them until the cottage looked like a florist shop. Something clicked into place inside me that time. I have always loved flowers, whether they are fresh or silk or made out of crepe paper. I love their colour, their shape and their smell. It's a joy to handle the stems, to cut and trim and arrange. And I suddenly realised that it's a love that had sprung from my mother to myself. I often wondered how much of me is really me and how much of me is really my mother or even my father? Do I own something that is solely mine? Where does the off-shoot of my own personality begin?

There was another thing which lightened my mother's spirit considerably on her visit to England. On the first day that we were out, her wrinkled eyes widened with surprise, her smile bemused.

"Ah Phine, ah," she said, "Look, there's an *ang mo* cleaning the streets."

"They're all Europeans here, Mak."

"A European cleaning the streets! Look, look, there's another one collecting rubbish. And he hasn't got a shirt on."

At that juncture, I had been out of village life for some considerable years. During that period, Singapore had gained independence through merging with Malaysia in 1963 and then going her own way in 1965. The industrial revolution had reformed the nation, pulling it out of colonial clutches and residual poverty and catapulting her into prosperity. Local businessmen employed local people and the face of employment changed, with the percentage of white bosses becoming fewer and fewer. So my mindset had already been altered for a number of years; brown as we may be, we proved to be as capable as the "White Man", capable of not only running our own country but of taking it to the heights of success. I had the advantage of education which fed me information of the Western world, its perfections as well as its imperfections. But my mother did not have that kind of exposure. She was still a frog under a coconut shell, her mind deeply etched by colonial supremacy. Initially, I couldn't understand why she was getting so excited about the idea of a White Man cleaning the streets. Throughout her stay with us, she kept on wanting to go out on drives. I knew she loved the hugeness of England and the lovely scenery but I was still suspicious. Only much later did I realise why. She wanted to absorb this new revelation: White people actually worked at jobs which were relegated to our people in our country. Wherever we went, she would smile and shake her head when she saw a white person working at ordinary jobs, like digging the road or serving us at the grocer's, butcher's or at the tea-shop. She actually laughed openly when she saw that the milkman delivering the milk was white and so was the delivery boy delivering the newspaper. It eventually dawned on me that her views of the White Man was that they were in a superior position and therefore would not have to engage in menial labour and seeing them doing so was to her tantamount to seeing the King work!

In 1932, when Grandmother arrived in Singapore with her 12-year-old son and four teenage daughters, Singapore was still a British colony. Except for a few people, mostly Chinese and Eurasians who came from the upper echelons of society and rubbed shoulders with the British and white community, the majority of the local population had little contact with them socially, only seeing them as their employers and leaders. It should have been no surprise to me that my mother, uneducated as she had been, could not see them otherwise. For Grandmother and her children, it was a time for a new struggle. Nobody spoke of the exodus for a long time, and then only in dribbles like a strangled tap. Neither Mak nor Great Aunt, Second Aunt nor Kanchil, breathed a reason. I never knew Fourth Aunt because she died before I was interested in familial connections and history. Was there really a fire? Did Grandfather die? Why won't my mother, aunts and uncle talk about it? Was theirs a mutual silence or a laundered memory? Do they not speak of it from shame or from inexplicable pain? I tried to put the pieces of verbal jigsaw together, bits of information gathered from Mak or one of the aunts. But that was not until many years later and, by then, they wanted to forget that it had ever happened. And even what I have pieced together may not be the way it happened, my siblings' and my variation differing on who had told us what, what we perceived as facts, and what we remembered. Kanchil eventually ran away to Australia — and later to America, a pioneer from the East, beginning his history anew, unfettered by the past.

Grandmother, in her late 40s, suddenly widowed and plunged from riches to rags, never recovered from her loss. There was the loss of her husband, and then the loss of all material comfort. Unknown to her, Grandfather's love of gambling had resulted in huge debts which sealed their fate. Or so Uncle Choong said. Uncle Choong was Grandfather's accountant. In the end, it appeared that Grandfather couldn't cope and ended his life in such a dramatic fashion. Grandmother must have held her pain at bay, kept her wits about her to flee the creditors. She ran away with some pieces of jewellery, her money belts and her daughters. With the help of Uncle Choong, Grandmother and her daughters were housed in Kuala Lumpur and then taken down to Johor by train, then into Singapore by car. My mother remembered the horrendous journey, recalled the dark and long hours hidden in this and that home. She remembered not liking Uncle Choong, who had a thin moustache and a manner that was simply too unctuous. He seemed keen on getting them out of the state and into another country; perhaps so that Grandmother could not know the real state of affairs or lay claim to Grandfather's estate or what was left of it. As the four girls were not literate nor understood business affairs and Kanchil too young, they never questioned Uncle Choong's authoritative plans. Of course, they never saw him again after they sought solace in anonymity in a new country. It was left to her daughters to mend their lives. Soon Hua, the elder at 19, sulked because her nails were broken and she had to fetch her drinking water from the stand-pipe a distance from their attap-hut they found themselves in. To bathe, they had to draw water from a well, something she had never done before. At night, she grumbled that her sisters' bodies were too close to hers in the small hut which was no bigger than their bath-house back in Malacca. Soon Chew sat on the platform bed all day hugging her knees because she hated the rats running around its base. Soon Mei was mesmerised by the sight of all the screaming children from the other families, dirty children in rags with spittle and mucus running down their faces. Kanchil sat with thumb in mouth, eyes wide as if the shift from an opulent house to this basic existence was a nightmare he was struggling to awake from. Grandmother sat wherever she was put, as if all life had left her, her eyes blank. It was Soon Neo who pawned their jewellery and it was Soon Neo who found them the hut on the edge of a Malay kampong. It was Soon Neo who went to the market to get food, who learnt how to start the fire in the clay stove, whose hands were chaffed from washing their clothes outside by the village well. Soon Neo was 16 going on 17. Slender, like the willowy bamboo, she had a grace that was not diminished even by the change in her station. Her face was soft, her eyes large, her hair plaited and coiled on either side of her head.

She gave the impression that she needed looking after, but a strong crust was slowly emerging — she realised that for the family to survive, she had to set aside her own grief. That was the first time she pulled herself up tall and stuck her chin out.

"We have to find husbands for you three," Soon Neo said.

"You think you madam or what, *ah*! Giving orders," Soon Chew remonstrated.

"Sure Chin Tuck will come for me, *lah*. Just because we have no money is not going to stop him. Mother is stupid to have run away."

"You know what is best, Third Sister," Soon Mei nodded meekly.

"Dream on, *lah*, you two. Find work, starve or get married. It's your choice. I'll see if anyone will pay me to do their washing."

"Aren't you stooping a bit low?"

" The men around here are such peasants."

"We're ruined and we've no dowry. We will be lucky if *anyone* want us."

"Dek-dek, how come you so tough all of a sudden, *huh*?"

The girls were young and pretty. That was enough to bring the suitors. There were many immigrant men in Singapore hoping to accrue enough money to start a new life or have enough to send back to starving families back home in China or India. Hardworking but lonely, decent men who would appreciate a little bit of home life. A man in his 30s came forward for Soon Hua. Recently widowed, he baited her with his *attap* house and a business selling chicken rice in Albert Street. Soon Hua accepted after all hopes of Chin Tuck coming for her were dashed. The man gave her four children and a lot of devotion. Soon Chew, Second Aunt, married a man who spent money like a sultan, only to discover that he was a gardener who gambled. Later, he had TB and succumbed to it after providing Second Aunt with two children. She then married an

Indian who gave her four more and a multitude of heartaches. Soon Mei was approached by a shopkeeper and she gave him a son and a daughter but did not live to see them grow up. Soon Neo held the family together with her sound mind and her diligence. She had just turned 17 when she married my father.

Chia Yong Tong, then 20, was cycling down the dusty *lorong* when he saw a pretty girl squatting by the village well washing pails of clothes on the wooden washboard. Although she was golden brown and was dressed in a *sarong kebaya* like his own mother, he knew she wasn't Malay. He had been on his way to attend the wake of one of his father's old colleagues when he saw the girl, whose skin was like burnished copper. He himself was fair complexioned, like his Chinese father who had come from China. The girl's head was bent down attending to her washings. There was something about the angle of her face, the long sweep of her neck and the small delicate ears which made him stop in mid-cycle putting his foot down in the dust scattering the chickens and ducks who clucked and quacked in protest. The other girls who were also washing clothes looked up and giggled, except *her*. She glanced at him briefly, then she modestly dropped her gaze. Twice more he cycled past that route. But he never approached her. Instead, he made enquiries and found out where she lived. He told his mother who arranged for an *Old Aunt* to make a proposal to Grandmother, but as Grandmother was not in a fit state to conduct such affairs, Soon Neo received the *Old Aunt* herself, which caused the old lady to frown.

"I will discuss these things with your mother."

"I speak for my mother and myself," said Soon Neo. Her voice was soft and deferential but she was leaning a force into it.

After seeing Grandmother and understanding the situation a little better, the *Old Aunt* outlined the proposal.

"I will not marry unless my mother and brother come with me."

"Young lady," the *Old Aunt* reproached Soon Neo. "There are many girls in your position who would die for an educated man like Mr Chia."

But secretly, the old lady knew that Soon Neo wasn't a peasant girl, she saw that from the texture of the girl's skin, her refined movements and speech. It was a match that would earn her a lot of money.

Yong Tong was third of five boys. His own father, years before on the brink of his own adulthood had fled from the squalor and famine of Swatow, in mainland China. Grandpa had heard about the island of opportunities, an island in the South China Sea. He left his parents, brothers and sisters in tears to journey on foot to the port to find a tongkang which would take him to Singapore. There were so many people on board that they had to sleep sitting up amongst the rats which ran about their feet. When the tongkang hit open waters, it heaved with the swells, some people were sick and the others had to put handkerchieves to noses. There were more men than women, men in pig-tails like himself, all seeking a new life. Just before they landed, a crowd of them stood on deck and in one heroic gesture snipped their pigtails off and flung them into the murky Singapore River. Grandpa became a coolie, carrying sacks of rice on his back, walking the gang planks between bumboats and warehouses. The work was relentless, bending his spine into his ribcage. The hot equatorial sun scraped raw his creamy white skin and bleached his blue-black hair. Lying on his wooden bunk in the cubicle which he shared with six other labourers, listening to the others cough and wheeze, he swore that the sacks of rice would break his back first before they broke his spirit.

I never knew either of my grandfathers. Nor my mother's mother. Nor their parents before them. I feel bereaved by this lack, a lotus floating on the surface of life without roots. My brothers and sisters seemed unconcerned about not knowing about our ancestry, but I feel it keenly.

I don't know enough about my ancestors to be sure about myself. When I was in school, the other kids made fun of me because I was so brown. "Are you Chinese or Malay?" They asked. Even now when I return to Singapore, people would say to me, "Eh, how come you so black, huh?"

I had a brief dalliance with a grandparent — Lao Ee, my father's mother. He called her *Ah Kou,* Aunty. Once I asked my mother why. And she explained that it was a Chinese superstition. If the gods knew that you had borne a son, they might take him away, so the simple folk tried to deceive the gods by making the son call his mother Aunty so that he would not be taken away. I must have been about 14 when Lao Ee died in her late 80s. It always seemed strange to me that we called her Lao Ee which meant Old (Maternal) Aunty. She lived with Fourth Uncle and his wife. When we visited them, Lao Ee was often on her platform bed reclining on her hard wooden pillow. She too was a prisoner of her mind and she smelled of moth-balls and Tiger Balm. She always used Tiger Balm for her headaches. I didn't like hugging her because she also smelled of urine. And sometimes, something worse. When she died, Mak sewed a beautiful long dress in cream lace to drape over her *kebaya panjang.* I still remember standing looking over the coffin wondering why Lao Ee had such an unnaturally stretched smile when Mak said, "I wonder who's going to make sure that when I die, I will go in something beautiful." And I promptly said, "I will see to it, Mak," although I could not imagine my mother dying or going anywhere without me. Lao Ee seemed to have come and gone without my even having noticed. Or cared. Then. Such is the callousness of youth. But I regret it now. She was my history but I've let her go without learning her.

Her husband let her go, too. Whether from choice or not, no one knew. He left after giving her a nice home and five sons. Grandpa had made good. From coolie to warehouse hand. Enough to get out of the cubicle into a decent flat, enough to educate his four boys. They had lost their eldest at birth. Then one day, when his two older boys had started work, Second Uncle, an inspector with the municipal and my father a store hand, he told Lao Ee that he was going back to China, take his mother twenty-four carat gold, take his father a handsome watch, money for his brothers and sisters. He set sail and never came back. No one knows what happened, whether the ship sank, whether he died on his journey up to the mountains or decided to stay on. No letter, no news. Suddenly, abruptly, Lao Ee was amputated of a husband. Another part of our history hacked off. Never to be spoken of or pried into. Perhaps this is one of the reasons for writing this story, to collect a history for myself and for my descendants and to etch it into memory so that we can recall it as though it has always been there.

But more important than documenting a family tree is the celebration of my mother's life. I don't want her grandchildren to remember this old, shrunken lady who acts funny sometimes, saying strange things or raving like a mad woman. I want to give them the gift of a wonderful grandmother whose life had been a selfless service to their parents without whom they would not be alive. I want them to read and capture the real portrait of a warm being not yet malformed by disease. It is easy to remember the bad rather than the good, easier to remember the deeds of Adolf Hitler rather than the deeds of Martin Luther King. The bad and the negative tend to over-shadow the good and beautiful. I want my brothers and sisters to remember not this troublesome old lady who havs tantrums and nightmares, who uses abusive words, but to remember her as she had been, tall, slender and beautiful; the same woman many of the villagers in *Kampong Potong Pasir* saw as an Angel of Mercy. They loved and valued her so much that when the shanty village was about to be razed to the ground to make the land available for high-rise blocks of flats, before the villagers were to be re-housed, they came and knelt at her feet and wet them with their tears. The most generous years of her life coincide with my childhood, so her story and mine are intrinsically linked, even though we were at the different ends of the spectrum of our mortal lives. Under all her wrinkled old skin, there is still a beautiful woman, intelligence behind her dull, opaque eyes. And somewhere inside her is her wonderful spirit, imprisoned now by her debilitating mortal mind.

Five

$\mathcal{M}$ak told me that when I was born in March 1951, a neighbour was dying. The eternal cycle of life. How many lifetimes do we need before our learning is completed? Who directs our learning in this earth-school? Our Higher Selves or a Supreme Consciousness? All I know is that my mortal education was made all the easier with my mother by my side because she showed me joy where there was pain, beauty where there was bleakness, richness in poverty. If it is ever said that angels do walk this earth, I would say I have the honour of knowing one. Whatever assaulted her physical, emotional and mental bodies, she had managed to keep her spirit intact. She was so rare a selfless being that I have not found another match. It was this nature of hers, more than her physical characteristics that made her radiate such beauty; even though her skin is wrinkled and her eyes opaque with cataracts. She had allowed nothing in life to beat her. Until now.

My mother in the throes of birthing could hear Kurumbia Vikaram's wife two doors away wailing as her husband entered the gates of death. Just as Mr Vikaram slipped into his soul, I slipped into my body. Mak described that day so vividly that I could see it as if I was an onlooker. This knack of hers to imprint her words into my memory throws me into confusion and I can't tell if what I know is what I personally remember or what I remembered from what she told me. For instance I can see myself, quite clearly, at six months, chubby, chuckling, my dimples showing. A Bengali woman was carrying me, a roll of fat visible between her *choli* and *sari*, a thick rope of well-oiled hair snaking down her back. She pinched my cheeks and said to my mother in Malay, "Very cute baby, very cute. You sell to me."

"No, *lah!*" Mak said. "My one."

"I make good offer. How much you want? You're young, strong womb, you have many more. You have three sons already, *what*. I have no children, I take many care of her. Give her everything."

"Ya, *lah*, why don't you?" Ah Tetia said later when my mother told him about the offer. "She's only a girl. We haven't got enough to feed the others as it is. Hara Singh has plenty of money, he will give her a better life than we can give her."

"No!"

My future was balanced on that single word. Histories are made on single words. If my mother had been any less forceful, I might have been raised a Bengali child, with kohl under my eyes and clad in Bengali costume, with a name like Indrajit Kaur, Surindar Kaur or something to that effect. Mak stood tall and erect then, not yet beaten by life or age. She confided in me once that she lost three daughters before me. But she could tell I would fight to live and she would live to fight my life. We are linked in more ways than one. Although she lived within the constraints of her species, she would show her mettle every now and again. This was the first but not the last time she fought my father for me. I remember many such incidents, carry them in my heart, my debts to her. She gave me a life I would otherwise not have had. Because of this, I give her a life that *she* definitely could not have: I learn languages, philosophy, literature, roam the world, hike, ski, parachute, and I describe to her each experience, each moment so that she can live my life alongside me. Her eyes would glow and her face would brighten as she fed on my living. That was after we have left the *kampong*, after Ah Tetia had died, releasing her, after I made my own escape from the man who fathered my sons.

Is it possible for a six-month-old to recall her memories? Is there an observer within the child? Ah, the age-old philosophical question — is a human being just his mind or is there another part of him which is more than his mind? I cannot say that I know the answer. However, I am still perturbed by the fact that I cannot sort out the ownership of the images in my mind — have they been placed there by my mother's suggestive words or are they a result of my own direct experiences? Does it really matter? I tell my story as the picture unfolds in front of my eyes.

My mother was 36 when she gave birth to me. I wasn't the first girl but was the first to survive. Ah Tetia assumed I was going to go the same way as the others, so he didn't consider registering my birth. When he eventually did, he was so flustered because the English clerk told him off for registering late that he forgot my Chinese name and gave only the Christian one. He was also so intimidated by the English clerk that he dared not disclose that I was born a couple of days before and gave my birth date wrong, so that I was made younger by two days by the State. From experience, my father learnt that if I should die without being registered, it would mean no unnecessary paperwork and no hassle. An unrecorded event. Just a personal tragedy. Mostly my mother's, rather than his. He wanted only boys to carry his name into posterity. "Girls waste rice," he said. "And then when they grow up will belong to someone else." His was a working man's philosophy. It didn't occur to him that if all men thought like him, he wouldn't have had a wife to marry.

By the time he married my mother, the three sisters were already married. My father had taken Grandmother and Kanchil into the fold of his household because he couldn't have had my mother without them. They weighed on his meagre resources, but he still sent Kanchil to school. My parents began their married life in a tiny attap hut in Genting Lane. From this moment until the time he died, my father had no privacy, sharing the one single room with the rest of the family. How he manoeuvred his way into my mother's bed without the others knowing, I cannot imagine. But he did, for my mother was pregnant every other year which added to their cost of living. Grandmother had long ago lost her spirit and soon her body followed. At 18, Soon Neo was mother to her own child and to her little brother. Even when pregnant, she drew water from the well, beat down the earth that made up their floor, washed her own clothes by hand and was still clean and beautiful for my father when he returned, her mother's words hammering in her brain about keeping your man at home. Amdist all her concerns, she worried about Kanchil, who seemed to have shrivelled up even more, saying very little and doing very little.

"Are you okay?" She asked him.

"I am hungry, *lah*," Kanchil said with his soulful eyes.

"Here, have some of my food."

When my father saw that my mother was giving away her own food when she was pregnant, he became concerned. But he never expressed that concern. Instead he said, "Why are you always giving him more food? I am hungry too, you know, and I have to work. Is it not enough that I give him a roof over his head and educate him?"

On bad days, he would raise his hand to her and Kanchil would register all this but said nothing. He felt responsible. He hated my father, yet was also obliged to him because of his generosity. When he was sixteen and a half, he left home never to come back until after my father died.

This period and right through the war is vague, because Mak found it hard to talk about the children she lost. In later years, the pain comes out in spurts like blood from a cut artery. Especially about the baby she was forced to give away because they could not afford to keep him. I don't know if my other brothers and sisters know about this. I never discussed it with them. My mother told me so quietly as if she was either ashamed or in such severe pain. It must be a particularly bad time for my parents because my father would never have chosen to give away a boy-child. My mother suffered anguish, she tried to busy herself, pretended she didn't care about his whereabouts, how he looked, how he was growing, whether he was well-cared for, whom he was calling *Mak*. Because we don't know the identity of our brother, I often wondered what would have happened if either my sisters or myself fell in love with a man only to discover that he was our brother. As though doomed to share her sorrow, I picked up my mother's pattern and knitted it into my own. When my first marriage disintegrated, I was forced to act in order to survive. I had no money, no means of bringing up my children on my own, so when I left their father, I had to leave them behind. And when I emigrated to England, the split became permanent. From then on, I trod on sharpened blades as I walked through life, always searching the crowd for children who could be my sons, my heart mangled by the heavy rollers of seeing young mothers doing small things for their little ones, like wiping ice-cream from their lips, tying their shoelaces. These ordinary acts were denied me. I did not have the sheer pleasure of a child's arms around my neck nor the simple joy of being called *mummy*. I was living in a hell of my own making. I wondered if my ex-husband made them call his wife, mummy.

My husband would have preferred me to remain the naive 17-year-old that I was when he met me. He tried to cage me to his opinions, walled me in because of his fears, possessed me because of his insecurities. And I wouldn't let him. Unfortunately, only after we were married did I see the same signs in him as I did my father. I couldn't let him do to me what my father did to my mother. I had to break out, for my children's sake, for my own — and for my mother's. But the guilt was enormous. I was a mother and *not* a mother, orphaned by the loss of my children. At least my mother had us, my brothers and sisters, to occupy the vacancy left by that other child. I had no such consolation. When I first arrived in England, I yearned to fill that void with my three stepchildren, but they were too old to mother and far too antagonistic to love.

My mother gave away her son because she wanted him to have a better life. I gave mine away because *I* wanted a better life. This is my sin for which I cannot forgive myself, guilt scraping me raw on the occasions of their birthdays, even though we are now reconciled. Each of their birthdays is a commemoration of my *birth day*, the day when the child who had fed and slept with me for nine months was ripped from me. Like my mother's spiritual bond to me, I am bonded to my sons even when I don't see their faces. People launched verbal attacks for my callousness, but they did not know the shadows within the marriage, the desperation of a trapped spirit. Only I know that I had tried to spare my children the same kind of scenes that had terrified me as a child, of one parent wielding his fist on the other. For years, I was haunted by the sight of my four-year-old screaming as his father and uncle wrenched him from me. My heart still shreds at the memory of the bewildered eyes of the younger one who was not quite a year old. They grew up believing the lies they were told, that their mother left them because she did not love them, that she died soon after, not knowing that a continual attempt at telephoning was censored, that frequent letters and presents lay in a solicitor's office, court cases across ten thousand miles dragging on. But that is another story.

Just before I was born, my family became Catholics. *Peranakans* were commonly Buddhists or Taoists. The white missionaries might have liked to believe that it was their God and talk of fire and brimstone which brought the pagan natives to the road of conversion, but in reality it was much more prosaic. Food. Hunger was a great motivator to accept a different God. The colonial government was not as giving as the missionaries in providing food and education. Aunty Mabel, who was a Eurasian, told my mother about it and she told my father.

"Our boys can be educated if they're Christians, *lah*. And we can get food — rice, milk, margarine."

"I suppose the food will come in handy," my father said.

On his day off, Ah Tetia took the family to church where they were greeted by a man in a black frock who watered their foreheads and stuck a pin in the pages of the bible to come up with their Christian names. My father became John and my mother, Catherine. My elder brothers became Jacob, Jeremiah, Matthew and Zacchariah. Mak could not say their English names properly, the English sounding foreign to her tongue, so she latched on to the endings of their names. That is why I am not a *Jo*. So 13-year-old Jacob was transfigured to Ah Cob, 9-year-old Jeremiah to Romia, 5-year-old Matthew to Maretiu and 3-year-old Zacchariah to Ah Iya. But even the solicitation of the Catholic God could not repair the damage that TB had wreaked in Ah Iya's lungs. He left before I came.

Perhaps three or four of Mak's babies had died in the war. She could not remember the number, only the pain. Once, she told me that when the Japanese bombs were exploding around her, she was exploding with the birth of a still-born child. She never spoke of it again and I had forgotten it, only to recall it now. It is very interesting how I can slip her words into folders into my memory and not even be aware of the information until years later, when I suddenly have access to them when an associated thought triggers them off. I know that in this writing of her story, I am illuminating bits of my brain for the memories that are crouching there waiting to spring up. In this writing, I am knowing her again so that I have more of her to hold before she leaves me forever.

"Your father was so foolish, *lah*," she said. "He kept all *banana money* in wooden chest. When British came back, Japanese money was totally useless!"

It was her one direct criticism of my father which I will always remember. If he had been wise enough to convert the Japanese printed money into commodities, like gold, perhaps we would have been spared the kind of childhood we had to go through. If they had been poor before the war, after the war, they were paupers. Ah Tetia found a small *attap* hut in *Kampong Potong Pasir; kampong* meaning village in Malay, *Potong* is to cut, *Pasir* means sand. It was thought that the name arose when a small hill was leveled to site the village. A river cut a broad swathe through *Lai Par,* the inner reaches of the village feeding the vegetable farms. Whenever Mak talks about the flood, she is remembering the flood caused when this river broke its banks in the late-50s. The hut they called home was not big enough for a proper bed. Instead, a wooden platform was raised off the mud floor where the rats and cockroaches ran about. This was where they slept with the four boys. There was no bathroom, toilet, running water or electricity. Mak cooked under a lean-to outside the hut. During the monsoons, when the heavy rain lashed the spindly wooden walls and soaked the clay stove, Mak had to cook indoors, causing the small hut to fill up with kerosene-induced smoke. The whole of the hut which was like a bedsit without either bathroom or kitchenette, was less than half the size of the kitchen in the bungalow my grandparents used to own in Malacca. Yet my mother cared for her home as if it was a palace. Each morning, she would clear the hut of mice and rat droppings, she would carry the chamber pot outside to the monsoon drain to empty its contents.

"As long as you have water, you're not that poor that you have to be dirty," my mother told me many times. It was one of her sayings which stole into my being and became mine.

In front of the hut were the *jambans* or outhouses which served all the villagers. On public holidays when the buckets hadn't been collected by the night-soil man, the wind would waft the stench into their hut and they would be unable to eat or sleep. Fortunately, before I was born, Ah Tetia was promoted to a store clerk in *Williams Jacks*, an English company selling industrial weighing scales.

"This unborn child has brought me luck," he said.

Our people are very *pantang*, shaping our activities around omens and superstitions. It was good that my father had a positive sign before he saw me. Otherwise, it would have been easier for him to have me sold off to Hara Singh and his wife. A short distance away from the smelly *jamban*, Babur Singh was converting a wooden cow shed into five living quarters. He exalted them by calling them houses. Each of these living quarters was about 800 square feet, comprising of a small living room, bedroom and kitchen. There was no door between bedroom and living room and he charged fifteen dollars a month for rent (about £2 when sterling pound was high). The roof of the kitchen was zinc, which turned the kitchen into an oven at mid-day. On rainy days, it was like living in the hollow of a drum and the rain was the drummer. A well surrounded by a wooden wall, which opened to the tops of coconut trees and the sky, served as communal bathroom. A quarter of a mile away was the standpipe which provided drinking water for the whole village. We had to use the same *jambans* that were in front of my parents' old hut.

In 1992, when I became the first Singaporean to win a prize in the UK Ian St James Awards for short fiction, I was interviewed by a young reporter when I went back to visit my family in Singapore. I told her about my life in the *kampong* and how we had to organise our visits to the toilet.

"You can't wait till you're really urgent," I told the young girl. "Because you might arrive at the *jamban* and find that there is a queue ahead. And then you have to hug your tummy and cross your legs. You see, we had to share the toilets with the rest of the village. Going to the toilet was quite an experience. You had to be careful of your footing or you might slip down the hole, especially at night, because there was no light and we had to use a carbide lamp. And when you are squatting over the hole, you have to grit your teeth and ignore the smell, the scuttling of cockroaches and rats. In some ways, it was better to go to the *jamban* at night so that you don't have to see the over-flowing bucket with all the rats running round the sodden and disgusting mess. We had to use cut-rectangles of old newspapers as toilet paper."

We were seated in the coffee house of a plush American-style hotel in modern-day Singapore, already one of the richest nations in Southeast Asia. The girl's jaw dropped. She was only 20 years younger than myself, yet seemingly generations apart. She stared at me in disbelief, unsure if I was spinning a yarn. I guess she assumed that someone like myself living in comfortable Surrey would have always been rich. She had also never seen a *kampong* in Singapore during her lifetime because by the time she was born, Singapore had gained independence and had propelled herself out of third world status through providing cheap labour for the manufacturing industry. The young lady had only seen sanitised versions of Malay villages smartened up for tourists. The reporter's eyes enlarged, "Josephine," she said. "You must have lived on a different planet!"

In contrast with my lifestyle today, it *was* a different planet. Back in 1951, it was upward mobility for Mak and Ah Tetia to move into 52B, the second last *house* that was once a section of the cow shed. This was where I grew up and I only left it when I got married. I can still remember the gutter in our cement floor that served as the urinal for the cows. Babur Singh had not bothered to fill this in to save on cement. The urinal, at the foot of the wooden walls, ran all the way along the north side of the houses, in some ways, uniting them. It was great for playing marbles. Us children, each in our own home, could play a game without seeing each other's face. We took it in turns to run our marbles down the gulley. We could also send notes and little toys to our friends along this cement-conduit. If you lay on the floor and tilted your head to one side in the gutter and the other kid did the same in his house, you can actually see each other. It was great. Wooden planked walls separated the five houses. We white-washed ours with *kapor* before we moved in, and every year after that in preparation for the Chinese New Year. Babur Singh skimped on the building of the separating walls, so there were gaps between the planks and we could quite easily look into our neighbour's home. As children, we had no qualms about peeping into each other homes. Oh, the things we saw! Of course, we heard everything as well because we had no ceiling and the wooden walls stopped short of the roof. We must have had many sick neighbours because in the night, we often heard lots of moans and groans. All the five houses shared one common *attap* roof shored up by timbers. Like my parents' other hut, this had neither bathroom, toilet, running water nor electricity. Washing up was done in a small area in the corner of the kitchen and all the waste water would run into a pit outside the house which we had to clear.

Usually the waste water became green and gungy. Babur Singh was really enterprising. This was where I was born and this was where I lived until I left to get married.

My mother was wrapping *nasi lemak*, coconut rice into squares of banana leaves when I prompted that I wished to be born. Every morning, she grated coconuts to squeeze the milk from them which she used for boiling the rice over a clay stove. The fragrance of this was unbelievable — it would tickle the soft palate and you could not stop salivating. Even today, I can still remember this smell and sometimes wake up in the mornings in England longing for it. One of the accompaniments with *nasi lemak* is fried fish, so Mak fried *ikan bilis* or *selar kuning*. She was happier here than in the previous hut because she could have a hen-house and a small stretch of rich loam soil which served as garden. One of the things she always talks about at Bernadette's beautiful house is her dream of planting herbs and vegetables, although we know she would be incapable of doing it. Then, she rejoiced in gathering warm eggs from the hen-house, fresh chillies and coriander from her garden. She made omelettes with the eggs, cracked them into bowls, thinning the mixture with water. She ground fresh chillies on her *batu gilling* or granite slab and fried it with tamarind juice to create a mouth-watering *sambal*, then arranged a portion of each neatly on the mound of cooked coconut rice. When wrapped, the *nasi lemak* packets were green pyramids, parts of the leaf wilted brown by the heat of the rice.

"My *nasi lemak* is well-known in the kampong, *one*," Mak used to say.

Little things can help her bridge the gap of time, a word, a memory, a favourite dish. The pride swells her voice, blooms her face as she captures her youth in fleeting moments. Unless you knew her before, you would not have known how capable she had been, how the other villagers looked up to her. Today, she is the one who needs looking after, struck witless by Alzheimer's. I am sitting with her eating *nasi lemak* with our fingers. These days, the rice is wrapped in oiled paper, it is possible but rare to find them wrapped in banana leaves. This is Singapore in the 1990s. *Nasi lemak* is manufactured in big factories and distributed around the island. It has the flavour and taste of cellophane wrapped bread. It is what people have become used to. Each packet deprived of its home-made goodness sells for $1.50 cents, sometimes more, whereas Mak used to sell hers for 3 cents. She used to make my eldest brother Jacob sell them to his school-mates in his missionary school during recess, until the school's principal forbade her to do so. After that, she paid one of the Malay boys in the *kampong* to hawk it.

"*Nasi lemak! Nasi lemak!*" The child would cry at the top of his voice.

In the mornings, he would be competing with other itinerant hawkers, some peddling their wares on bicycles or tricycles, some in baskets slung on bamboo poles across thin shoulders: curry puffs, noodles, *thosai, roti prata, lontong,* and a myriad of other foods which served as breakfast. Villagers were roused from their sleep by the crowing of the cocks, dogs barking, sparrows twittering and the hawkers shouting out their wares, the bicycle bell of the *chye tow kway* lady, the clack-clack of the noodle-man's bamboo clackers. These were the echoes of rural life, sounds that my ears stretched to hear when my eyes opened in the mornings.

On the morning I was born, my mother forfeited her sale of *nasi lemak*. She was cooking, standing and squatting by the clay stove right up to the moment I was going to emerge. I announced my intention to begin my journey from inside to outside by causing my mother severe cramps. My father was at work and the elder boys had gone to school. Four-year-old Matthew was sitting on the threshold of the door, filling and filling his bucket with sand. Mak lifted him and put him in a home-made cot, wooden slats nailed together, just a square wooden fence on the cement floor. She gave him some broken toys to play with, a dismembered train, some wooden blocks, a rattle, all discarded by the rich English families living at the top of the hill. Another cramp seized her and she had to steady herself on the bed-post. There wasn't time to call a neighbour. She quickly spread the absorbent rice paper on the bed, heaved the heavy metal bath-pail, filling it up with warm water, got her scissors and cotton-thread ready, squares of her old sarong serving as nappies. How could I see this so clearly when I was inside her? Or was my mother's telling so potent that the scene entered my mind and stayed imbedded as my own memory? Is this the sort of thing that constitutes *false memory syndrome*? But what does it matter whose words shaped the tale? Its contents remain the same. She stacked the pillows on the bed and sat herself down in the birthing position. I was coming too quickly, she was in so much pain, she couldn't call out to Mak Ahyee next door. She would have to manage on her own. Still, she was not unaccustomed to delivering her babies by herself, she had done it so many times before, for herself and the villagers. It was simply one of those things which was a woman's lot.

Counting the number of children living, I was probably her fifth. But if I were to take into account the babies she told me about, I must be about her tenth or eleventh. There is no way to verify this total, no way of discovering how much she erred in her summation. All I know is that my mother would not lie, had no reason to lie. If I was her 11th, then Agatha was her 12th, Bernadette her 13th and Robert her 14th. There were 22 years between my eldest brother, Jacob, and my youngest brother, Robert. Perhaps all of my brothers and sisters, dead and alive, had sapped Mak's strength because by the time Robert was born, he had little immunity.

He contracted a fever when he was a few weeks old, which damaged his brain and made him a spastic, unable to sit, unable to walk or talk. She was 43 when Robert arrived, and 67 when he left.

"I delivered all my children myself and there was no problem. But I had a professional midwife for Robert and look what happened!" Mak would lament.

But she had no midwife nor friend to assist her in the delivery on the day I was born. She lay on her bed as soon as her waters broke. She was sweating so much, the bed-sheet was drenched. And it was not just from the tropical heat. Her hands gripped tight the headboard of her bed and she grit her teeth. Her hips, so used to childbirth, opened easily, so I came out fast. Only once, did she cry out, for Mak Ahyee to come to her aid. But nobody heard her. For, two doors away, the drumming had begun. When the wife of the great Chinese philosopher, Chuang Tze, died, friends going to offer their condolences found Chuang Tze playing the drum. "How can you be so happy when the woman who has been your life companion has just passed away?" They asked. "Why should I grief when she is now freed of her mortal bonds?" He said softly. On that humid, equatorial day in March, just as Mr Kurumbia Vikaram was loosening himself from his mortal bonds, I was tethering myself onto mine.

Six

$\mathscr{B}$ernadette had her son, her only child, when she was 36. Mak was exactly the same age when she had me, although I was not her first nor her last. Andy is eight, a week older than my stepdaughter Sadie's little boy, whom I would have loved to dote on as my own grandchild. When we heard that Sadie had her baby, David and I rushed to the London hospital, proud to be first-time grandparents. Sadie was lounging in her *Dawn French Fashions* outfit on the hospital bed. If she smiled, she would have look really lovely, but her young face was always expressing disapproval and bitterness, making her cheeks drag down. With great joy, I scooped the newborn babe into my arms and nuzzled into him. For me, there's something especially precious about a newborn's tender skin and its lovely baby smell. It makes my insides melt.

"Smile for Grandma," I said, tickling his chin gently. "Smile for Grandma."

"He has two grandmothers already. He can't have another," Sadie snapped.

Though I have already known her sharp tongue, I was still staggered. It was clear, that I was not kin to her, and never would be. David's family seem to believe that he had gone out to the Far East and had been disarmed by the tropical moon, fell headlong in love with an Asian floosie twelve years younger than himself, who staked a marriage claim as soon as she learnt that he had a country mansion and a Rolls Royce. They don't want to be reminded that I had been self-supporting, had two degrees and a successful career. I have learnt that it's impossible to fight prejudice. Money breeds greed. I realise that part of their rancour is due to the fact that I am a threat to their inheritance. No matter how I act, the image they have of me is already deeply ingrained in them. (I shall always be grateful that at least one member of the family turned up at Heathrow after our wedding in Singapore to welcome me with a bouquet of flowers, and that was David's younger brother. Unfortunately, his wife doesn't like David so we don't see much of each other.) Of David's three children, only the elder twin, James, allows his generous nature to overcome prejudices and so he has always been civil to me. The only thing to do is to maintain equanimity. I don't want to prevent my husband from seeing his family, but will no longer crave for their love as I once had. So I seek familial love in my friends and keep myself emotionally distant from my stepfamily. It's the only way to survive.

Naming a child was so important in Chinese communities in the old days. Family before self, so surnames came before one's own. An astrologer was usually consulted as to the most auspicious name that should accompany a mortal incarnation. Naming was similar to a fairy godmother bestowing a baby with abstract gifts of love, beauty, kindness, etc. There were meanings in names, potentials to be realised. My mother's was Soon Neo: "New Bride". That combination of innocence and anticipatory pleasure. A freshness of view. She lived life in accordance to her name, she approached everything with new zeal, innocent of duplicity. She found ways to spur herself forward even when the landscape of her days was bleak. It's a wisdom that I extract to plump up my own life.

These days, it's fashionable to give a child a western name, only the traditionalists plod on with the old custom, reluctant to lose their culture to the West. So when Andy was born, Bernadette gave him a Christian name. The name he was given must have been popular, because right across the world, without one or the other knowing, Sadie gave her baby the same name. However, except for the two boys sharing the same birth year and name, they are as different as coffee and butter. Sadie's little boy has curly golden hair and looks like one of cupid's angels, his blue eyes vacantly benign, whilst Bernadette's boy has the devil in him, coppertone in complexion like me, rather than like his mum who is fair-skinned. The Asian Andy has eyes like black marbles which speak volumes and gleams whenever he is up to something. He is so quick-witted and bright that I shake my head in amazement. At eight, he reads English and Mandarin books more suitable for someone at least three years older than himself. He is very small like his dad and is a natural on the computer, getting into the Internet and sending e-mails like a pro, working easily on Windows 98 when I am still struggling with Windows 95! The previous year, at a special concert staged by his kindergarten to welcome the local minister, he was appointed master of ceremonies, where he presented the whole programme. His parents caught it on video for me. He spoke into the microphone as though he was born to it! He definitely has Bernadette's way with people and her bubbling personality. He is an all-round livewire, asking endless questions all the time so that one can get exhausted just listening to him. But he is truly lovable.

Because Bernadette works full-time and I am there in the house on holiday, Andy and I get to do a lot together that I had missed out on with my own sons when they were his age. I take him to the playground, take him to the pictures, buy him ice creams. Since Bernadette can't swim and isn't an outdoor or sporty person, Andy and I go swimming a lot and it is an activity he identifies with me. He even comes in to my bed so that I can read him his bedtime stories. Sometimes he pretends that I am his mother, putting his little arms around me and calling me *mummy*. I know that he's not replacing Bernadette and never will, but I believe that he does it because he's an old soul who understands my suffering and is calling me mummy because I had missed out, thus giving me a unique gift. He is truly special. But he can be bothersome when I am trying to keep Mak company because he keeps on interrupting. Talking to Mak and Andy at the same time, I bat between our *Peranakan* Creole and English.

Mak and I are sitting on the settee facing the French windows. I am sweltering in the humidity, sweat gathering under my armpits and my back because Mak cannot tolerate the cool air-conditioning which hurts her legs. Her knees are now disjointed, swollen out of proportion, her hips bony and out of kilter. The large living room which is an atrium that goes right up to the ceiling normally circulates with air but today it feels as though its walls are stuffed with heavy blankets. Once again, Mak is telling me how she came to buy this house. Even her voice is getting frail. Andy places his Thomas The Tank Engine colouring book on the marble floor and is pressing his crayons hard into the white spaces. He soon tires of this and brings out a writing pad.

"Aunty Phine, I'm going to write stories like you. Can you spell for me?"

"Okay."

"How do you spell, 'creature'?"

I spell it for him. He writes down the sentence, "The aeroplane is a creature." I raise my brow thinking that he has misused the word.

"How do you spell, 'transforms'?"

I am amazed that a child his age even knows the word. I spell it for him. His face is a picture of concentration, eyebrows knitting. He looks up and asks me to spell another word, then he painstakingly writes it down. I am full of admiration for his perseverance and more, for his imagination. Gradually, the story builds up. He tells the story of an aeroplane who is a flesh and blood creature who had to transform its body into metal to protect itself. What a gem! A budding science fiction writer.

Bernadette has always been a career lady so before she had Dolores working for her, it was Mak who got up in the night to bottle-feed him, sat with him through a fever, toilet-trained him, watched his first few stumbling steps, played with him when he got bored. She was the typical old-fashioned grandmother: sweet, gentle and loving. Her personal goals were twinned with the family's, not separate. Her life was an offering to us. All my brothers' and sisters' children were nurtured and brought up by her; Andy was the last because when her memory started to fail, Dolores was brought in from the Philippines.

"*Aiiyah*! She keeps on giving me food, *lah*!" Andy complained when Mak tried to give him his dinner again for the fourth time. That was when Bernadette noticed that things were not right with our mother. Now Mak looks quizzically at Andy, who keeps on leaping up onto my lap every now and again to hug my neck and kiss me or to ask me to spell something. This is a child she had watered and pruned, yet the memory of him has somehow slipped away from her mind. She turns to me and say, "He has a delightful nature this boy, always smiling. But what's he doing here, *huh*? Who does he belong to?"

When I was eight, I could not even read, let alone write. I remember seeing a green Milo tin and thinking, "Those squiggles mean something." But why didn't I know what they meant? I was distraught that there existed a world beyond my comprehension. I felt stupid. When your father batters you with the idea that school is not meant for you, the idea digs into the tissues of your mind. You begin to believe that ignorance is bliss. But my mother, despite not having been educated herself, went beyond the reaches of her mind and saw education's potential for me. So despite earning my father's wrath and mockery, she continued to try to get me into school. Although I was a Catholic and named to honour St Joseph, I was somehow refused entry into the convent. The nun tried to explain it to Mak in English, except that Mak could not understand a single word. If she had to be converted to another religion to get me into school, she probably would have done so. Ah Tetia had no part in the endeavour to get me into school because he objected to schooling for me. "Education is bad for women," he often said. "Poisons their minds. Makes them less meek." Both my husbands could well agree to that. In my down days, I am sorry that I am not meek and mild. How peaceful and uneventful my life would have been if I could simply acquiesce and accept whatever I am told, instead of forming my own opinions and fighting oppression.

"If she is schooling, she need not be answerable to any man, *what*," my mother said in a voice I didn't usually hear. But I never forget her words. I try to live my life never being beholden to a man. And that causes problems. A man has an innate tendency to control women, whether it is through his opinions, money or power. He can't help himself. Just as a woman can't help herself and feels she has to apologise for her needs.

I used to think that it was her boldness which made my father let Mak have her own way occasionally. Only in later years did I know the truth. When I got married, she told me about it. She called it, "pillow talk". "Learn to hold your tongue till right moment," she advised. "Whisper quiet-quiet into his ear in softness after love-making. You will more get what you cannot at other times." Unfortunately, I have no such patience, shooting from the hip whenever I want to say something. Instead of rewards, it often earns me abuse. I should really try to learn. But I don't have either my mother's grace or patience.

My mother was very eye-catching when she was young. She was tall and slim-hipped even after having so many children. Her face was exquisitely shaped, her features so fine. When she married, she combed her coal-black hair into a single bun instead of the two coils on the side of her head, which were more appropriate for the young maiden. Her hair when loosened would reach her waist and I used to love standing behind her back and running the comb through it. When newly washed and dried, her hair would squeak. To maintain its gloss, she would smother her hair in freshly squeezed coconut cream and then wrapped it with a warm towel. Before I suffered from malnutrition and anemia, she used to do the same with my hair and, for a while, my hair too was as rich as hers had been. I imagine that she would have looked lovely with her dark hair spread out against white pillows, her arms and legs nut-brown and slender, capturing my father's desire. I have seen men look at the way she walked in her *sarong kebaya*, the way their eyes followed her hips swaying to an inner rhythm. What was lovely was that she was totally unconscious of her beauty and therefore she was at ease with her body, unlike women who behave in a stiff and arrogant manner because they *think* they are beautiful.

It must have been a major expedition for Mak to try and get me into school when she could neither speak English or read the written word. To say that she was a very determined woman would probably be an understatement. She put my two younger sisters and our youngest brother in the care of a neighbour and she dragged me from school to school. I was apprehensive about this new world she was going to introduce me to and yet was filled with excitement. She made me wear shoes for the occasion. Now being forced into shoes meant it *had* to be a special occasion! All the kampong children did not wear shoes. I was no exception and I particularly enjoyed kicking rainbows out of puddles, feel the grains of sand between my toes, the coarse grass sinking under my soles. This inclination to go round barefoot was inherited from the Malay side of our ancestry, so that feet could breathe and find their natural shape, unlike the Chinese who bound their women's feet to keep them from growing so that they remained dainty. But for the school-finding trip, my mother made me wear white, frilly socks with shiny black shoes which squeezed the breadth of my feet and squashed my toes. My toes are so spread out that no shoes have yet been made which can fit my feet comfortably.

"And what big feet you have," said David in his mock Red Riding Hood voice when he first saw them, making me self-conscious of them from then on. It hadn't occurred to me that Westerners would have different feet, narrow, toes pressed tightly together, sometimes with the little toe overlapping the fourth. No wonder they suffer so much from ingrown toe nails and athlete's foot. My toes are so widely spread out that the wind whistles through them, blowing dry any moisture or sweat, not allowing fungus to grow. My feet were a shock to him as his were to me. He looked down at them and said, "In actual fact they are absolutely *prehensile*."

English humour takes getting used to. The trouble was I proved my toes' agility. I usually used them like fingers only in the secrecy of my boudoir, but on that fateful day, we were at a restaurant at EPCOT in Disney World, Florida. David and I went into the Chinese restaurant for lunch. I placed my sunglasses on the table. While we were eating, I accidentally elbowed the sunglasses off the table and they fell onto the floor. Without thinking, I automatically slipped my right foot out from my shoe and used my bare toes to pick them up and in one quick sweep returned them to the table. The American guy at the table right next to us, chopsticks frozen in mid-air, said, "Gee, that's a pretty neat trick. Can you do that again? My friend didn't see it." David flushed crimson red. And it wasn't from the spicy Szechuan Chicken either.

On the day of the school hunt, my feet were hurting in my plastic shoes made for daintier feet. My mother believed that if I looked presentable, I would be accepted into school. But there is presentable and there is *presentable*. I still grow hot with embarrassment when I recall what Mak made me wear. To get me prepared, she washed my hair with Sunlight soap and combed it into two thick plaits. She even permitted me my hoop gold earrings, which I was only allowed to wear during Chinese New Year. She must have had some jewellery left over from her better days, because she pawned hers to buy me mine. A year or so before, she had my ears pierced by Inchik Kassim, the authorised village Ear Piercer. This was in the days when there was no automatic gun piercer nor alcohol swab, and ear piercing was only for girls. The only boys who had their ears pierced were those who had a problem with their testes descending. You knew which testicle had not descended properly by the side which the earring was worn. It always amuses me these days to see men wearing one-sided earrings because it reminds me of what we used to believe! I wonder what Inchik Kassim would make of it if he is still alive. The Malay man was well-liked in the village and though he was quite large in his body, he had very soft, gentle hands which kneaded the ear lobe to prepare it for taking the needle or safety pin. Most of the village girls had their ears pierced by the time they were six. So when I was due to have mine done, it was natural for Mak to engage Inchik

Kassim to do it. He began by rubbing fresh garlic juice onto my ear lobes. I was filled with horror when I saw him burn the sharp end of a silver sewing needle over a naked flame. My mother clamped me with her legs and her arms circled my body as Inchik Kassim's hand approached me. He sent the hot needle through my ear lobe and I howled and peed in my pants. Worse was to follow as he used a piece of garlic stem to force the hole to open wide. I howled and peed again. He stopped only when the garlic stem was properly lodged in my ear lobe. Then he repeated the whole procedure again for the other ear. And I repeated the whole procedure again, howling and peeing in my pants, the sand at my feet, soggy with pee. When the holes healed, he tied a red thread to the end of the stem and pulled the thread through to tie it in a loop. I am amazed today what Inchik Kassim probably knew or guessed instinctively, that garlic juice could help fight infection. Only after the pierced holes were clean and neat and not weeping was my mother given permission to put the earrings in. They were the only pieces of gold I owned which Mak intended should form part of my *pia-kim*, my wedding accoutrement. Only 24-carat gold is cherished because it has a reddish quality much loved by the Chinese and is a symbol of good luck and is reckoned to ward away evil. Warding away evil is a big thing in Chinese communities.

I also knew school hunt day was special because Mak made me wear a proper dress which she had sewed. Store bought things were a luxury. When I was a teenager, I used to leaf through old copies of *Her World* and looked at the beautiful bras and panties that were advertised and promised myself that one day, I would be able to afford them. Today, one of my pet indulgences is buying beautiful bra and pants sets. Home sewn panties did not hug to the shape of your bottom and their leg holes were so large that you have to be careful how you sat. Made from cheap cotton, they usually bulged and billowed under a dress, so figure-hugging dresses would look ghastly. Until I had my period and had small swellings on my chest, I used to run around bare-chested. How I loved it when it rained, when I could go and stand under the pouring sky, twirling and swirling, feeling the rainwater drench my hair, touch my face, my body here and there. It was magical. On cooler days, I might wear a short A-line shift. We had dresses made for the first day of Chinese New Year because it was lucky to wear something new. I remember a lament of my mother when Chinese New Year was creeping up, with its superstitious demands for new things around the house and new clothes.

"New Year coming and don't even have on cent," she said sadly.

In those years, the boys had one new shirt each from the flea market. Flea markets were dumping grounds for rejected, stolen and second-hand goods. My mother believed that a person transferred his energy to his clothes, so she would not buy us second-hand clothes worn by other people even though we were very poor. But she was not opposed to buying us new, though imperfectly sewn clothes or clothes discoloured by the sun. Flea markets were noisy affairs with hundreds of open stalls, laden with all sorts of goods, from clothes to household items to food. The most famous one was at Sungei Road and was also called *Robinson's Petang* and there were others at Macpherson's and Six Mile on Serangoon Road. Except for *Robinson's Petang* , most of the stalls tended to be open only in the evenings because it was cooler and such open markets were called *Pasar Malam* or Night Market. Usually, a noisy generator provided the electricity to light up the bulbs that were strung above the stalls. Some of the more affluent stallholders had a tent-roof but more often than not, the stalls were right in the open and if it rained, there was a rush for sheets of tarpaulin to cover their wares. Throngs of people visited such markets, their voices loud, chattering loudly; stallholders and potential customers bargaining furiously.

My sisters' and my dresses were usually made from the previous year's curtains. When I was a teenager and saw Vivien Leigh as Scarlet O'Hara in *Gone With The Wind*, pulling down the green drapes to make a new dress for herself, I recalled my childhood years and thought that such a situation was not just Hollywood dramatisation and could happen in the 1950s in Singapore. You can make grand ballgowns from curtains. Especially when you have a mother like mine, whose long, graceful fingers could snip and cut with dexterity and flair. Mak had an artistic eye and could copy a pattern from an old copy of *Her World*, a local woman's magazine. (She herself never wore anything other than the *sarong kebaya*.) She always dressed us three girls like identical triplets. People thought it was because she wanted us to look like sisters, but actually it was for a more practical reason — our dresses were cut from the same length of curtain. This was usually from the drapes that separated our living room from the bedroom. It was one thing to wear dresses in identical material with your sisters, but quite another when your brother's shirt, too, was made from the same curtain! Poor Matthew, I wondered how he felt.

So we set off that important day with me in my Chinese New Year's dress that had a full skirt, with a can-can underneath which was horribly warm and scratchy. Mak knew that can-cans were in fashion and she thought it would give the impression that we were fashionable and were not simply country bumpkins. She was definitely out to impress.

From our house to the main road, there was at least half a mile of sandy track called a *lorong*, a track which the heavy monsoon rains had dug out in places creating huge pot-holes. Fortunately, on that day, as we were making our way out to the tarmac street, Abu Bakar came by on his bullock cart and offered us a ride. Abu Bakar was one of our neighbours and he earned a living by gathering hay or cutting fresh grass and selling it to people who kept livestock. He also sold cow's manure and sometimes his open cart was piled high with hot steaming manure. He was a common sight, trundling up and down our dusty *kampong* road with his bullock cart making deliveries. Inchik Abu Bakar was in his 40s and had a firm, brown torso which he revealed because he hardly ever wore a shirt. Generally, all he would be dressed in was his checked sarong with a *songkok* on his head, as he was the day he picked us up. Fortunately, too, on the day he picked us up, he was only carrying hay.

Mak sat up-front with him and I sat at the back fidgeting with my can-can, which was causing rashes on my skin because it was such a hot day. I must have looked a sight, dressed in my Sunday best, perched on the edge of a bullock cart, my legs dangling, with hay piled up behind me and mud clinging to the wheels. He whipped the curved back of the bullock gently with a cane to get it going. The cart smelled of cow dung and I worried that the smell might transfer itself to my outfit. Still, it was such a neighbourly thing for Abu Bakar to give us a lift and my mother innocently accepted the offer. She could not have known what the consequences were going to be. The bullock's hooves and cart-wheels kicked up dust as we passed Kakar's provision shop where the scent of fragrant spices piled high in the sacks rose to meet our noses; Nenek Boyan's *kueh* stall, her colourful cakes beautifully arranged, her renowned *mee siam* in a heap in the large enamel basin. We also passed Ah Gu's bicycle shop where Ah Gu was sitting on the wooden stool outside his shop plucking at the hairs on his chin. He saw Mak sitting next to Abu Bakar and he frowned. Every evening after he shut his shop, he would come into our house to have a smoke and a pint of Guinness with Ah Tetia and they would discuss politics and put the world right. I waved to him but he did not wave back. Just at that moment, the bullock stepped into a pothole and the cart wobbled, throwing Mak against Abu Bakar who reached out to steady her. Flesh against flesh. Unknown to us, Ah

Gu was watching all this, registering it, saving it up as if for a feast. I toppled backward and the mound of hay collapsed over me. I spent the rest of the journey coughing out hay and brushing it from my dress. Further along, a waft of fishy smells reached us when we passed the fish ponds where the fishermen were bringing in the nets, the fish all bundled together, still wriggling, some escaping through torn parts of the nets. The marigolds were bright yellow, looping their vine in and out of the chain-linked fences. Maniam was by his push-cart selling ice balls, children in a queue and I was jealous of them. He was shaving the ice block across metal scrapers. Then he stuffed cooked red beans into the centre of the shaved ice and quickly compressed it into a ball and deftly tossed it around one hand as he swirled a variety of coloured syrups and evaporated milk over the sphere of ice. When Ah Tetia struck the 4-Ds, he would treat me to one and it would be the highlight of my week.

My mother had only one thing in mind that day, so she was not conscious of how she looked sitting on that cart with Abu Bakar. Her destination was Cedar School, a couple of miles away, which she had heard was very encouraging to *kampong* children and not just to children of town parents. I often wondered what gave my mother such determination to get me into school. We couldn't afford a taxi and the buses did not run from our village to the school. So after disembarking from Abu Bakar's bullock cart at the boundary of the village, we had to walk through Senette Estate, which was a housing estate. At that time, living in an *attap* hut in a shanty village, the houses here looked grand, rows and rows of concrete houses, really big houses with electric lights and fenced off gardens. I had heard, too, that they had water piped into their houses. I thought they were all millionaires, locals as well as English. As we walked, Mak's *char kiak* (wooden clogs) clacked rhythmically on the cement pavement, her body so fluid. She admired the beautiful flowers

and talked about how she would like to have them in her garden —
jasmine, frangipani, roses. She honoured the small bed of loam soil in
our yard by calling it her garden where she planted chillies and *pandan*.
As it was a long walk, Mak had brought a basket laden with two packets
of her *nasi lemak* for our lunch and ice cream soda in an F & N bottle.

Alkaff Gardens was located just before Cedar Schools, both
secondary and primary, so Mak decided that it was a good place to stop
for our packed lunch, although the gardens had a restaurant. Indeed, it
was a very scenic area designed like a Japanese tea garden, with a
restaurant, tea kiosks and an artificial lake to emulate old Japan. There
was even a little hillock which was supposed to represent Mount Fuji.
The gardens were developed by Shaik Alkaff of the Alkaff family who
came over from Indonesia in 1852. The family was originally from Yemen
and they made their money in the sale of spices, coffee and sugar and
also in the property business. The Alkaffs sailed their boats on the lake,
trained their horses in the neighbourhood and raced their bicycles and
motorcycles on specially built tracks. Years later, this place became quite
a beauty spot and also the location for the production of many Shaw
Brothers films, one starring the famous P Ramlee and his glamorous co-
star, Saloma, both of whom were my mother's favourite film stars. All
their films were like musicals, with them singing the main leads, and
Mak particularly loved P Ramlee's deep voice. But just before the war,
the British requisitioned the gardens to build a camp for the Indian troops.
In 1949, the Alkaffs sold the gardens to Sennett Realty Company. I was
not aware of the historical significance of the gardens nor their eventual
fate when we sat there for our lunch, but I loved the place. Weeping
willows stood around the lake and on the surface of its water bloomed
bright pink lotuses. Sparrows and swallows flitted about in the air without
care; butterflies and dragonflies fluttered above our heads as we sat on

the grass to eat our *nasi lemak* with our fingers. When we finished, we washed our hands in the lake. Years later, when the gardens were torn apart to build a school, they called the school *Willow Avenue Secondary School*, perhaps after the weeping willows. The hillock was dug up to fill up the lake to become the school's playing field.

Alkaff Gardens was my Eden. There I was still unconscious, my mind green and unplucked. Once I walked through it and arrived at the school which was just round the corner, I ate the apple which told me of my nakedness. I finally understood why Mak was so insistent about school. Children younger than myself in nicely starched white blouses and dark blue pinafores were not only chanting and writing their own language, they were speaking English, reading English, writing English. The very language that conquered nations, made rulers of men, built ships and aeroplanes, a language understood by many and not just a few. I was staggered. How small I felt and how ignorant. There was a place called a library where there were books, books and books; knowledge, wisdom and new worlds to be pulled out from them by the knower of the written word. There were old and new worlds compressed amongst the wood pages and suddenly the world seemed gigantic to *me* — the *katak* (frog) under the *tempurong* (coconut shell). My mother had no key to all these, yet she had brought me to their threshold. I felt humbled.

Mak asked her way to the principal's office. For someone who could not read, following directions which included signs, were not easy. So we got lost in long corridors, unpeopled rooms. Teachers and pupils looked at us in askance and I heard sniggerings in the background. What must we have looked like to them, a woman, wearing *char kiak*, a mark of the peasant, leading a child wearing a full-skirted dress with can-can underneath on a hot afternoon? By this time, my mother's brow was breaking out in nervous sweat, her hand clutching mine was clammy.

Eventually we were put out of our misery by a kindly Indian peon who led us to the principal's office. The principal was a Eurasian spinster called Miss D'Souza. She was plump, her face pock-marked and her hair short. She looked so stern that I lost hope of being admitted the moment I set eyes on her. Fortunately, she spoke fluent Malay and could converse with my mother.

"Are you Chinese or Malay?" She asked gruffly.

It wouldn't be unlike my mother to say, *Peranakan* because I knew she was as proud of her heritage as I am. But lately, she had heard that the Chinese were calling us *pariahs* of the race because we diluted their purity. The Malays did not want to own us either because we ate pork and worshipped Chinese Gods. As far as the British were concerned, we were plain Chinese. My mother instinctively knew that her answer would make a difference as to whether I was accepted into school or not. So she blurted out, "Chinese."

"What's the child's name?"

"Josephine," my mother said. She pronounced my name as *JosJosFien*. "We are converted Catholics."

The principal frowned when she heard the corruption of my name and must have been trying to work out what my mother was saying. My heart thumped at the severity of her look. Eurasians like Miss D'Souza were usually Catholics, so my mother's mention of us being Catholics was probably a point in my favour. I saw my fortune change a little, for now I was as anxious as my mother to get me into school.

"Has she got a Chinese name?"

"*Ya*," my mother lied quickly. "But I don't know how to write it, *lah*. I have no schooling. It's not in birth certificate because my husband forgot to give it to English clerk."

"Why is her father not here?"

Mak seemed to be suddenly reduced in size. She shifted uneasily and was quiet for a bit, seeming to inspect her clogs. I suspected she was thinking up some lies but fortuitously decided to tell the truth, her speech stumbling over the rocks of her illiteracy, words that are seared forever in my memory.

"My husband stern-stern man. He thinks girls no need to study, *what*. Don't study very terrible for me. So want my daughter to be educated. I don't know anything. Very *bodoh*. Stupid. Cut off from so many things. Can't read road signs. Not even my name." Her voice thinned and seemed to tear. "Must make my daughter able to read words on signboards: *Come, Stop, Go, Wait, Careful*. Read newspaper. She must not be like me. Stupid. If educated, she can work, earn own money. No need to ask from man. No need to *makan darah* (eat blood)."

Miss D'Souza sat very still, so still, I thought she had not heard my mother. Her face grew hard like stone and her mouth worked wordlessly. Was she angry at my mother's rhetoric? Did she see me as peasant stock unfit to be educated? I thought my career had ended before it had a chance to begin. She seemed to be examining my mother, weighing her words. Then I heard her heave a loud sigh and thought I noticed a moistness in her eyes — could it be due to the waft of chillies and *asam pedas* emitting from the school tuckshop? When she found her voice, she said, "Men like your husband are still living in the dark ages. Do you see any boys in this school? Am I a man? Nonya, you have a lot of courage to defy your husband. I'm only sorry that you missed your chance but let us help you to ensure that your daughter will make you proud of your efforts. Get someone to write her Chinese name and bring it to me and she can start school in Second Term."

My mother was so moved that she could only keep bowing and bowing in gratitude, her head bobbing up and down like one of those

Chinese clay figurines with a hinged neck. She pulled me out of Miss D'Souza's office as if she was afraid Miss D'Souza might change her mind. But still, she didn't speak.

"I will make you really, really proud of me, Mak," I said afterwards, dancing alongside her on our walk home. "I shall read you stories from books!"

My mind was filled with the image of the library and all the books I will soon be able to read that at first I did not notice that Mak had gone quiet. She should be triumphant since she had achieved her goal of getting me into school. I did not know that her mind had raced ahead worrying about where she was going to find the money to buy the school uniforms and books. Father had said he would not contribute.

"Want to go school, must work first. Get money to pay for uniform and books," she said. "I must sell more *kueh*. Maybe can take in the neighbour's washing. You can help me before you leave for school or after you come back."

"I'll help, Mak. I'll help."

We stopped at the shophouses before our village. Along the five-foot-way, there was an old fortune teller sitting at his little wooden stall papered with red and gold rectangles of Chinese characters, his fortune-telling bird twittering and hoping in its cage. When he had a customer, Ah Pek would rattle fortune sticks in a bamboo container. He would release the bird who helped to pick out the stick which told the customer his future. Then Ah Pek read the oracle and provided the interpretation. Ah Pek was very thin and had no hair on his head but had a long wispy beard and he spoke with a rasping, smoky voice. I was curious as to why my mother wanted to consult him on this particular day.

"Ah Pek," she said to him in Teochew. "Can give my daughter a good Chinese name or not?"

She meant an auspicious name which would bring luck. Then she proceeded to tell him why she needed it.

"What is your family name?"

"Chia," my mother said.

"Nice. It's *Xia* in Mandarin. It means gratitude. You call her what name, now?"

"Ah Phine," she said.

"Josephine," I interjected. "My name is Josephine. It's from a Christian saint."

"Phine sounds like *fen*, fragrant. Your daughter has a bright face, like *Yue,* the moon. Why don't we call her *Yue Fen*, Moon Fragrant? (Fragrant Moon)."

He spoke the name in Mandarin, the literate language of the Chinese which was what I had to learn now that I was classed a Chinese. It would be foreign to my tongue for no one in my family spoke the language, our Peranakan Creole being a hybrid of Malay and Teochew, a Chinese dialect. As in Malay, nouns come before adjectives.

"Yes, that sounds lovely," my mother said.

I had already been used to being called Ah Phine, so I was not particularly interested in using another name. Would having a new name change the way I was? Is naming a kind of branding? I decided to amuse myself and tickled the bird under its chin. With meticulous care, Ah Pek spread out a clean sheet of rice paper. He dipped his Chinese brush into the pot of black ink then held his hand poised in mid-air as if he was waiting for inspiration. When it came, he let it flow through his arm into his hand and into the brush so that hand and brush moved in symphony to each other and my new Chinese name flowed from his fingers expressing itself in beautiful calligraphy onto the rice paper. As far as I was concerned, it was without doubt lovely brushwork but it had nothing to do with the essence of me. The name did not connect. Neither Mak nor I could read what was on the paper and I was thinking: This is going to be hard to write.

And I still can't write it today.

Seven

$\mathcal{B}$efore I went to school, I was a frog under the coconut shell, my *kampong* was the coconut shell. After I went to school, the coconut shell became bigger. But I was still a frog, limited by my upbringing and attitudes. Schooling shifts the walls of the coconut shell but doesn't make them disappear. Unless you break free, dare to search and venture outside the shell. We know who we are in the confines of the coconut shell, but once we step outside, into the larger world, under the open sky, we lose ourselves in the crowd, lose our clear space, our sense of who we are, and perhaps our sense of importance. For that security, we confine ourselves. Prison walls can be made of different things.

My mother is now a frog imprisoned under the coconut shell of her debilitating mind. Her world is limited to what she can grasp at any one moment. Nothing exists for her except what her Self makes up. *Cogito, Ergo Sum* — I think therefore I am. Can she think about who she really is? She *believes* she is what she thinks, but those who have known her know that her perception of herself is inaccurate, that her thinking is flawed. She construes a Self which is really a conglomerate of supposed ideas of herself, her life a hotch-potch of what she remembers. In her make-belief setting, the Self she creates is real. It is fiction at its best. Her belief is absolute.

The first time I suspected that something was wrong with her was on one of my trips back to Singapore when she told me, "I went to Australia on holiday on my own, you know. Oh, I had good-good time!"

Mak still cannot construct a whole sentence in English and can only string some words together, words which she borrows from listening in to our conversations, TV soap operas and sitcoms; sentences without articles nor tenses as in the languages we speak. With her usual determination, she had been intent on conversing with David in his language when they first met. He recalled the day when we had lunched at a smart hotel in Singapore. I had gone to get the car and David was waiting with Mak in the hotel lobby. Mak pulled up her *sarong* to expose her knee and she grumbled to David, "My leg very trouble, *lah*." With such limitations and no travel sense, I could not imagine her going off to Australia on her own. She would not know how to go about buying herself a ticket, let alone board a plane. Her knowledge of the world is limited to the coconut shell of her life. Bernadette confirmed that the trip was a construction of Mak's imagination. Bernadette had told her of her own trip to Australia and somehow my mother had seized the experience as her own. When you are desperate for new memories, you steal from others. That was the beginning.

I watch her now with a feeling of deep sadness as she plays out her tragic comedy because in some ways, the things she makes up are funny, in others, pathetic. How deep do her emotions go? Are her emotions like her memory, only skimming the surface of her heart and mind? She is animated one minute, full of joy, and the next she is sullen, full of complaints. It can't be easy for Bernadette and her husband, especially when they have guests for lunch. Mak is extremely voluble, talking to one of their friends, Kenny, who is also a *Peranakan*. She talks to him in our *Peranakan* Creole in a voice which is louder and more shrill than usual as though someone else and not herself has taken control over it. She talks as if she has never had a chance to talk before and now that she has a captive audience, she has to bare her heart. If you did not know the true story, you would believe some of the things she says because she is so convincing. She acts like a petulant child and seems almost malicious in intent which is totally unlike my mother. She tells Kenny that Bernadette and her husband do not talk to her all day, that Dolores chats over the fence to the neighbour's maid rather then look after her, that she has been discarded to the ground floor room next to Dolores' as though she were the servant.

"*Apa nak buat? Sudah tua, apa.* What to do? So old, *what.*" She laments.

In reality, Bernadette allocated that particular room to her to save her climbing up the stairs. Initially when they moved in and her mind was still in working order, Mak had been overjoyed with her room because it had ensuite facilities and had easy access to the kitchen and living room. For a woman who has lived most of her adult life in make-shift huts without proper sanitation, water or electricity, to have an entire room to herself for the first time with bathroom attached, running water and electricity, she has indeed been reinstated to the glory of her parents' wealthier days. Why she should then consider that she has been relegated to the position of a servant is difficult to understand. She has always been such a positive person with such a lovely nature that this dark side seems out of character. It appears that Alzheimer's is the culprit for these personality changes. But whatever the cause, the reality of having to deal with these strange manifestations of dark moods is a living nightmare.

Later, Bernadette's husband says to me, "You see that's why we can't invite business colleagues to the house. Kenny understands because he's a close friend but people we know casually in business might not understand. Especially when Mak makes it out that we ill-treat her."

Her sense of being neglected and ill-treated seems a large part of her make-up now. My heart bleeds that she should feel like this. I want so much for her to be happy and comfortable in her old age, as I am sure my brothers and sisters want her to be. I want her to feel loved the way she has loved me and cared for me. But an unspoken sorrow inside her makes her sit down and weep sometimes and I know there is nothing I can say to console her. Every now and again, she gets it into her head that someone is coming to steal something from the house and she will go to the French windows to keep watch. To Bernadette's continuous frustration, she would collect ornaments that Bernadette has placed around the house to put them away in the cupboard in her room so that whoever comes into the house would not be able to steal them. What we didn't know was that our mother was also putting away food, presumably for leaner times. When Mak was in hospital, Bernadette opened the cupboard to retrieve her ornaments and found the shelves full of ants because Mak had also put away fruits and food for goodness know how long, food which she couldn't remember was hidden. No words can reassure Mak that she is being fed and looked after when she gets into that sort of mood. I pray that deep inside her, she knows she is being loved and cared for, that there is a part of her which still remains wholesome and beautiful. I sometimes wonder if this need to save food and things comes from her days of deprivation, and whether her sense of persecution stems from my father's treatment of her. I have a memory of an incident which will not go away. I remember that on the day I was told I could go to school, I had been elated but my father spoiled the day for me. I remember pressing my face into the folds of my mother's *sarong* in a bid to comfort her as she sat huddled in the corner of the darkened kitchen with the tears sliding silently down her cheeks. That one time, I felt the air thick with her sense of hopelessness, so thick that I wanted to take a *parang*, wield it to slice through the thicket to free her. I felt so responsible because it was her endeavour to get me into school, her dream to want something different for me, that had caused her the trouble.

My father was a volatile man. My eldest brother exhibits this same trait and impatience. There is a bitterness in him that scrapes him raw. Perhaps experiences with our father has marked him like this and I wish that he can let go of the past. Perhaps he is also bitter about the opportunities he had lost because he helped put us through school. This is understandable but, grateful as I am to him, I also feel that it wasn't too late for him to improve his lot if he really wanted to — and he should have, and could have, because he was very intelligent. But then again, perhaps marriage intervened, its responsibilities, the need to support wife and children. How much are we a victim of circumstances and how much are we our own person? Although Jacob is darker skinned than our father, I see our father in him. Ah Tetia was so smitten by my mother's beauty that he thought all other men would look at her in the same way that he looked at her. He wanted her where he could be assured of her fidelity. If she strayed from his field of surveillance, he would get edgy, his imagination going wild. This trait of his was exactly like my ex-husband's. KC always insisted that he drove me everywhere. If I was lunching with a girlfriend, he would drive me to the meeting place and at a specified time, turn up to pick me. He was terrified that I would appear attractive to other men, so he made me button up my blouse to my neck in all this heat and humidity, made sure that he selected my clothes so that they were not sexy, and made sure that I wore no make-up. He was a prison guard, rewarded me when I behaved, bought me food, nice things, took me on holidays. But I had to obey his rules. I could not crave for the outdoor or sunshine if he was not there to watch over me, could not crave to stretch my legs or my mind without his sanction. When I was pregnant with my younger son, he said,

"I wanted you to be pregnant so that you won't think of leaving home."

And I saw my mother's fate becoming mine, a child every other year, a baby still in the arms and another on the way. I saw myself bloated, a beached whale unable to reach the open sea, and was terrified. I needed to swim. And then one day, I snapped. I was working as a conventions co-ordinator for an international hotel and KC phoned my secretary to find out which restaurant I was at for my luncheon meeting with a male client. He came and sat in the same restaurant throughout my meeting, to keep an eye on the predator, as if all men were interested in his wife. But that is another story.

My mother's story was already written the moment she was born. She was born a woman, in a day and age when only a man could determine a woman's fate. Her life was in his hands. It was this she wanted to change for me. Education is the key to undo the lock that men have over women. If I could break out of the stronghold, I could write my own life story. I don't have to play the part a man sets out for me. I can write my own part. This is what my mother has given me, a pen to write my own story. But she was skillful, brought talent to her part, brought her own individuality to the role my father prescribed for her. Though she remained a dutiful wife, she played other roles in the village. The village folks called my mother *Nonya*. Even with her multitude of chores, she always found time for others. One of the things she was good at was delivering babies. Professional midwives and doctors were not readily available then. My mother's training came from the delivery of her own children: she never went to hospital when she brought us into the world. Only Robert, her last child, was delivered by a professional midwife. Therefore, it was ironic that of all her children, it was Robert who became damaged, his brain filled with water when he was a few weeks old and it swelled disproportionately to his wasted body. He spent his 24 years of life imprisoned in his body and mind, never learning to sit, crawl or toddle. He came as a child and left as a child. Yet he taught us so much, with his quick chuckles, his wordless voice, his eyes which flashed brightly whenever I sang him a song. Till today, I can remember the songs which gave him pleasure. One of his favourites was Simon and Garfunkel's *Sounds of Silence*. All his life, he could only swallow baby food. But he would not eat if someone did not sing to him or if the radio was not switched on. He signaled his approval of a song by thumping his permanently clenched fist vigorously on the mattress or by rocking his congenitally crossed legs. My third elder brother, Matthew, was most affected by Robert's death, though he knew it was for the best. Usually a placid character not given to raising his voice or criticising others, Matthew was pushed into renouncing Agatha because she refused to attend Robert's funeral on account of the fact that the death "energies" would interfere with her own. But before Robert came and tied my mother to his daily needs, Mak served as the village midwife. My father could have shown a little pride of his wife's natural expertise, but like a lot of Chinese men, praise from him was rare. Instead, he seemed to enjoy putting her down.

"You think you come from a university or what, *huh*? You can't even write your own name. If you make a mistake, you could be sent to prison, you know."

In a sense, my father was right to caution her, babies snatched by death at birth were not uncommon in those days. There were no pre-natal check-ups for the *kampong* women, no tests. Perhaps the high mortality was due to poor maternal health which resulted in a sickly child, poor hygiene or the lack of aftercare or the lack of proper nutrition after the child was born. Who knows? Carrying a child to full-term in that era wasn't a guarantee of a live birth. I can remember seeing the corpse of an eight-month-old foetus, a perfectly formed child who arrived too early and did not survive. The mother wrapped him in cheap cotton layette and placed him on a table whilst we all sat around to mourn the clipped life, the mother wailing the loudest. Surely my mother was aware of all this, but she paid little attention to her own welfare or what might happen if the babies she delivered were to die. She was that sort of special person. She felt it her duty to assist other women in deliveries, when many could not afford either a midwife or doctor. Mak seemed to have a capacity for beating off my father's words, her face simply remaining serene as she went about her self-imposed vocation. The trouble was that babies tended to arrive at all hours of the day and night. Her departure from home late at night always ignited Father's jealousy and wrath.

"Are you sure you're not meeting a man?"

"Why don't you come with me, *lah*?" She suggested in a quiet voice.

When I was the youngest, she would take me with her whenever she attended to a birth, so long before I knew how babies were made, I knew where they came from. The first delivery I witnessed made such an impression that I can never rub it from my memory. It was when Petai gave birth. Petai was a huge Indian lady who did not look any different whether she was pregnant or not. At that time, she seemed rather old to me, but I expect she was no more than thirty. The voluminous sari that she wore was adjusted accordingly as the pregnancy progressed. She was so black that the Malays likened her to the bottom of a claypot, *macham pantat belanga*. In response, she would laugh showing off her false teeth which gleamed whitely like a toothpaste advertisement. She had sent for my mother in the late evening, the niece banging loudly at our front door. When we left the house, Ah Tetia was not at home. We only had a carbide lamp to light the way through a darkened *lorong*. I clutched my mother's hand tightly as I stumbled along the rutted path, the carbide lamp hissing and spitting. In typical Indian melodrama, there were scores of relatives at Petai's house, all talking in excited tones when we arrived. The house smelled of curry and spices. There was so much commotion that no one noticed me going to sit cross-legged, in the room underneath the table opposite the bed where the delivery was to take place. So I watched it all. I saw Petai's folds and folds of ebony flesh, her huge belly exposed, naked. Lying there on the bed like an over-turned cow, her legs straddled, her arms threshing the bed. Petai moaned a terrible moan, making me cover my ears with my hands. Yet, I heard her cry, first in spasms, then in a piercing scream. Besides hers, my mother's voice was gentle, calm, coaxing her, instructing her. And then I clasped my mouth in horror as a flash-flood of fluid and blood came from between Petai's legs to be caught in several enamel basins by my mother and her helper. Petai screamed. I thought she was going to explode. And then, this small, wet thing emerged, rushing down the sluice of blood and water. My mother put her fingers in the baby's mouth to clear it, then turned it upside down and gave it a sharp smack on its bottom. I was surprised, wondering why Mak needed to make the baby cry. All that time, Mak was cool and efficient, cutting the cord that was strung between baby and mother. She handed the boy-child to the helper to be washed, then she pushed hard into Petai's belly, kneading it till Petai complained. And then it came, that ugly mass of blob that looked like liver, covered in dark blood and scum. I hated eating pig's liver for months afterwards, not that our family could afford much of it anyway. When we went outside to show off the baby, everyone congratulated my mother for her work.

Looking at my mother now, you would not believe that she was the same woman who was so efficient, so calmly delivering other people's babies, the same woman whose mind today cannot even remember if she has eaten.

Going home late, she had to deal with my father's wrath. When he came home from the cabaret and found that she was out and not waiting up for him like a dutiful wife, he unleashed drunken words which tore at her self-esteem. It was perfectly acceptable for him to amuse himself with the ladies at the cabaret in New World, but if he thought that she encouraged a man to look at her, he would not let her be. His jealousy was legendary.

On that auspicious day when I had cause to celebrate getting into school, he was intercepted by Ah Gu on his way home. Ah Tetia usually goes to work on a bicycle that Ah Gu had sold him. When passing Ah Gu's shop, he would ring the bell to signal to Ah Gu that he was home so that Ah Gu could come around and the two of them would carry weights in the sandy yard. He cycled more than twenty miles a day for his work and carried weights every evening. He didn't have much hair but he had a superb body. Unfortunately, he poisoned himself with numerous cigarettes a day and that was what got him eventually, at the age of 57. He loved to talk politics like most men, so Ah Gu and him would have a drink together after their workout. Mostly, it was Ah Gu who drank Guinness, while Ah Tetia smoked. Unlike my mother, my father did not have either Malay or Indian friends. He mixed with foreigners only when he was obliged to, like at work. That evening, Ah Gu was waiting outside his shop, his face a tabloid of melodrama.

"What's wrong?" my father asked.

"Did you know what I saw today, *huh*? Your wife sitting thigh to thigh with that wretched Abu Bakar."

Their exchange was revealed to Mak later in Father's heated, over-wrought voice. It was this incident, his treatment of her that woke something in me, something dark and malcontent. After all, aren't I my father's daughter, too? Can we escape our genetic inheritance? On that day, we knew from the moment we heard him arriving that he was upset. His bicycle screeched to a halt in the yard. He must have run over a rat because we heard it squeal in agony. The wall of our kitchen was made with wooden planks up to about four feet high and above that were simply wooden slats so we could see him from inside. He was certainly in a state of agitation. Usually, he would lean the bicycle neatly against the kitchen wall, but this time he simply let it fall and we heard it crash.

"Are you alright or not?' Mak asked as he strode into the kitchen, like an enraged bull, his nostrils flaring, his eyes narrowed.

We had just sat down on the kitchen floor in a circle to begin dinner. Since we did not own a dining table, the enamel plates holding our food were placed on the rough cement floor in the centre in front of our crossed legs. In one corner of the kitchen was our washing-up area, a ridge of concrete separating it from the rest of the kitchen, where the water ran under the wooden wall into a cavity in the ground outside which we had to clear daily. Alongside this area which measured no more than two square foot was a giant earthern-ware Ali Baba type container called a *tempayan*. This was for storing drinking water fetched from half-a-mile away from the standpipe and it had a wooden lid over it to prevent the mice and rats getting into it. Next to it stood our meat-safe, which was a free-standing larder. As we had no refrigerator, this was used for storing the cooked food. Inside the frame of its two doors were fine wire-meshing, which let in the air and kept the food cool. Under each of the four legs of the meat-safe was a small saucer filled with water so that ants could not pass from floor to the legs of the larder.

Four-year-old Bernadette was on Mak's lap and Mak was using her fingers to put rice and meat into her own mouth to chew and soften before bringing it out of her mouth to feed it to Bernadette. Her intentions were good; most mothers and grandmothers did this at that time to make sure that bones did not get into a child's food and that it was soft enough to swallow. Years later, when Mak was looking after Agatha's children, she used the same method to Agatha's disapproval..

"You're feeding my children germs from your mouth! You'll make them sick. You better stop this filthy habit, *ahh!*"

We were seven on the kitchen floor that evening. All of us, except Bernadette, looked up when Ah Tetia came in through the door. He cursed in Teochew and I felt my mother react by drawing herself inward as though her instinct bade her to protect herself from what was to come. I have never heard her retorting and most times I wished she would. Sometimes, I was disappointed that she would be so passive in the face of his temper. Only later did I learn that if she had reacted, if she had responded, she would have fueled his anger more. Sometimes he might come on all loud and abusive but after a while, he would trail off into sullenness, but this was not that sort of time. There was no reprieve in store that evening. In his madness, he strode into the room, reached out with his foot to kick our plates and dishes. Everything went flying, enamel plates clattering, bits of food spreading. Shocked, Bernadette started to cry. Ah Cob who was then in his late teens leapt to his feet to restrain Ah Tetia as he made towards my mother.

"How dare you lay a hand on your father!" Ah Tetia said, punching Jacob in the face. As Ah Cob reeled backward, he knocked the wooden lid off the *tempayan*. His bottom sank down into the jug. My father fished him out roughly and kicked him out of the house. Next, he shoved Jeremiah and Matthew out of the kitchen and bolted the door. Everything happened so fast. He snatched the baby from Mak, and shoved Bernadette in my arms. Then he pulled my mother's hair and her bun loosened. Her face that day is imprinted in my mind forever, a look of utter fear as he dragged her into the part of the house which was our sleeping quarters.

"*Chow Chee Bai!* (Smelly cunt!)" He swore, though I didn't know what the words meant then. He slammed the door hard. Agatha started to whimper and I told her to shut up. I was shaking from terror and from a new rage that I did not understand. Something was germinating in the deep well of my being. I heard my father's angry shouts and the sharp slaps, the dull kicks, a body crashing into the furniture, things falling. But not once did I hear my mother cry out.

It seemed to last forever.

It was not the first time nor the last. Jacob had tried to stop that sort of thing happening. Time and again, he would bear the brunt of our father's fists. I believe that it was eventually the cause of his marrying early and leaving home. And yet, of all my brothers and sisters, Ah Cob seems the least tolerant of our mother's debilitating mind. He loses his patience when she says things that are, in his opinion, wrong. He argues with her, probably not understanding that it is the disease that is making her act peculiarly. There is no doubt of his love for her. After all, he was a filial son and supported her financially after our father died. But Ah Cob is a man who has difficulty in expressing his emotions and does not exhibit any outward show of love. Perhaps in his mind, he thinks that by arguing with her, he is keeping her sane and from degenerating so rapidly.

On that day when my father let loose his anger on my mother, something rose from the deep seat of my being. My sense of injustice framed itself in blasphemous thoughts. Was it not enough that he belittled her as he belittled us? His words used to make me weep. He said to me many times in Teochew, "*Bor eng kai! Chiak leoh bi!* (Worthless! A waste of rice!)" or he might say, "*Anai ou! Bor nang ai!* (So black [therefore, by implication, ugly]! No one wants (to marry)." For my mother and myself, I imagined myself with an arm that rippled with muscles. I saw myself thrust my manly fist into my father's face. It would force him to make up excuses like my mother had to do to neighbours: "Oh, I ran into a door"; "You know, I totally missed that jutting pole"; "I slipped and knocked my head on the edge of the table." These were the same kind of excuses I made in my later years. A woman is shamed when her husband beats her up, as if she feels herself unworthy and at fault. Today, I know what that feels like. But when I was a child and did not known this, I couldn't understand why my mother did not retaliate. I was so furious with my father, and saw only that my father was to blame entirely. It was the one time I wished I was a man. Then I would do to him what he was doing to my mother. But I was *not* a man and my child's fists would hardly wound him. I could only cower on my side of the door and listen with fear. But a huge wave of feeling was washing over me. That was when I knew I hated him. My father never even gave us the chance to tell him about my acceptance into school.

Eight

$\mathcal{M}$y mother's perseverance got me accepted into school, her fortitude kept me in it. At that time, I didn't understand what a tremendous achievement it had been. Today, I marvel at her source of strength. Where and how did a woman of such illiteracy gather and pool her resources? Where did her intelligence and resilience come from? How did she manage to get my father to accept the situation? Perhaps she simply stood her ground on the issue? When she eventually summoned the courage to tell my father that I had been accepted into school, he shrugged then said, "*Aiiyah!* Do what you like. But don't expect me to pay for anything. If I find out that you are using the food money for the child's books, I'll belt you!"

"I'll help you, Mak," my eldest brother Jacob said. "I can give Maths tuition to the village kids after school and earn a bit of money."

Ah Cob was already 21 and undergoing training at a Teacher's College. Thank goodness, not all men thought in the same vein as my father. He was a very good brother, concerned about our welfare though he was strict and could be hard like our father. Ah Cob was forward thinking and he, too, was instrumental in my receiving an education. For that I will always be grateful to him. He persuaded the neighbours to part with $5 a month. He told them that the children had to be good in

Arithmetic even if they were simply going to be hawkers and shopkeepers. He gathered his pupils, aged between six and fourteen; found some empty orange crates to use as stools and desks and there began his tuition school on our cement floor in the living room. I can still hear the younger kids saying in unison, "Good morning, Sir!" followed by their chanting of the multiplication table, in highly accented English, "TU times TU is FOR; TU times TREE is SIKS." Jacob was an excellent teacher but his sternness made us frightened of him. Anyone, including myself who didn't get things right, got our knuckles rapped by his wooden ruler. He told me that my capacity to learn Arithmetic was minimal, which was true and that I get all the English tenses mixed up, which was also true. Like our father, Ah Cob did not mince words nor give compliments. When I said I was going to be a writer, he laughed.

"You're joking! You can't even string a sentence together properly!"

I burned with shame at my preposterous dream. Firstly, you need talent, and secondly, you need money to write. It seemed that I possessed neither. However, I am still indebted to Ah Cob, without whose efforts to bring in the money, complementing my mother's, I would not have been able to go to school at all and thus would not have even begun to live my dream as a writer. When I told my mother my dream, she did not laugh like Jacob, instead, she said, "Work that calls is guided by soul to express spirit. It is work that will bring you greatest happiness. But never forget to thank those who help put you on path."

It was her way of telling me to be grateful to Ah Cob because she knew how he and I clashed sometimes. So when I started working, I always bought him gifts; and when I moved to England, I sent him an air ticket to join our wedding party and gave him a good holiday. My eldest brother is thirteen years older than I am. Like all my brothers, he is very handsome. My family falls in two categories, the dark and the fair. Jacob,

Matthew, Robert and I have our mother's complexion whilst Romia, Agatha and Bernadette inherited our father's fair complexion. When we three sisters stand together to pose for a picture, no one would believe that I am related to the other two. My schooling set a precedence for my two younger sisters so that when their time came, my father did not even bother to protest. But even Jacob's tuition money was insufficient to buy books and uniforms and all the other necessary things for school.

"Ah Yee's mother is pregnant and she can't squat down easily," I volunteered. "Since I am in afternoon school, I can do the washing for her before school. And when I come back from school, I can do the ironing."

"Alright, *lah*. I shall help you with the saris. I will show you how to fill the iron with coals."

Mak had to wash the clothes of nine people everyday by hand. Up until then, helping her with the washing was a game for me. After all, I was only eight and a half years old. She gave me the little things to wash, underpants, knickers, handkerchieves. Now I would have to learn to wash clothes properly. My education was hard-earned and not just by myself. That is why I appreciate being educated so much, as so many other people's dreams sit upon my shoulders. My fulfillment is also theirs. It was not all hard work because my mother had a way of making every chore seemed an undertaking of the spirit and she would do everything joyfully and I had picked up this trait from her, singing whilst doing my chores to lighten the load. We'd carry the pails of washing to the bathroom and took turns to draw water from the well, always careful not to pull up the catfish that lived at the bottom of the well to eat up the algae and mosquitoes. We sat on our low, wooden stools and scrubbed the clothes on wooden washboards. We washed the clothes with Sunlight soap until we could afford a better detergent like FAB. The corrugated zinc bathroom had no roof, so we sat under the warm open sky, the tops of banana and coconut trees visible, birds flying overhead. The bathroom door would be flung open so that we could keep an eye on Bernadette and Agatha playing Balloon (hop-scotch) in the sand. Mak sometimes strapped Robert to her back with a sarong or left him in the oval metal bucket which she lined with a folded bed sheet. Mak always used this time to entertain me with her days of plenty in Malacca. I loved listening to her voice, to the happiness which made it glow when she talked about her family and her privileged life in Malacca.

"You know, Mak. I will study very hard and when I finished school, I will earn a lot of money and I shall take you to Malacca to see the place where you used to live and anywhere you want to go."

She fell silent at this and she looked down to concentrate on her washboard.

My mother took me to *Robinson's Petang* to buy the material for my school uniform. *Robinson's Petang* parodied *Robinson's*, the plush English department store at Raffles Square with the status of a *Harrods* only in its name. One was in the posh part of town, the other in the slums. One sold goods imported from England and America, the other leftovers from sales and goods that fell off the back of a lorry. As a Christmas treat, Ah Tetia would take us to the real *Robinson's* to window shop. We would take a rickety *Tay Koh Yat* bus or sometimes STC's number 18 to Finalyson Green, then walk a short way through Change Alley, known for its bazaar of moneychangers, mostly South Indian immigrant men who haggled in loud voices and expressive gesticulations. In the alley, stalls selling local crafts of Chinese and Malay dolls, basketwork and batik prints to tourists spilled onto the narrow alley, making it seem even narrower.

In the big store, most of the clientele were Caucasians. My sisters and I would gawk at the Christmas decorations and the beautiful displays of things beyond our reach. There is a sense of awe when one looks at things unattainable, but it also gives you something to work towards. At that time, so far removed as I was from that world, I did not even harbour any hope of attaining any of the beautiful things and was envious of the children who queued to sit on Santa's lap to whisper what they wanted for Christmas, kids whose clothes looked princely. I fantasised about being play companion to some rich kid so that I could share in her luxuries, even if they were not mine to own. How greedy I was! In our excursions to *Robinson's,* I noticed that the security guard kept on following us everywhere. He must have looked at our clothes and decided that we could not afford anything there. But when I was a child, I thought he was concerned for our safety. Once, when I was about four or five, I actually got myself onto Santa's lap only to be pulled away roughly by my father. I thought the presents that Santa was giving away were free. Years later, even before I could afford to shop there, a tragedy occurred. The store was destroyed by fire and some people were trapped in the lift, which became their crematorium. The store was then rebuilt on another site in Orchard Road, and later moved to its present location a few doors away when the store expanded. One of my pleasurable memories was when I was able to walk into its Orchard Road store with my mother for her to choose a present for herself. After her long struggle to educate me, I was able to repay her somewhat by buying her some of the nice things she grew up with. But that time of her life was so distant from her many years of deprivation that she found it hard to spend money on trivial things.

"How much is this?" She pointed to an Italian ceramic posy.

"$180. Why don't you have it?"

"What? That's a year's rent for our house in *Potong Pasir.*"

"Mak, you're not in *Potong Pasir* now. You live in a nice HDB flat. Have it to put on your coffee table."

"What about this? How much?"

It was a display doll with blonde hair and blue eyes.

"$80. Mak, would you like it?"

"I just like to know how much they cost."

She spent the entire afternoon pointing to different things and asking their prices, being thrilled to bits that we could actually afford to buy them. She beamed at her good fortune, infecting me with her joy. This was one of her characteristics which was very endearing: she was always thankful and never took anything for granted. In the end, she chose a musical box, a ballerina in a delicate tutu poised on the toes of one foot. When the music box was wound, the ballerina twirled round and round.

"*Aiiyah!*" She said with a child's delight and naivete. "How does it turn-turn, *lah*? Where is music coming from? People are so clever nowadays, *hor*?"

But in the early 1950s, our family shopped at street stalls. A special outing was to *Robinson's Petang*. A Malay name meaning Afternoon or Evening Robinsons, the thieves' market on Sungei Road was a multitude of outdoor stalls sprawled alongside the river or *sungei*. Since the market was in the open, the vendors chose to set up their stalls in the late afternoon to take advantage of lengthening shadows, away from the blazing equatorial sun. For this same reason, outdoor markets can be seen all over the island in the cool of the evening at dusk and these are called *Pasar Malam*. A night market could have stalls spreading over half a mile long. More often than not, the general populace shopped at these night markets, not at the High Street in town with its expensive shops. At *Robinson's Petang*, as with the night markets, food stalls compete for custom with stalls selling clothes, household products, vehicle parts and everything else that could be bought and sold. The origins of some of these items were suspicious, giving rise to its name thieves' market. The sounds and smells were varied. My favourite was always food. I loved the atmosphere. Even now in England, I would seek out market stalls to remind me of my childhood. Although my childhood was a time of deprivation, it was also a time when I felt that people living in the village were friendly and had genuine warmth for each other. I have a favourite market in England, *Blackbushe* in Hampshire, where a thousand stalls are sprawled over the site of a former airport each Sunday. David thinks I'm mad because on most days, the wind howls through the open air market and the rain comes down in sheets, but I love the market prattle of the stallholders, the interesting stalls and the foods. Whenever I hanker for a bit of Singapore, I'd drive to Blackbushe, 45 minutes away, eat at my favourite nooddle stall in Row D, stop for lunch at Asian Foods for my vegetarian bryani or chappati with mashed spinach. I pay £3 for a huge bag of potatoes which I can share with my stepchildren or neighbours and £1 for a box of mushrooms. In the shops, I would pay 60 to 70 pence for a sheet of wrapping paper; at the market, I can find those of a similar quality at £1 for 18 sheets! Today, I have a choice *not* to go to the market to buy things, but I still can't see why I should pay store prices when I can buy the same thing of the same quality from the market at 20% or 50% less.

My friends in England say, "Phine, you're always so glamourous!"

They think that my clothes are expensive and I would proudly say, "I bought these from Blackbushe. Guess how much this outfit cost?" And they'd guess £70 or more and I'd say, "It cost me £15." This is the way I still am, not that I don't allow myself nice things from nice places; but if I can, I am just as happy to wear something from the market. But all those years ago, when my mother was struggling to put me through school, we had no choice but to go to the market to look for material for my uniform. To celebrate my getting into school, my mother and I shared a bowl of *laksa* between us, which cost about 30 cents. Sungei Road was famous for its *laksa*, spicy noodles in coconut milk done *nonya* style. Modern stalls these days would claim that they originated from that particular stall. As food is so much a part of the lifestyle in Singapore, people will go to great lengths to get to a special place that is known for a particular food.

After eating, Mak stopped at a stall to finger a bolt of dark blue cloth. The material was affordable on Mak's meagre budget and looked very much like the blue required for my school pinafore. *Very much* are the key words here. She couldn't have been more wrong. On the day that I arrived for the school assembly, I stood out like the flame-of-the forest flowers in the jungle. The children in my new school sniggered. It is terrible to start school in the middle of a year and to be nearly two years older than the other kids in Primary One. And worse, to turn up wearing the wrong shade of blue for the pinafore. I slunk into the back row, feeling like the real country peasant that I was. But I would rather tolerate the taunts of my new schoolmates than break my mother's heart by telling her that what she had made so much effort to buy was the wrong thing. There was no way that she could afford another few yards of cloth to make two sets of uniform. Already, when I accompanied her to the wet market, I noticed she asked the vegetable sellers for the scrap vegetables, the cut-offs of meat. I lodged the observations in my mind, reminding myself that one day, I would repay her for all these, buy her the freshest vegetables, the juiciest of meats. It is my mother's dreams sitting on my shoulders and her belief in me which continually presses me to succeed.

"Oii! *Sua ku*! (Mountain tortoise)", someone might shout out in

Hokkien to denigrate me for my rural ways. In school, you can be bullied for all sorts of reasons. I was bullied because I was the oldest in my class but the most stupid and I wore the wrong uniform. A month later, Miss D'Souza, who was not only observant but kind, gave me two sets of uniform which came from the parents of a girl who had left school. Only then did I tell my mother the situation and she altered them to fit me.

The first thing I loved about school was the toilet. Not knowing about flush toilets, I had not expected any difference in school and was amazed when I asked for the *jamban* and was sent to this large room (bigger than my entire *attap* house), with a row of sinks where water came out magically from taps, where there were many small rooms, all with doors. I was really a *sua ku*.

"But where is the toilet?" I asked my new friend, Elizabeth.

She looked at me in puzzlement. Elizabeth came from a middle class family and lived in a lovely brick terraced house in Sennet Estate, which I thought was Millionaires' Row. She wouldn't recognise a *jamban* if she saw one, in the same way that I couldn't recognise a flush toilet.

"There," she pointed to one of the cubicles.

I walked in there and it smelled beautifully of disinfectant, had a very clean ceramic squatting bowl with a chain; no foul smells, no sign of other people's faeces, no rats and no cockroaches. It was so vastly different from what I was used to that I could not believe that this could be a toilet. I walked out again, quite non-plussed. In case the other girls in the lavatory heard, I said to Elizabeth quietly, "I can't find the toilet."

She walked me into the toilet and pointed to it. She was a wise girl because she suddenly realised that I wouldn't know what a toilet would look like. She was puzzled but she didn't make me feel small. "Here! You place your feet on these pads, *lah* and squat down. When you finish your job, you pull this chain and the water will flush it away."

"You're kidding!" my eyes widened. At first, I thought she might be making fun of me because I was a kampong girl but she was such a nice person that I didn't think she would be that sort of person. She left me to it and I tried it out and, lo and behold, water came out from under the ceramic bowl to wash away my pee! I forced another pee and pulled the chain again to see if it would work one more time and it did! I thought it was great. I wondered what Elizabeth must have thought, waiting for me outside the cubicle when she heard the flush going on a few times. For *bigger jobs*, Elizabeth explained, I could use the toilet paper which was on a roll. I couldn't believe it! The paper was soft and malleable and felt like cotton wool on my bottom, not at all like the coarse newspaper squares which we used. Sometimes when we walked in the rain to the *jamban*, the newspaper squares might have gotten damp or wet and we ended up with newsprint on our backsides! But this toilet paper was without newsprint and was pure white and soft. There was even a tap in the cubicle for us to *chaybok*, wash our bottoms properly after wiping it. It was quite an experience for me, this introduction to a flushing toilet — it was pure luxury! I wanted so much for my mother to share my good fortune instead of having to squat in the smelly *jamban* where the flies swarmed around and the rats ran underneath. Sadly, I couldn't take the flush toilet to her but I could steal the soft toilet paper for her, so I unrolled a yard of it, folded it, and stuffed it into my rafiaed school-bag to take it home to her. I thought her eyes looked moist when I handed the soft, toilet paper to her. But she said, "Don't steal anything, *huh*. To take what is not yours is debt to your soul."

My form teacher told us that we had to put up our hand to ask for permission to go to the bathroom. So I kept putting up my hand all day on my first week in school. Until she said to me, "Josephine, do you have a stomach problem?" I nodded, not daring to tell a lie but also wanting to enjoy the pleasures of this new found luxury. But eventually, I was afraid of being found out, so I went less often after that. Since I discovered those clean toilets, I tried to control my bowel movements and saved all my *big jobs* for school so that I didn't have to go to the horrible, smelly *jambans* in the village. If you want to control yourself, you have to stop whatever you're doing, count slowly and be very still until the spasm in your abdomen has passed. School started at seven in the morning, so I always tried to practise control until I got there. I was really cross that my father didn't save *his big jobs* for his workplace because he was fond of doing them at night into the chamber pot. My poor mother had to clear its contents every morning and when I was ten, it became my job. I dumped the mess he made into the nearby monsoon drain. But since we did not have a separate room where the chamber pot was placed, whenever Ah Tetia did his *job* at night, the smell would premeate the whole house. He always started his *big job* by passing wind and his farts would echo in the empty enamel chamber pot like firecrackers going off. And of course for the rest of the night, the whole house stank. So the introduction to a flush toilet was a milestone in my life. When I learnt to read, it was such enormous pleasure to be able to take a book into the beautifully clean and luxurious lavatory. Sometimes when I got up, my legs would be all pins-and-needles! Years later when I moved into a flat with my first *throne* or sitting toilet, I was so overwhelmed by the sheer luxury of it, I'd sit on it and read a whole book. When I moved to England and learnt that the English called a toilet a *loo*, I dubbed my toilet a *loo-brary.*

"*Xia Yue Fen, Xia Yue Fen,*" the teacher called out during Chinese class.

This was Miss Tang, the teacher who taught us Mandarin. She was Chinese-educated herself and spoke highly accented English. She had all of the charactistics of a Chinese-educated person with her old-fashioned and severe demeanour. The *cheong sum*, which hung loosely around her rigid body, made her look painfully thin, her arms like sticks protruding from the short sleeves. The spectacles had numerous rings on her thick glasses, which gave her a weird gaze. Her grey-streaked hair cut in a page-boy style seemed rather incongruous with her age. She stood at the front of the class repeatedly calling out the name, looking round the class for a hand to shoot up in acknowledgement. She grew more and more impatient when no one responded. No one got up to receive the homework book from her. It was my first few weeks in school and I was sitting right at the back of the class but I could already feel the tension building up in the room. I had been too shy to make friends, conscious of my ignorance and of my upbringing, and except for Elizabeth, no one in the Chinese class had approached me to be friends. The other girls were unsure if I was Chinese because I was so dark in complexion compared to them. To make matters worse, I didn't understand what they said.

The Mandarin teacher's voice was getting strident and all my classmates turned in their seats to look at the back of the class. I thought perhaps they were looking for a girl behind me, so I, too, turned to look but there was no one else behind me. An unnatural hush fell over the class as Miss Tang strode down the aisle between two rows of desks carrying the brown exercise book. Her mouth was a tight moue. She stopped at my desk.

"Why didn't you answer me? Isn't your name *Xia Yue Fen*?"

"My name is Josephine ..." I stammered. She looked so fierce, I was terrified.

"It says here on this book that it's *Xia Yue Fen*. Did you write this?"

As I did not know how to read the Chinese characters, I was not sure and did not answer her. I looked down at the characters on the book and dimly recognised the scrawl. She repeated her question again. And this time, I felt pushed to give her a reply.

"Yes, Miss Tang."

"So why didn't you answer me?" She slapped the book across my face.

My face stung. It took a while before it dawned on me that perhaps, she was calling me by the name that my mother had got from Ah Pek, the old fortune-teller. Of course, I didn't remember that that was supposed to be my Chinese name. I couldn't recognise the characters since they were mere squiggles to me. I had simply copied Ah Pek's brushwork onto all my exercise books for Chinese lessons and then completely forgotten about it. And the worse thing was that I still couldn't read the words because I didn't recognise the Chinese characters which were foreign to me. At home, we only spoke our *Peranakan* patois and Malay, and Teochew with my father. At Miss Tang's repeated question about whether the name on the book was mine, the rest of the class giggled.

"Quiet!" Then turning to me, she said. "What kind of a girl are you that you don't know your own name? Are you Chinese or Malay? I'm going to see Miss D'Souza about you. If you are not telling me the truth, you are going to get a few Order Marks from me! As far as your work is concerned, it is total gibberish! What did you think you were writing?"

There was some sounds of strangled laughter, hands cupped over mouths. I was so ashamed, I dared not say anything. The exercise she set us was to form sentences with selected words which she gave us. The rest of the class was a term ahead. How could I explain to her that the Chinese characters didn't make any sense to me? Afraid to ask because I did not want to appear stupid, I scanned a storybook, looked for a similarly-formed character and simply copied the sentence with the character in it. I hadn't any idea what the sentence said, whether it was at all a full sentence or just a clause, I just copied to where the line ended with a Chinese full stop, which was like a tiny circle. That was the only clue I had that the line was complete. Miss Tang was probably right that it was gibberish. As the months went by, she despaired of me. My comprehension of the literate Chinese language was nil. I could not understand the meaning or usefulness of a stroke and therefore could not construct a word. I was so frightened to ask her that I couldn't learn anything. At the end of the year, I failed her subject. The worse thing was that I had to go home to tell my mother.

"You do what?" She said.

My mother hardly ever raised her voice. But that day, she did. She looked at my blue record book and on the page of lines which she could not read, she saw a word written in red. Scarlet letters, condemning me. I knew I could be scalped or feathered-and-tarred for this sin. Or both.

"What does that say?"

I could hardly bring myself to say it, "'Failed.'"

"After all that I'm doing to send you to school, you've failed! I give you chance to be somebody and you failed! I got to suffer your father so that you can go to school and this is how you repay me."

Her words and her broken voice lacerated me. Still, she took the dreaded *rotan*, the length of cane which was hooked over a protruding nail on the wooden wall. The rod was the penalty for childish misdemeanours. My mother would not tolerate laziness and bad manners. If we were rude to our parents or answered back or repeated a word that other village children had said, which was not supposed to be repeated, she had one sure way of making us remember. She would take out her mortar-and-pestle and pound the searing hot *chilli padi*, the hottest of all chillies. Then she would hold us tight and force the hot chilli paste into our mouths. And our mouths would burn for hours! Even though I realised that I deserved it, it was the one thing I didn't like about my mother. She could be really cruel until we learnt our lesson. For other childish pranks or not doing our chores properly, we got the cane. That day, when I took her my school report, she caught hold of my arm and whacked me hard on my bare legs.

"But I tried my best!" I yelled in defence.

"Best? No good best if you fail! If you want something so bad-bad, you got to dream it, sleep it, live with it. Let it be part of you, not outside you."

I didn't understand what she meant. All I wanted at that moment was to escape her beating. She whacked again, this time harder, as if her disappointment in me had transferred itself to the cane. With my wrist imprisoned tightly in her one hand, I danced a jig around her trying to avoid the cane, eventually letting out a howl. Then with a cry, she threw down the *rotan* and sat huddled on the floor, burying her face in her hands. At first, I was relieved to be spared further affliction and sat down to nurse the striped weals of red coming up on my legs. It was some while before I noticed that Mak's shoulders were heaving. Then I realised that she was sobbing and it made my heart sick because it was I who caused her to grieve.

"Mak, I'll do better next year. I promise."

Promising was one thing, but trying to keep the promise was another. There was too much going against me; my classmates didn't like me, neither did Miss Tang. I didn't look Chinese. I was dumb. There was no one at home or in the village to practise the language with. Mandarin was still the language of the educated. There weren't many in our sector of the kampong. There was an all-Chinese school further in the village but the kids there didn't mix with us kids in the Malay part of the kampong. So I failed in my promise and didn't do well in Chinese, although I was okay in English and the other subjects. I loved English, loved the sound of its vowels, the precision of its tenses, *sing, sang, sung; take, took, taken.* It was wonderful and made a lot of sense to add an "s" to make a plural instead of our language, which repeats the word to make it a plural. I could say, *book, books*, not *buku* to become *buku-buku*. In Malay, we also repeat our words for emphasis or to make a gerund and it fascinated me that you didn't have to do that in English, you'd say *walk-ing* instead of *walk-walk, play-ing,* instead of *play-play*. What a thrilling adventure learning English was. But to Jacob's frustration, I also failed mathematics. So he gave up on me and I was flung out of his tuition class. Fear is a great block to learning, I think. I feared Jacob, my Maths teacher, Miss Gupta and Miss Tang. And worse, because we couldn't afford new text books, I was using text books that belonged to Jacob. The books were 13 years out of date. I could hardly ever follow the lessons in class because the pagination and content were different from the current text. Also, it seemed ridiculous to me to be learning about pounds, shillings and pence when I didn't know what they looked like. It was inevitable that my inability to add and subtract earned me a red mark on my report book until I took my Senior Cambridge examinations when I was 16. Today, I joke that I can only count up to 21, the total in the game of Blackjack.

Thank goodness, I was more capable in English and the other subjects which pulled my grades up. I came in 16 in a class of 32. My mother didn't seem as upset when I failed in Maths. The following year, I failed Chinese every single term. It just seemed that I just had no aptitude for that written language. Now, it was not only the Chinese teacher who despaired of me, but my mother and Miss D'Souza. Eventually, I was sent to see her. She looked enormous behind that desk of hers in the principal's office. It was an ordeal even to walk pass her office, let alone be in it. I felt small in the chair opposite her. I was praying that she was not going to say that my school days were ended. But her tone was exceedingly kind.

"Do you know how much hope your mother places on you?"

"Yes, Miss D'Souza."

"She is a fine woman, your mother. With a very sharp mind. If she lived in a different era, she would be a great success, I tell you. She wants the best for you, you know that, don't you."

"I know that, Miss D'Souza."

"Does anyone speak Mandarin at home?"

"No, Miss D"Souza."

"Your mother spoke Malay fluently. Are you the same?"

"Yes, Miss D'Souza."

"Then I can't see why you need to go on taking Chinese, even if you are classed as one. I'll speak to 'Che Siti. It will be the first time she has a non-Malay in her class. But I'm sure you'll get on very well. I don't know why I didn't think about it before."

"Oh, thank you Miss D'Souza, thank you so much."

If only there was a similar solution for Maths. The Malay taught in school is the Romanised script and not *Jawi*. So it was a case of learning to put familiar words together with the English alphabet. 'Che Siti was a lovely lady, who moved so fluidly in her *baju kurong*. When Miss D'Souza took me to see her, she welcomed me with her soft voice and her smiling eyes. I felt so at home in her class. It was helped by my classmates who treated me like one of them and we chatted in the same language from the first day. When I joined their class, I was way behind because although I was in Primary Three, I had not learnt Malay formally. 'Che Siti took extra time over me and my new friends were very helpful with my homework. Except for a difference in religion, I felt very much as if I was one of them. Until today, I identify myself more with the Malays than I do the Chinese, who always seem quick to criticise my dark skin and love to hear of mishaps. 'Che Siti would be proud to know that I read Malay linguistics and literature up to my third year at University. In her sweet and gentle way, she gave me a love for the language and encouraged me by giving me a part in the year-end school play, which was performed entirely in Malay. At the end of the concert was a prize presentation and I was totally surprised when I was awarded a prize for coming third in Malay. It was a small Malay-English dictionary but to me, it was as if I had won a million dollars. I ran all the way home so that I could show it to Mak.

Nine

*T*here is so little now that my mother is capable of doing that it is easy to imagine that she has always been this way. Like when you look at very old people and somehow find it difficult to imagine them as young and sprightly with powerful brains who have raised a family or commanded a business enterprise or was a well-respected professional. It's as though someone with a weak body, wrinkled skin, an ambling gait and a forgetful mind could not have owned another kind of body, mind or life. But if you look closely into those opaque fish-like eyes long enough, you may see the life that was once there, that the same wrinkled face once had a strong jaw-line, taut skin, those same eyes had once sparkled like precious gems, filled with love, wit and mischief.

As my mother's once were. Besides her figure, her eyes were once her best asset, though you wouldn't know it now. Due to our mixed heritage, her eyes were large yet with a hint of an Oriental tilt. Except for a slight spreading of her hips, she has remained slim unlike both her elder sisters, who developed bodies that showed neglect and indulgence. Soon Hua, Great Aunt who had dreamt of marrying her millionaire husband but forced to marry a chicken rice seller, turned out well because the man doted on her. She discovered what it meant to be an *old man's darling.* Her husband had been a widower and was nearly 20 years older than she was. He bought her a two-storey brick house in Alexander Estate. Soon Chew had a love-marriage after her first husband died, which was unusual for her generation. She had no parents to stop her from doing what she liked, no brothers to run her life. Her Indian husband was a garbage collector and was assigned living quarters in a bricked-terrace house. Soon Mei, Fourth Aunt, married and died in a few short years and her husband took the two children away and never kept in touch. Ah Tetia wasn't particularly fond of my two aunts and he never visited them, but on the few occasions when Mak took my sisters and I to visit my aunts, I thought they were very rich because of the brick houses that they lived in, compared to our *kampong* hut.

I used to believe that anyone who lived in a brick house had to be rich. Long before my mother had the courage to defy her husband and take us to visit her sisters, I was given an opportunity to see the inside of a brick house. Elizabeth was my first friend in school. Unlike the others who ridiculed me because I looked Malay and spoke Malay but was a Straits Chinese, Elizabeth accepted me as I was. She was seven, a little more than a year younger than I was when we met. She was a grand looking girl and when she made me her friend, others took me into their circle, too. Elizabeth knew that I lived in the shanty village down the road from her. And I think she felt sorry for me.

"I was named after the Queen of England, you know or not?"

"Is the Queen of England as beautiful as you?" I asked in all innocence and that must have endeared me towards Elizabeth. At eight and a half, I wasn't flattering because I didn't know how. To me, the girl from the *kampong*, she *was* like a queen. Her pierced ears were graced with 24-carat gold studs and on her wrist was a bracelet with small gold hearts. Her uniform was the right colour, was always properly pressed, her canvas shoes were bought from a department store in town and well blanco-ed. Her hands were unbelievably soft and creamy. She wasn't very tall but she was petite; such grace and poise in her mannerisms and walk. I quickly learnt that the rich had a certain confidence when they speak or do something because they expected to be listened to, and all my other schoolmates seemed to bow to Elizabeth. As I was in the morning school session and my brother Romia in the afternoon, he would cycle me to school on the bar of his push-bike but I had to walk the couple of miles home. So it was with envy that I watched the chauffeur taking Elizabeth to school in an expensive motorcar every morning. There were many bicycles, trishaws and bullock-carts in the village, but if a motorcar should drive down our rutted road, it was still an occasion for all the children and even some adults to come out to look. Motorcars were definitely for the rich. Elizabeth had everything. But she had such a sweet nature and was exceedingly kind to me so I could not really be jealous. When I learnt that she was a ballerina, I was really impressed. Piano-learning and ballet dancing were only for those who did not have to spend every available cent on food and clothing.

"You want to come to my house for lunch or not? Maybe on Saturday when there's no school," she said.

It was like being invited to the *istana* (palace). I was very excited. My best friend in the *kampong* was Parvathi and I told her about it. Paravthi was an Indian girl three years older than I was. Her family was so poor that she was sent out to work at the paper factory when she turned twelve a year ago. The paper factory manufactured stationery and envelopes and all the envelopes were folded manually so they employed youngsters like Parvathi as cheap labour. Besides the paper factory, our *kampong* also boasted a rattan factory, huge piles of long rattan outside waiting to be shaved and cleaned and sent to other factories to be formed into furniture and baskets. Parvathi had no hope of an education and when I started school, I became her teacher, teaching her the English alphabet. When I told her that my classmate, Elizabeth, had lessons in ballet and piano, she said, "Wahhh! Her family *chap wang* (print money) or wat-huh?"

I told Mak about the invitation and she was so pleased for me. Perhaps she was remembering her life of plenty when everyone took pains with their clothes and appearances when they visited each other. She set about preparing me for the visit. As my hair had gone back to being straight, she released her *Tontin* money for my permanent wave. She believed that curly hair was more sophisticated than straight hair though she never indulged in it herself. *Tontin* was like a kind of fund where each person participating puts a certain sum into the fund and could take out the whole group sum in an emergency. Against my protests, she marched me to the village hairdresser and subjected me to an ordeal of hot wire rods that stuck out like Medusa's head of snakes. The old-fashioned perming rods made my head, face and neck look like a boiled crab. When the rods were released, my artificial curls sprang out like I had had a fright. Worse still, the hairdresser back-combed and hair-sprayed them. In those days, hair spray was not as fine as what we have today and it made my hair look lacquered! I came out of the salon with this huge crown of stiff curls.

"Don't disgrace me," Mak said. "You must be well-mannered and behave properly. You better go in your best clothes."

I thought, oh no, she's going to put me in that Chinese New Year dress again. After all, it was my best and only really smart dress. The one with the awful can-can which I hated! And I bet she would make me wear those horrible, black, plastic shoes which squashed my toes. But I guess Mak was right. It certainly wouldn't do to appear at Elizabeth's posh house in just my homemade knickers or my well-washed A-line dress. I guess a bit of discomfort would be worth it for the pleasure of the visit. I was excited but nervous, too. I hadn't been in a brick house before. I told Mak how Elizabeth was so rich she could take ballet lessons and also play the piano. These activities were so beyond our circumstances that the thought of someone able to do them was such worthy news.

"I used to play the piano," she said in a soft voice.

Perhaps my mother had wanted to talk about her piano-playing days, and share them with me. But I didn't give her the opportunity to open her heart because I was too engrossed about my visit to my friend's palatial house. A child is a child because she can't see beyond her own wants. How easy it is to miss emotional opportunities! Through simple non-attention. Our minds can be engaged elsewhere when our mouths are opening in conversation. Does it mean that there are two of us? Why is it that the significance of my mother's words made no impact on me then and yet can cross time barriers to touch me today? How is it that what she told me flew past my attention then and yet today, I can recall what she said? Or am I imagining it? She had told me that she was tutored to play the piano, like her two elder sisters. Their family piano sat in the living room, which opened out to a verandah which looked out to the sea. I can see her as she must have looked, young and slender, sitting with her back straight on the piano stool, her dark head tilted forward, her beautiful eyes looking downward. Like the ripples of waves outside, her supple fingers made the piano keys ripple in delightful tunes. What pleasure it must have been for her and for those who had the good fortune to hear her play. She would be so absorbed she wouldn't feel the sea breeze gently playing with her hair. Why hadn't I thought of buying her a piano when I could afford it? When her fingers had not yet been arched by arthritis? Especially when the musical notes were still in her voice and in her head? What good is money if it's not to feed the desires of one's loved ones?

How I regret it now. The music she loved is no longer hers to capture. Occasionally, I hear her humming in her room as she combs her scanty hair. I had bought her a tape deck but she finds it difficult to operate a mechanical thing that holds no meaning for her. So she holds the tunes in her head and she tries to sound them with her voice, but the voice that ensues from her old throat is worn and cracked. I remember all this now, yet on that day when I had told her of Elizabeth's invitation, all I could think of was my excursion to my friend's beautiful house in Sennet Estate. I didn't think of my mother and how she had longed to tell me about her piano playing days.

Elizabeth's family lived in a terraced house. Today, I would probably look at it with different eyes, but back then, with my experience of life in a *kampong*, being a frog in the coconut shell of my existence, I thought they lived in Millionaires' Row. I hadn't been in a brick house before. I felt small in front of the huge front door, which looked like an entrance to a palace or something. I stood there feeling nervous, dressed in my best, the Chinese New Year dress with the can-can underneath which I had worn on my school-hunting day. And of course those toe-pinching shoes. My mother had baked a small cake for me to bring because she said it was not polite to visit someone's home empty-handed. She had spent half the morning baking the cake over her clay stove. She put the cake in a small wicker basket and it was difficult trying to hold the basket, keep my skirt with the can-can underneath down and maintain balance on Romia's bicycle.

"Have fun," he said, when he dropped me off. "I'll be back at three."

I knocked and knocked but the wood of the door was so thick that nobody heard me. The door of our own house was only a plank-thick and even a small fist like mine could make an impact. Then I noticed a button by the door and pressed that and I nearly jumped when I heard the sound it made right through the house. An electric doorbell! I was impressed. You can't have electirc doorbells when you don't have electricity. A woman dressed in a crisp, white samfoo and black trousers opened the door and she looked at me, standing there on the doorstep wearing my Chinese New Year dress with the can-can underneath, with a basket in my hand.

"Hello, Aunty. Elizabeth invited me," I said in English.

Without saying a word to me, she turned her head to face into the house and yelled, "Lizzabet! Lizzabet! Your friend is here." I thought she was Elizabeth's mother, so I handed her the basket with the cake. She looked at it with a wrinkling of her nose, closed the front door and then walked away with it in an ambling gait. I quickly took off my shoes and lay them neatly, then stood in the cavernous room in total amazement that a room could be so huge. The floor was in colourful mosaic, smooth and level, unlike our undulating cement floor with the vestigial urinal for the cows. There was even a staircase! I have never seen a house with a staircase before and I was staring up at it when Elizabeth glided down the stairs, like a queen, in a pretty but simple, store-bought dress. She looked at me standing there in my Chinese New Year dress with the can-can underneath and she said, "You look different without your school uniform."

"I brought something for you. I gave it to your mother."

"That's my amah, silly," she said.

I had heard of people having servants but this was the first time I had met one. She showed me into the hall cum living room and to me, the room was enormous, bigger than our whole attap hut. I was stunned. Then I saw it, the baby grand piano whose surface was so shiny that it showed my surprised face. The price of the piano would probably feed my family for a year, if not longer. And what would the lessons cost?

"Can you play that?" I asked, with incredulity in my voice.

"Of course, *what*." She said with the confidence of the rich. "Want to hear me play?"

I nodded and sat watching with admiration as her hands moved like magic across the keys. To me, it seemed incredible that an innate object like the piano could be persuaded by clever fingers to exude such heavenly music. I had never seen a real piano being played before, never heard such glorious music live. I wanted to laugh and cry at the same time. It was then that I remembered my mother telling me about her playing the piano. What a loss it must be for her not to be able to run her fingers along its keys. I recalled her description of Grandfather's bungalow by the sea and I imagined her sitting on the piano stool as Elizabeth was sitting, her slender fingers making the keys ripple, her back straight as the sea-breeze lifted her beautiful black hair. So this was what it was like to be rich, you did not have to worry about anything but the making of lovely music.

I didn't want her to stop but she did, to show me around her house which seemed a trillion times larger than our attap hut. All the furniture and ornaments were so expensive looking! We walked through so many rooms and we were still downstairs. In the end, I couldn't keep from asking, "May I climb the staircase?"

Elizabeth looked oddly at me and said, "Okay, *lah*."

She led the way. For me, each step upward was an exciting journey. My hand caressed the polished wood of the bannister. When I reached the top landing, my triumph was equal to that of a mountaineer who had scaled the peak of some famous mountain. The summit of bedrooms and bathroom was a virgin landscape to me. I stood and surveyed this new land of *personal* bedrooms and *personal* wardrobes and *personal* space. Elizabeth and her younger brother had a bedroom each, whilst her parents shared one! I could not believe the luxury of it. In our home, my father slept in one bed with my two elder brothers. Where his bed ended, my mother's began and she slept in it with my two sisters and myself. When Robert arrived, I moved out onto a fold-up canvas bed with Matthew. When I had my period and became self-conscious of being so close to Matthew's body, I chose to sleep on an old mattress on the floor where the rats scuttled around at night. Until today, I can remember the squeaking of the mice and rats as they emerged from the drains to burrow through the holes in the ground into our houses. Though it was hot and humid, I would tuck my blanket carefully and tightly around my feet, all round my body and over my shoulders. Sometimes a curious mouse or worse, a rat, might sit on the edge of my pillow to peer with curiosity into my face, its eyes gleaming in the dark. I'd be so terrified, I would have no voice to scream.

"Aren't you afraid of being alone in such a big room?" I asked.

"What's there to be afraid of?" she asked in the voice of a child so used to being secure, to owning things

"Where's your mother?" I asked.

"Oh, she's probably playing *mahjong*. My amah takes care of me all day."

She showed me her beautiful toys, the kind that you get from the real *Robinson's*, the kind that Santa Claus handed out; everything was store-bought and properly made, not like my homemade rag dolls and doll-houses made from shoe boxes. Here at last was the Rich Kid I had been dreaming of, who might need a companion! I hoped that Elizabeth would ask me back again. Downstairs, there was a room totally dedicated to dining, with an enormous rosewood table with mother-of-pearl inlay and matching chairs. At our home, our family sat on the kitchen floor for our meals; when we had visitors, they sat on empty orange crates. We were too small to reach the table, so the amah piled cushions on the chairs for us to sit on. Then the amah brought out plates and plates of food. It was a feast fit for an emperor.

"Who else is coming?"

"I hope you like the food."

Like? I hadn't had meat for a week at least and there was all that wonderful chicken and beef laid out in front of me — I thought I had landed in heaven. There was a dish of fried chicken, black bean shredded beef, chilli king prawns, steamed fish and wholesome vegetables, none of the type discarded by the vegetable sellers to be used as pig's swill. And as much boiled rice as I wanted. The rice was a full-grain variety, not the broken rice that we normally ate, which families like Elizabeth's would feed to their chickens. It tasted wonderful. My friend acted very nonchalant and played with her food, hardly eating, confident that there will be another meal if she wanted. I daren't let the opportunity pass. I was vaguely aware that she was eyeing me, probably with regret for asking me but I could not resist stuffing as much food as I could into my mouth and belly. When you wake up in the morning and are not sure if you are going to be fed, you eat when there's food. Today, when people tell me they are on a diet or when they say they're too busy working to have time to eat, I know they have not been really hungry. True hunger is not from choice. True hunger is a stone mill grinding away in your stomach, but with nothing to grind but acid. You hold your tummy and double-up with the agony, your face is pinched, the tears crouching behind your lids ready to fall. When we were lucky, we had a whole fish to share with the whole family, some over-ripe vegetables which Mak skillfully disguised with spices or curry powder. Sometimes, Ah Cob and Romia would bring in the eels they catch, they would steal the leaves from someone's *ubi kayu* plant for vegetables or Mak would cook an unripe papaya. On bad days, we ate our boiled rice with a sprinkling of soya sauce and nothing else. Elizabeth would not have survived.

My brother Matthew, just a few years older than I, was a survivor in the wilderness of our deprivation. He had a small build with a head that reminded me of an elf's. It was he who taught me how to fish for eels so that we could take them home for Mak to curry. He showed me how to look for warm eggs, when ducks and chickens had strayed from their coops. And it was he who taught me how to scour the rubbish bins for half-eaten sweets, apples or blackened bananas.

"Don't ever plunge your arm into the bin," he warned me when I was five. "There might be broken glass inside. Slowly remove each layer of rubbish and work your way through."

The rubbish bins of the rich, like those of the English people at the top of the hill in their mock Tudor houses, were treasure coves. I was too small to look into the bins without standing on my toes. Matthew taught me how to hold my breath, how to swat the flies and ignore the cockcroaches as we rummaged our way through the things discarded by the rich. What things we would find, torn comics and picture books and broken toys! What did it matter that a doll had only one arm or that a fire engine had no wheels? They were toys we would never dream of having in a hundred years. Matthew and my second elder brother, Romia, were good with their hands and could repair almost anything. So a doll with an empty eye socket might be filled with a coloured marble, a toy-puppy with a leg missing might be invested with a piece of wood.

There is a day I can never forget. A day that will rush back to me in my nightmares. And sometimes in my waking moments. The memory of that day came flooding back to me once when I was walking up the hill in Guildford, Surrey (comfortable Surrey, people call it). I suffered such a panic, that the sweat ran down my back and I trembled from head to foot. I had to tell myself that I did have money in my wallet, that I could actually walk into any restaurant there and pay for a meal of my choice. When you've been hungry for a long time, the fear still crouches in the corner of your mind, waiting, waiting. The day which keeps coming back to haunt me was the day Matthew took me up to the top of the hill where the English people lived in their white-walled houses with fake black beams.

"The *rambutans* will be out," Matthew said. "The branches will be drooping over the fences with the weight of the fruits. All we have to do is pluck them."

Amongst all the things that he had taught me, Matthew taught me how to steal fruits from people's gardens. But hunger had no conscience. So I was willing to be led. Besides, we were only kids. It was not an easy climb for my short legs up the hill to where the big houses were. To our dismay, all that remained were fruits which were still green. The gardener must have picked the ripe fruits that morning. I was particularly hungry and ready to cry. The rubbish bins, too, looked clean as though they had just been washed, so there was nothing to pick. Just as we were about to turn away, a servant came out of the house into the garden with an enormous piece of steak in her hand. Pets were to us a phenomenon of the wealthy. After all, who could afford food to feed to pets when human beings were going hungry?

"Loger! Loger!" The *amah* in her white samfoo and black trousers shouted for the family pet in Cantonese-accented English. The huge Alsatian dog bounded from the back garden and the *amah* threw the steak on the ground. There was only a chain-linked fence between us and the dog — and the steak.

"Oh, look at that piece of meat!" Matthew said. "It could feed our family for a week."

"Mak could curry it," I said, drooling.

The servant turned on her heels and disappeared back into the kitchen. The dog eyed the piece of meat critically. The dog might be fussy but we weren't. I imagined what Mak could make with that piece of meat, marinating it with spices and stir-frying it. The juices ran in my mouth as I saw myself biting into that piece of lovely meat.

"I could put my hand through the fence and grab it from the dog," I said.

I looked at Matthew. He didn't say anything but I knew he wanted me to. His arm was much larger than mine, so I knew he could not do it.

"Be careful," he whispered.

I knelt on the ground near the fence, balled my hand into a fist so that I could put it through the chain-link. The Alsatian suddenly looked our way and saw us. He must have smelled what we were up to because he looked at us suspiciously. As my hand inched its way towards the piece of meat, the dog sprang up towards it. His barking was so loud that I shook with fear. I was so terrified, I forgot to curl my hand and it got stuck. The Alsatian was coming fast towards the fence.

"Quick! Quick! Make your hand into a fist," Matthew said trying to pull my arm.

The dog snarled and bared its rows of teeth. Just as he reached us, I balled up my hand and drew it through the chain-link. Matthew was pulling me so hard that we both fell backwards to the ground. The dog's nose came through the fence but thank goodness nothing else. His head loomed large, his eyes like fire, his bark loud. His jaw was open, his tongue hanging out with saliva dripping from it. For a moment, I saw my hand ripped and bloody between his teeth. I started to tremble and

Matthew dragged me up and we scampered hastily down the hill.

Once I made the mistake of confiding this incident and my recurring fear to my stepdaughter Sadie. I entertained false hopes that by being friendly and spending some time with her, sharing confidences would bring us closer. Even though she was already in her 30s, Sadie still harped on the fact that her parents had neglected her on *exeat* weekends when she was in an expensive public boarding school in the West Country. She was brought up in a mansion in Buckinghamshire and never really had to work for a living, giving up a job as soon as she found it tiresome. After all, her material needs were supplied by a doting father and then by a husband. Her idea of deprivation is that she and her family didn't have more than three holidays a year.

"Shouldn't be a problem now, right?" She said, drily. "You've got my father."

Old fears are hard to loosen from one's psyche. They cling to you like your own shadow. For that reason, I am afraid to stop working, reluctant to be financially dependent on someone else. But how can someone like Sadie understand? She has everything money could buy. She has never known a single day of hunger and has made herself rotund by her love of food but not exercise, so that even designer clothes could not disguise it. Even when I had provided the best sleeping arrangement for her sons that I could manage that Easter, she had complained. Apparently, she did not think it was adequate that her young son should sleep on garden cushions on the carpeted floor of a plush suite just for a short visit. I wanted to tell her how I slept, for years, on someone's discarded mattress on the cement floor with rats running around. But I didn't. I don't know what triggers off the memory of the day the Alsatian bared his teeth to me. But it came as I sat at Elizabeth's beautiful dining table with all the wonderful food spread out before me. The utter fear of being hungry again gripped my insides. I felt lucky being able to feast as I was feasting in this house, on food which I had only dreamt about. I was only sad that I could not pack the huge leftovers for my brothers and sisters, particularly for Matthew and Mak. Elizabeth was pure Chinese, so she ate her rice daintily with chopsticks. Although Peranakans eat noodles using chopsticks, we eat rice using our fingers. I scooped the food out of the dishes with a spoon but used my fingers to eat. Customs differ in different cultures, even those that are within the same country. So it must have seemed really strange to Elizabeth to see me eating with my fingers, gobbling and gobbling down all the food. As she watched, her eyes grew larger and larger. I was not too surprised when she never asked me again. I must have seemed to her like a pig at a trough.

Ten

I know now that my mother often sacrificed her share of food for us when we were children. I was so greedy and so ready to take it from her that I never stopped to think that she might be hungry too. Aren't children thoughtless? My memory of the past comes sliding back into the present like films on rerun. I don't know why this is so. Perhaps it's because I have the capacity to think more deeply now then when I was a child. Somehow, my subconscious must have stored the impressions and the images from those times and replay them to me now as my mind focuses on that particular period. I can *recall* (can it be recollection when I wasn't aware then?) seeing my mother push her plate aside when she saw we didn't have enough to eat. If my father should remark upon it, she would say that she was not hungry. She would fill her stomach with bulk food, like rice or noodles to spare us the fish or the meat. She was truly the epitome of the perfect mother. I regret that she was everything I was not, so selfless in giving to her children. Those opportunities I could have had to prove myself such a mother were not mine to have because I chose to run away from the father of my children. It's the little things I have lost, a child's first words, his face when he opens his birthday present, me reaching out to clean ice cream off his cheek, feeling his breath on my skin, hear him call me

Mummy. Little things which would have plugged up the hole of my emptiness.

But this is my mother's story. I remembered her giving her food to me, so when I started working, I tried to redress the situation by buying her her favourite food. I would never go out and return home without something for her to eat. It might be a packet of *hokkien mee* or *satay* or something really small, like a steamed *pau* or *siew mai*. But it would always something that she liked or had expressed a *nafsu* or desire for. I would go out of my way to a hawker centre which was famed for that particular food so that she got the best. I had the privilege of money and transport and the ability to read signs, so no distance in Singapore was too much trouble to take something home for her to eat. It is the one thing she remembers to this day. That is why when she's caught in her state of confusion, she always says to Bernadette that it is only I who feeds her. This is not so, but she remembers it like that because I was unfailing in my daily ritual until I left the village to get married. But Matthew, Agatha and Bernadette are the ones buying her the food now that I am so far away. Once she fed us, but it is our turn now to feed her. And it's not just food.

If I could, I would also take her out further afield to places which sold the special foods that she loved. Since I am back home again in Singapore, I suggest an outing to a wet market in *Geylang Serai* and then to a hawker centre near Haig Road, so that she can eat her favourite *nasi bryani*. Because the hawkers are no longer itinerant and no longer hawk their wares, hawker centres are now called food centres, though I am too entrenched in old terminology to change. Bernadette had generously put her car at my disposal so that I can take our mother there.

"You're so clever," Mak says. "How come you can still remember Singapore roads when you've lived in England for so long, *huh*? You know

I used to go to *Geylang Serai* by myself before. But now, I'm so useless, *lah*, roads have changed, buses are different. Even buildings have changed. I can't recognise anything. And bus fares! Wah, they're so expensive now, more like prices of taxis."

My mother is one of the walking wounded, people out of their time, suffering because they were young in another era. Most old people are like that, all over the world, out of sync with the new, with technological developments outside their ken; sometimes made to look stupid by the youngsters because they cannot keep up. For someone like my mother who had no freedom to do what she wanted when her husband was alive, she never even came close to achieving her potential, let alone realise them. A woman's ability to drive was to her a huge achievement. It represented everything she could not have, could not be. It's a measure not only of success and attainment, but of freedom as well. When she visited David and I in England, I drove her around the twisty country lanes where one couldn't see around the corner. She was very impressed by that and rather proud of me. I was pleased to make her proud. I know that given the chance in her youth, she would have loved to learn to drive. So when I drive a car, I'm driving for her, her desire has seeped into mine. Sometimes, I feel that I *am* her, as though our spirits overlap. Don't ask me how I know. It is just so. I ache when I see her looking so tiny in the front seat of Bernadette's BMW, a shrivelled brown leaf fallen from some great tree. It is not just that the lustre has gone from her once beautiful eyes, but the fierce energy that was once there has also dissipated. Her body which had once stood erect with confidence is now sagging with weariness. It is almost as if her spirit is begging to be released. The thought clutches at my heart fearfully. I am not ready to let her go.

Geylang Serai, where most Malays live, is Mother's favourite place to shop for the kind of outfit she wears and the spices she loves. It is where they sell batiks for the *sarongs* and embroidered voile for her *kebaya*; where there are special tailors who still know how to sew a *kebaya* the *Peranakan* way. Although the *sarong kebaya* is Malay in origin, the *Peranakan kebaya* is shaped slightly differently and needs an expert tailor for the technique of *ketok lobang*, where a series of holes is *punched* into the fine seam of the material from shoulder to hip. *Geylang Serai* was once a *kampong* like the one we had lived in but now, it too has been overtaken by towering blocks. These changes have affected my mother's generation a great deal, a way of life they know and love, swept away too suddenly by modernisation. In September 1963, Singapore gained independence from the British and became part of Malaysia but in August 1965, she broke away to become an independent nation. It was a traumatic time of uncertainty. That uncertainty entered people's souls, made them concerned for superficial wealth, made them fear to be solitary so that they congregated opinions and thoughts. Today, people live in closer proximity in the tower blocks than they ever did in the villages, but their hearts are miles apart. Every home has electricity and running water, but the quality of life has changed.

A wet market still exists in *Geylang Serai,* where numerous stalls sell fresh food and vegetables and Malay food. When we weave in and out of the stalls, Mak is voluble, making remarks and talking to total strangers as she did in the old days. She asks people how they are, if they have eaten. The latter is a common subject in Singapore, like the weather in England. People are so concerned with food here that they would be shocked if you said you were on diet or have not eaten. My mother, suddenly plunged back into an atmosphere that she is comfortable in, is capturing her past when people were neighbourly and everybody talked to everybody. So her greetings would not have seemed strange or eccentric before, but these days when people are used to being cocooned, when people wrap themslves up with their own concerns and opinions, they get uncomfortable at such a display of open friendliness. Some respond briefly whilst others totally ignore her prattling, looking at her askance. Once or twice, I make a move to stop her but I realise that she is happy again, reliving her life in the *kampong*. So I step aside and try not to be embarrassed. One of Mak's indulgences is *bunga rampai*, a mixed cluster of fresh petals of roses, *chempaka, bunga melor* and other flowers. She loves to have this on her Catholic altar where its lovely fragrance fills the house. If I am ever near the market, I will always try to buy the potpourri for her. For me, the scent of the *bunga rampai* is synonymous with her, especially the yellow *bunga chempaka* which she used to thread into a chain to twist around her bun on special occasions. She also uses flowers like a good luck charm. If we need to pass exams or were sick, she would bath us with seven varieties of flowers. It is interesting how the image of her, all dressed up, her youthful face powdered with *bedak sejok*, her eyes soulful, is permanently printed in my mind. I wish I had a camera then to capture her beauty so that I can show you today how elegant and fine she looked. In the market, Mak loses some of the dejection that seems ever present in her eyes. The sounds and aromas of people chatting, the sizzling of food being fried, of spices and food, must have transported her back to a time when she had been in greater control of her faculties. Being amongst familiar objects reminiscent of the life she led, she is somehow restored in herself, the sense of loss that she must sometimes feel is left behind in the other world of fast moving cars, skyscrapers and changing landscape.

"Look! A *kueh baolu achuan*. I haven't been able to find my old one, perhaps I ought to buy another."

She talks as if she can remember how to make the kueh. She picks up the cake mould and look it over. My mother used to make the most lovely cakes in the village. In the days before electric cake mixers, she would whisk the eggs by hand and gently fold in the flour to pour into her heated iron-cast mould that had individual pools in the shape of animals and flowers. Standing there in the market with her as she examines the mould, the wonderful smell of her *kueh baolu* being baked comes back to me, the hot coals on top of its lid and in the clay stove, serving as oven. Remembering, I can almost taste its lightness as each *baolu* melts in my mouth. My throat tightens when I think of how proficient my mother had been and how utterly incapable she is now. I wonder sometimes if I might be grieving for my own imminent loss now that I am middle-aged. Do we all look at elderly people and think sometimes how life seems such a waste that for all our achievements and endeavours, this is how we are going to end? Even I, who believe in an after-life sometimes despair, what about those who don't?.

"I'll look for your old one at home, Mak. They don't make the mould as good as yours." I didn't want her to buy something she would never ever use again. "Meanwhile, if you want some *kueh baolu*, there's a *Peranakan* shop in Katong which sells very good ones. I'll buy you some."

I regret that I never got her recipes for her cakes because they were superb. It could be that I, like my sisters, was tired of spending weeks before each Chinese New Year slaving over the hot clay stove making cakes. Although we sometimes had very little to eat, there was a ritual of mother's which she kept up all the years she lived in the village. She would scrimp and save so that every New Year, she would be able to get *new* dresses for her daughters, even if they were from last year's curtains; and distribute her variety of cakes and favourite dishes to the neighbours. My sisters and I had to each carry a tray laden with small plates of the different items to deliver to each of the neighbours in the *kampong*. It was a reciprocal arrangement and during *Hari Raya*, the

Malay neighbours would bring their cakes to us; during *Deepavali,* our Hindu neighbours would send us their food. So everybody's New Year was a time of excitement for everybody else. Life in the kampong was like that.

We had no oven and had to bake over a clay stove using an aluminum pot for an oven, the hot coals below it and on the lid. (When I started work as a nurse and had saved enough, I bought her a *Baby Belling* to put over our kerosene stove, but she never learnt to use it.) Every process was long and tedious, with no mechanical assistance. We had to pound the mung beans by hand and pressed them into moulds manually for the *kueh koyah*; for the *kueh tart,* we had to grate the pineapple and fry it in *gula-melaka* or palm-sugar till it caramelised, then pinch decorative patterns on every single pineapple tart with pincers. We grated numerous coconuts to squeeze the milk from them to make the *kueh bangkit*; rolled the thin crepe hot as it came off its mould to make *kueh belanda*. The *kueh belanda* or love letters was her piece-de-resistance. Legend has it that lovers in the olden days, when love was not openly permitted, used to smuggle love letters in the rolled up crispy crepe to send to their sweethearts. So to emulate tradition, a strip of paper was placed on the crepe before rolling it up, usually with a blessing or prophecy. (That is probably the origin of fortune cookies.) The technique of making love letters is very precise. A thin film of batter made from mixing flour with coconut milk is poured into the mould and as soon as it is cooked, has to be lifted gently off the mould and quickly rolled into a cigar-shape before it hardens. It meant that by the time we have done a few, our palms would be blistering from the heat.

"I used to make the best *kueh*. Look at that decoration on that *kueh tart,*" she says, pointing to a batch of machine-made pineapple tarts. "It's so coarse, too hastily done."

For her, artistry is the key. She never cuts corners. Even if a cake is tiny and will be consumed in minutes, it had to be done properly. In all things, she taught me to be fine, that to be coarse is to be no better than being an animal. It is better to eat in a refined manner from a banana leaf than to eat out of expensive china with no thought for the food. It is better to live in a hut with mud-packed floor where the hut is clean than in a brick mansion where there is filth. It is not the clothes you wear or the way you live that marks you as a fine person, it is integrity. The way you would behave even if no one is watching you. You can't lie or cheat yourself. You can pretend to others, but never to yourself.

"You are talking about a different person," Agatha has said to me many times since my return. "You are romanticising because you don't see her as she is now."

My younger sister has the knack of putting me in my place. Like children who always feel they are children in their parents' presence, no matter how old they are, I always feel like the younger, inexperienced, unsuccessful sister in Agatha's presence. It is strange how all the stories abound about my mother's bad behaviour and yet, she hadn't exhibited it since I arrived. I have seen Mak raving though I have not seen her mouthing the swear words that both Agatha and Bernadette claim can ensue from her mouth. But it won't change my perception of my mother even if I did, I know my mother for what she truly is, a wonderful woman who has lived a life of service to her family and to others. Even if the disease causes her to mutate into some kind of monster, I will always see her as she was. I may not like what I see in her today but that won't stop me loving her, I shall take it that her damaged brain is simply suppressing all that is fine and good in her.

Deep in thoughts, I have lost sight of my mother. She is like a child who needs looking after and is easy to lose in a crowded market. I experience a moment of panic. If she should discover that she is lost, she will panic and will not be able to find her way home. I remember losing my younger son, who was then six, at the newly opened Changi Airport and when I found him, relief turned into cross words because I had feared for him. Our relationship was newly founded and brittle in the early stages of our reunion and I remember the bewilderment in his little eyes. Oh, the mistakes I make in life! Is there a way of retrieving them to sprinkle some fairy dust to make them turn out right? I scuttle round to find my mother, telling myself not to be cross with her when I do find her. She is so frail and small now that she curls into herself so she is not easy to pick out in a crowd. Where she would have stood out in her *sarong kebaya* in the Chinese community, here amongst the Malays who wear the same type of outfit as herself, she is not readily distinguishable. In my urgent haste, I push people out of the way and receive a backlash of rough words. Then I hear her animated voice, which I recognise immediately above the din of the market-place. It's like when your child cries in the night and you wake up even when you have been sound asleep; or when you hear your own name being called in a crowded, noisy room. She is my child now, mine to look after. I can afford to slacken my pace. I do not want to convey my distress to her. She is talking to a wizened old man, the skin on his bare chest, ribbed and brown. She must have tuned in to my presence because she turns to face me without surprise, as if we have not been separated. I am amazed how many times she exhibited this link with me, even when we are thousands of miles apart — I know when to phone her, when she needs to hear from me.

"Ah Phine, ah, look what I have found. This *datok* here knows all the herbs that I have used before. *Datok*, this my daughter, this my daughter. Come all the way from England to see me." She speaks in Malay for the benefit of the old man.

Datok. Our people address the elders like honorary relatives. We never call them by their first names as in the West. My sons call David, *Uncle David*, whereas his children call me by my first name. In the East, his children would be seen as unmannered, it would be seen that they do not hold me in regard. In the days when I was growing up, the manner of addressing elders was more structured, the very way in which we address a person in Chinese, for example an aunt, told the observer *exactly* whether the aunt was a sister on the mother's or father's side and which rung in the family ladder she was on. My Great Aunt, for instance, was called *Tua Ee*, this meant she was the eldest of my mother's sisters. If she was my father's eldest sister, she would be called *Tua Kou*. These days, the manner of calling has been simplified and anglicised, an older man is an *Uncle*, an older lady, an *Aunty*. But in Malay, the traditional language is still retained, an old man like the one my mother is talking to is *Datok* or *Grandfather*. Mak has discovered an ally in the old man, someone who, like her is out of his time, tending a stall of dried herbs which few people have any use for. The walking wounded. In their heyday, both *Datok* and Mak were respected for their expertise, they healed with herbs and poultices, not with pills and injections. Amongst her many skills, my mother was the village herbalist. I don't remember the names of all the herbs she used, but I remember the *dokong anak* because she always got me to collect it from the fields after she had taught me how to identify the herb.

Our family rarely went to the doctor. Firstly, it was because it was expensive; and secondly, because my mother was a naturally gifted herbalist and healer. It was Agatha and Robert who required the most medical attention, Robert because of the infection which damaged his brain, and Agatha because she had rheumatic fever which affected her heart. For someone who spent her lifetime being ill, Agatha is admirable in not letting her illness get the better of her and rising to be the most successful member of our family. She has a shrewd mind and an acute business acumen. Compared to her, I am hopeless in managing my finances whilst she has investments in strategic companies and homes in many places. For both Agatha and Robert, Mak spent a great deal of time to-ing and fro-ing the hospital. Only once was it for herself, when she had to go into hospital to have her goitre removed. I remembered the occasion well because Robert was already born then and she folded her used sarong to place near him and when I asked why, she said that her spirit was caught in the web of the sarong and would help Robert go to sleep.

If we had a fever, she would mix herbs and flour to extract the fever from us. If we had stomach ache, she would boil some foul-smelling herbs or the scrotum of a goat. I carry a scar on my right foot where ankle meets foot. Today, I am surprised that I still have my foot. Then, I placed all my trust in Mother's skill. My big brother, Romia, earned his allowance after school by bringing in drinking water for the neighbours. The nearest public standpipe was about a quarter mile away. People use well-water for washing and ablutions and some of the old and infirm could not manage bringing in the drinking water from so far away. So they paid a few cents for their water to be brought to them. When he was not working, Ah Cob used to do it, then Romia, then Matthew. They cleaned out two kerosene tins and fixed each with a handle, roped them to a pole and they could carry two kerosene tins of water each trip for 20 cents a tin. I must have been about ten or eleven. All of Ah Cob's efforts and Mak's efforts and my own was not bringing in as much money as we needed when Agatha was also in school. My exercise books were running out and I needed some new ones. I thought if I sold some pails of water and charged perhaps 5 cents a pail, I could buy my school exercise books.

The metal pail was almost as tall as I was. The base of the pail was a raised ridge. Without anyone knowing my plan, I carried the pail to the standpipe. When I filled up the pail, I had to use both hands to lift it. It was heavy. The water sloshed about and I lost most of the water on my journey home. I thought, well, I may not even get 5 cents for it but someone might pay me 3 cents for it. A quarter of a mile was a long way for a little girl with a huge pail of water. But I was determined, though I grunted and groaned. My arms felt as if they were coming out of their sockets. I had to stop now and again to regain my strength. A few yards from home, I was near jubilant. And then it happened. After a short rest, I lifted the pail up but my arms were so weakened that the pail came down almost immediately. The problem was that the pail came down with a thud to land on my right foot and the metal ridge sliced cleanly through my ankle. I screamed. Rani came running out of her house and in true Indian fashion, she wailed, "Ah, yo, yo! Ah, yo yo! *Apa lu buat!* What have you done!"

The sand around me was soaked with blood, my foot was nearly dangling from my ankle. I did not pass out but I seemed to have floated away from my body to watch the commotion like a spectator. Someone brought a towel to bind my foot which quickly coloured red. Abdullah, one of our other neighbours, carried me straight to my mother who let out a shrill cry when she saw what had happened. In all honesty, I cannot recall being taken to either a doctor or a hospital. I was completely treated by my mother. How she sealed the gap of my wound, I don't know. All I remember is that she bound my ankle tightly with smelly herbs for weeks, changing the bandages and herbs regularly until I could walk properly again. All I am left with to remind me of my foolishness is an inch-wide scar across where ankle meets foot.

The first time I ever remember seeing a doctor was when the World

Health Organisation (WHO) sent a health team to my school to give all the pupils a medical examination. The doctor declared that I was suffering from malnutrition and fed me a diet of pills, milk and cod liver emulsion. The latter two were equally disgusting to me. The pupils who were considered in need of vitamins and medicine had to queue up to drink the milk at school supervised by the teachers. I nearly threw up when I drank my first pint of milk which was made from powdered milk. The next day, I brought a packet of sugar to put into the milk before I could even manage to keep it down. There was no such solution to the cod liver emulsion. This was usually dispensed by the nurse who came to the school and she would pour out a tablespoonful and each of the malnourished pupils had to line up to be spoon-fed. There was no escape and we had to swallow the emulsion before we were allowed to leave in case we spat it out. The emulsion was like thick cream but had a horrible fishy smell and just as horrible a taste. It felt like torture to be given it rather than a boon. As we stood in line, we tried to scheme to find a way of escaping it but we couldn't. We felt our stomachs become squeasy at the thought of that emulsion and we made faces as we swallowed it. After a few months of these and various other vitamins, my cheeks puffed outwards and my waist disappeared. The medical team was very pleased at my progress but I wasn't. I was so fat that the kids in the *kampong* started to chant a limerick every time I passed by:

Fatty, fatty bom-bom.

Malam, malam churi jagong.

Bom-bom was supposed to be the sound of the earth moving as I walked. And the second line said that every night (*malam*), I stole corn (*jagong*) to eat, which was the reason why I was so fat.

Mak and *Datok* compare old notes, discussing the various herbs they had used for the different ailments. She takes the herb he proffers, smells it and cogitate about it. A smile when there is an agreement, a wave of her hand and a sidelong look when she disagrees. Whether the two of them are hallucinating or play-acting or they genuinely remember their past, I cannot tell. I just rejoice in their animation and their brief companionship. It is so fascinating that my mother who, occasionally, cannot remember the name of her son or grandchild can recall the names of herbs from 30 or 40 years ago. But she has come alive, surfacing from the mildew of her cave and it is enough for me that she can still find a small measure of joy. Joy scalps age from a face more easily than a surgeon's scalpel.

"Must go now, *Datok*. I'm taking my daughter to eat *nasi bryani*. She can't get it in England, you know."

She is suddenly sure of herself, leading rather than being led. A little trip out of the house, back into an environment she can cope with has given her back some confidence. I had noticed that when I took her out to places familiar to her.

"Why don't you take her out to these places more," I asked Bernadette once.

"*Aiiyah*! You think I've got nothing to do all day. I've a business to run, you know. It's so easy for you to talk. You don't live here. And when you are here, you're on holiday. Where have we got time?"

Since Bernadette and her husband have gone into business together, Bernadette has developed a different personality, one that is more suitable for the work she had to do, commanding a staff, making important decisions. A little bit more like Agatha. It is possible that worries over financial matters makes her more harassed and her voice has become shriller. These days she is prone to losing her patience but underneath it all, she is still a kind person, genuinely caring, unable to see people suffer.

We cross the road to the Haig Road food centre where Mak's favourite *bryani* stall is. I notice more and more that she walks with a shuffling gait as if she has little strength to pick up her feet. Like me, she loves the bustle of people around the food centre, the rows of stalls selling different foods with their colourful neon signs, showing pictures of the food they sell, unlike the basic stalls of the old days. I order the *bryani*, mutton for Mak because she loves it, and fish for me because I don't eat meat. The saffron-flavoured Basmati rice is served in the traditional way on a square of banana leaf. In deference to modernity, the banana leaf is placed on a dinner plate. Mak's appetite has dwindled over the years so though she eats often, the amount she eats is birdlike. She scoops up a portion of her rice with her fingers and puts it on my banana leaf. It's an act of love, a habit she has not outgrown, always giving us a portion of her meal in case we go hungry. She has stopped doing that with Agatha, who is strict on hygiene, as she would tick her off.

"It's good to see that you still know how to eat with your fingers, *lah*. Except for Maretiu, no one in the family does that anymore. Do you eat with your fingers in England?"

"Yes, but only at home, when we have good friends. Not when we have business associates or people who don't know me well. I don't want to embarrass David. It seems peasant-like to Europeans to eat with our fingers."

"They don't make love with forks and knives do they?" Mak laughs at her own jocularity. "You know what Grandmother used to tell me? *'Feel with your fingers. You eat with them and you make love with them'.*"

I am astounded. It is as if the years have not fled from her mind and in that moment she is once more the mother I knew. She had repeated those same words to me so many times when I was a child that they were etched in my heart. But I have not heard them since. The waters of her life have carved away so much from the banks of her mind, so what bait had she used to lure a fragment of memory to the surface of her diseased brain?

Eleven

A close friend of mine in Haslemere, a private nurse, nurses a man who had suffered a severe stroke which left him half-paralysed. The tragedy is that this man was once one of Britain's top cardiologists with a thriving practice in Harley Street. One would have thought that an eminent cardiologist would know enough to prevent himself from being struck by such a disease. Sadly, that's not the way of nature. Healers are not exempt from the diseases they are skilled at healing. This must be one of life's greatest ironies. My mother, too, cannot stop or fight the disease that is gripping her own brain, although she has healed many people through her own efforts. It is interesting that looking back at those years in the *kampong* through the telescope of an adult eye, I can see her role as a healer, yet had accepted it as not being anything particularly special when I was a child. Having resource to New Age beliefs these days, I am led to believe that my mother was truly a natural healer (after all, she was neither tutored in the use of herbs nor in the art of healing), but she has never set herself up as one nor allowed anyone to proclaim her so.

"I just do my best to help," she said.

Perhaps true healing is an instinctive thing and medical science only augments that natural skill. Perhaps, also, the milieu of the *kampong* where medical help was not easy to come by and where people were largely uneducated was an environment where my mother's skill could come to the fore. The village people trusted her and I have a vague feeling that trust is a huge factor in the healing process. The Malays were usually the last to come to her because they have their own resource, the *bomoh*, a kind of witch-doctor who prescribed potions and herbs to accompany specific rituals. Mostly male, the village *bomoh* could help you beat fevers and colds and make you sexually attractive or repellent, as each case may have required. Through the thin wooden walls of our hut, I once overheard a woman confiding in a neighbour that the *bomoh* helped her save her marriage through a potion and daily ritual. I did not understand the meaning of *secret garden*, but the words sounded mysterious and they pulled my ears to the gap between the wooden planks.

"He made me stand naked over a steaming bowl of rice and then asked me to feed the rice to my husband. The *bomoh* said that the steam from the rice entering my *secret garden* would keep my husband attracted to me."

Of course, we have all heard about *bomoh* rituals. Village folks were careful where they discarded their nail and hair clippings, old clothes and other personal items — these were said to be potent for making spells work. Pak Hassan, who was our village *bomoh*, was so thin that his belly was a hollow cave under his bony ribcage. He usually received payment in kind for his work: a couple of chickens, some eggs, vegetables and fruits or a new *sarong*, depending on the service he rendered. (The *sarongs* presented to him were patterned differently from those of females', usually in stripes and bold checks unlike the females' which tended to be designed with trees, flowers or birds.) Pak Hassan had no real need of money since there were no rates to pay as he was just like everybody else, without water and electricity in his hut. When he needed a wash, he availed himself of the village well. He housed himself in an *attap* lean-to in the shelter of the sweeping *angsana* trees. If the monsoon rain should batter his fragile *attap* roof, he might get donations of freshly stitched *attap* or a sheet of corrugated zinc. Most of the time, he would be bare-bodied, wrapped only in his *sarong*, sitting cross-legged and staring into space, which I came to learn signified that he was meditating. He was a figure of ambiguity because although he was a healer, it was said that his knowledge of healing came from dark forces. He was reputed to *simpan polong*, ie nurture a *familiar*. He would sit in deep meditation until the *familiar* left his physical body at night to roam across roof-tops to steal souls. That was why many villagers fixed a cactus on their roof-tops so that the needles of the cactus would snag at the *polong* as it passed by. Knowing this, anyone who *simpan polong* would shave their heads to prevent their hair being caught on the cactus. All bald-headed people were suspects. So when Pak Hassan shaved his head, it reiterated the belief that he did indeed nurture a *familiar*. I remember my mother being very convincing when she told us the story, although I am not sure if she used it to keep us indoors at nights.

"Folks swore that they had seen *polong* leave his body," she told us. "One evening, two boys creep-creep to Pak Hassan's hut where his empty shell of a body was sitting upright on the straw mat. *Jahat sekali!* They were so wicked! They leapt under the lean-to and turn-turn body over. Next morning, when *polong* returned, it could not re-enter body from top of head because body now not upright, *what*. So it let out such a wail that goosebumps rose on flesh of *kampong* people, including flesh of bad-bad boys. After long-long, one heroic villager went to hut to re-position body. So *polong* could return home. For weeks, bad-bad boys suffered from raging fever that nearly killed them."

It was the kind of rumour to make the village children wary of

Pak Hassan. Children would scatter whenever he approached them, myself and my friend Parvathi, included. He was the bogeyman of the village. Our hearts would thump as we hid behind doors to watch him shuffling in his wooden clogs down the sandy paths creating clouds of dust. He became more and more eccentric and his methods of curing became quite bizarre: for instance, for heavy period flows, he recommended a drink of fresh blood from a newly slaughtered chicken. I have seen the poor chicken thrashing about on the dusty ground, its throat cut, its head lolling about uncontrollably. (The image came back to haunt me years later, and was one of the factors which turned me into a vegetarian.) People preferred more conventional methods of cure, so they turned to my mother.

"*Nonya, ada sakit, lah!* (Nonya, I'm ill!)" The villagers might say and my mother would put everything aside to tend to them, a Florence Nightingale who provided hope and comfort, if little else. Besides tending to complaints of stomach aches, headaches and other aches, she tended to babies with bloated bellies, women with runaway husbands, men with battered egos. Where she got her knowledge and her wisdom from has always been a mystery to me — this uneducated, illiterate woman who could read no books. The wonderful thing was that she was entirely unassuming about her skills, it was as if she was passing on what was simply flowing through her from a higher source, expecting no returns. My friend Parvathi and her family, who received her closest care, lived only three doors away from us. If I had ever considered moaning about our family's dire straits, I would only have had to look at my friend's family and would realise how lucky we were. Sleeping with rats was nothing compared to the way this family lived. Parvathi, who was the eldest, had eleven brothers and sisters. The floor of their hut was earth-beaten, with neither beds nor furniture. They slept on straw mats. Once on one of my trips to *Atas Bukit*, Top-Of-The-Hill, where the rich English people lived, I saw an old mattress with pockets of broken springs, discarded lying by the rubbish bin. Matthew, Parvathi and I dragged it all the way down so that her sick brother, Gopal could sleep on it. Their mother, Letchumi, was in her 30s and always pregnant and listless. She had a part-time husband who turned up like a bad omen every now and again. Rajah would bring with him a waft of toddy which came out from his breath and pores. The smell of the illegally distilled alcoholic drink made from palm-sugar oozed out from him like slime. Usually unshaven and dressed in clothes that had been slept in, he would stagger into the village, calling for his wife in a drink-sodden voice,

"Eh, Letchumi! Letchumi! Your husband is here."

How they manage to copulate on the straw mats with all the other children in the same small space was an interesting feat. It must have been a particular skill of men living in the *kampong*, because my father too was very virile and got his own way often, although he and my mother did not share the same bed. From the number of pregnancies that my mother was supposed to have had, she would have had to have a child every two years since she got married at the age of 17. Many women in the village were in the same situation as my mother, being objects of their husband's sexual urges and the instruments for bearing their children. Necessity, rather than love, kept these women where they were. Since Rajah paid the rent and bought the food, Letchumi had little choice but to make her body available for her drunken husband. He gave her babies and left her to rear them herself. Her youngest, Gopal, suffered from epileptic fits and my mother often had to attend to the little boy holding him whilst he thrashed about wildly, his mouth foaming. Letchumi was unable to cope with this and would just watch and cry. The visiting district nurse supplied Letchumi with some sleeping tablets for little

Gopal. No one could have anticipated the tragedy that was to occur, a tragedy that is seared into my brain. Sometimes, a word, a name, an image would flutter through my mind and I would recall that very sad and painful day.

Parvathi was Letchumi's eldest daughter and hope. She was a very pretty teenager with huge eyes and shiny black hair which snaked down her back in a single plait. Parvathi worked in the paper factory in the village ever since she was twelve, cutting, pasting and folding envelopes. It was amazing how such seemingly harmless work could result in such pain for her. Paper slices thinly like a sharp razor and her fingers and hands would often bleed from her work. Like her other collegaues, she was paid according to the number of envelopes she finished per day, so in her rush to complete more, she could not afford to pay undue care, resulting in little nicks all over her hands, small but deep nicks, which were not helpful when you then had to scrub the family's washing. Although she was three years older than I was, we were the best of friends. When I began school, I became her teacher. Not all the village children was as privileged as I was to go to school, in fact the majority didn't. Parvathi and I would sit in the hissing light of a carbide lamp and I would teach her how to read and write English. If you knew a carbide lamp, you would know that it spat and spluttered so that the flame was never constant. So your eyes had to chase the light to the illuminated part of the book so that you could read the words. The long-term effect of this was to make your eyes go funny. Perhaps that is why I have one lazy eye which manifests itself when I am tired. *Juling ayer*, it was called. Though Parvathi never went to school, she spoke Tamil and Malay, the latter being the language that unified the villagers. The village folks were largely uneducated, but many were bilingual. This is a fact that puzzles me today. Do we humans have this natural capacity for language, for healing, for listening?

"Paper. P-a-p-e-r," She would repeat slowly after me.

At nearly nine, I learnt what a responsibility it was to be a teacher, your pupil expecting that what you teach is the truth. You become an authority. Of course, she envied me being able to go to school. It was only natural. After all, she was just a little over 12 years old. Two people shared my school days intimately with me: my mother and Parvathi. Through me, they too learnt. I stored each thing that happened in school to bring home as a gift to these two hungry minds. But my mother did not learn to read, she simply absorbed my words and my experiences at school. My first visit to the school library was a memorable occasion which the two of them lapped up voraciously. It was not a big library but it was the first I had seen, six short bookshelves crammed with books that you did not have to pay to read. As soon as I could read, I borrowed all the number of allocated books, which was two a week and finished them before the week was out. My cousin George, twice removed or something, told me about the National Library in town, where there were thousands of books waiting to be read. It sounded like paradise to me but up until then, I had not been allowed out on my own without my parents or my brothers to chaperone me. So a visit to the National Library became an ambition. Youngsters today don't realise what a milestone it was for us to go out on our own, visit the library or cinema when they have all this freedom today. This is such a modern world of internet, e-mails and Bluetooth devices that to imagine a world without electricty, just a couple of generations ago, must be unthinkable for them. Reading by poor light was the cause of my bad eyesight today. In the evening, our house was lit by a hurricane lamp and after ten o'clock it would be replaced by oil lamps. Because we shared one big room, the lights would be put out when it was bedtime, so that those who wanted to sleep could go to sleep, and late reading was not exactly encouraged. When I started sleeping on the floor in the living room where the orange crates were, I was more able to read into the night in candlelight, and when we eventually had electricity in 1965, when Singapore finally became independent, I used the electric table lamp. Between the two periods, our house was lit by a flourescent lamp powered by a village generator. The generator had its own personality and every now and again, it would throw a tantrum and refused to work. So we kept candles and oil lamps handy.

The publisher for my first novel took me out to lunch one day on one of my trips to Singapore and he brought along one of his colleagues. The lady was well-dressed, heavy 24-carat gold earrings with diamonds in her ears, a thick gold chain around her neck, a multitude of rings on her fingers. She spoke with a polished, buttery voice. My publisher told her that I had been brought up in a Malay *kampong* and he asked me to tell her about it. I described to her the kind of life I had led, with no electricity and no running water, but I tried to make it sound humorous than pathetic because I don't have to live that kind of life now. The woman sat disbelieving, then tossed back her mane of jet-black, shoulder-length hair and said, "Were there really *kampongs* like that here in Singapore? I thought they existed only in Malaya."

If she had been at the age of the young reporter who had interviewed me when I won the prize in the Ian St. James Awards, I would not have been surprised, but she looked nearer my age, which meant that the *kampongs* existed in her lifetime. I then thought she that she might have been educated abroad and had therefore been shielded from the harsh realities of her own country.

"Did you grow up in Singpaore?" I asked her.

"Yes. Around Holland Road," she said.

Well, that explained part of it. Holland Road is to the ordinary, local people in Singapore, like Knightsbridge or Mayfair to the English. Only Europeans and extremely wealthy local people lived there. If I thought my classmate, Elizabeth, was rich, this lady and her family must have been hugely wealthy. Subsequently, when she began to talk about her family and the bond-maids they had, I *knew* they were (and probably still are) hugely wealthy. Bond-maids were servants bought from poor households, who rendered a lifetime of service. Like slaves really. And this lady was telling us that her family had them until the 1960s! Now, I became disbelieving that people could pluck young children, usually pre-teen girls from China or Malaya, from their own families to serve theirs. Certainly, the likes of this woman wouldn't have dreamed of venturing near *kampongs* such as ours for fear of disease, plague and dirt. But I was still surprised that she thought everyone in Singapore lived like her, that she could be so unaware of the poverty that surrounded her in such a small country as Singapore.

She couldn't have understood what it was like for me, a *kampong* girl, to take my first step into the school library to realise that these were books I could take home to read for free. She would not have known the impact of the idea that between the leaves of books were worlds waiting to be explored, when all the world I had until then known was the shanty-village I grew up in. All it needed was a capacity to read and one could be transported to new places — to someone who had no means of travelling, no hope of knowing other places, other worlds, like the rich and privileged, it was a phenomenal step. But never mind, she must have been a really good person in her past lives to have deserved being born into such privilege. Even if I had been bad in mine, I was okay in this lifetime because I was given the opportunity of going to school and I did learn to read. I was given the chance to borrow books. Since we were a British colony, most of the books were stories about England and I travelled to that faraway place through Enid Blyton's books. I took them home to share with Mak and Parvathi. My mother was happy on two accounts: one, that I could read; and two, that she was given a way to escape the coconut shell of her existence through these books, too. Mine was a shared edcuation, brightening the lives of others as I learned. So when I started reading the daily English newspapers, I began to share them with Mak, too, pointing out to her relevant photographs pertaining to the article I was reading. It was a habit that lasted all the time I lived with her and I know she treasured it, too. Many of the housewives in the village did not read either and Mak might relay a tid-bit of news to them the following day. It was amusing to watch her as she held out the newspaper and pointed out the photographs to them and talked about the article as if she could read.

"You see," I heard her say to Mak Ahyee once. "That's how Bukit Timah canal looked yesterday, *lah*. Rushing water was muddy and overflowed to flood the road. Very many trouble for people and cyclists. This motorist was blind-blind by rain that he drove straight into canal. That is his up-turned car here. "

"Wahh!" Mak Ahyee exclaimed, and I couldn't be sure whether it was a response to the incident or the fact that she thought Mak could read the newspaper.

On her days off when we were not reading, Parvathi and I played at *masak-masak*, cooking over a small clay stove and pretending to be wives and mothers. We crouched behind a lean-to, cooking and beating off mosquitoes. Parvathi's mental years did not match her physical years. It was not something I noted then nor was I bothered by it, she was just a good friend with whom I shared lovely times and impossible dreams. When she returned home from work with her fingers bleeding, I would tend to them as if I was a nurse and that made her very happy. We had five good years together where she learnt a great deal from the books we read together. When I turned fourteen, and Parvathi, nearly seventeen, we started reading romances by Denise Robins and Barbara Cartland. We had salvaged the romantic novels from the bins of the English people at the Top-Of-The-Hill. Because my father would kill me if he found out, we wrapped the covers with brown paper and read it in our secret hideaway. Once there, we would unwrap the covers and drooled over the bronzed muscular bodies of the handsome heroes. We learnt of strong, handsome men who would come and sweep us off our feet, take us away from the village to live in their wonderful castles. The books inspired us to dream about falling in love and marrying for love. It was not a concept we were used to, but we could hope. For brief moments, we would pretend that we would be allowed to fall in love and marry the men of our choice. But this was not to be for Parvathi. That was the pivotal point when everything changed for Parvathi, and for our relationship. If her life had been luckless before, it was to get worse. She had a visit from her father, then came calling me in huge distress, tears streaming from her face.

"What is it, *huh*?" I said. "What is it?"

We held hands and walked together to our secret hideout, a place hidden from view by a coconut tree brought down by the monsoon rains, its trunk resting on the ground, its fronds creating a shelter. The fact that my best friend was distressed made me distressed but I let her cry for a bit, rubbing coconut oil into her hands.

"My father got make match for me, *lah*."

"Oh, no, *lah*," I said, in disbelief that such a fate was going to befall my friend. But I had not heard the whole news yet.

"And more-more bad. The man my father chosen me is my father's brother! Imagine, my own uncle! He is fat and ugly, *one*, and he is 40 years old, *lah!* And I am not even 17!" She bawled.

I had caught a glimpse of her uncle before and he was not a pretty sight, a man with a pockmarked face, with teeth all brown with betel nut juice stains. I tried to imagine having to let such a man kiss or fondle me, and it filled me with disgust, so I cried with her; fearing my own destiny, the fate that my own father had spoken of many times, of finding the right man for me when I was old enough. Someone he said, who would give him a sizeable dowry for me. But I had planned to run away from home before he inflicted that fate upon me. I didn't know what I would tell my mother when the time came, but I was sure she'd understand. But it was Parvathi, not I, who stood at such a crossroad.

"What did your mother say?"

"Ah, she's only a woman, *what*. What can she do? She said him to find a younger man for me, *lah*. But my father, he said her to shut up. He making the reason that my uncle, his wife just dieded. And they have four little-little children. So of course need new wife quickly-quickly to look after them, *what*. He promiseded to pay my father plenty money for me. But what *for, huh?* Money won't last long; same night will be used for toddy, *lah*."

When I told Mak about it, she sighed.

"That's why I want you to go to school," she said. "Then you can earn your own living. You don't have to be ruled by men."

Was she laying the ground for me to defy my father? Was she suggesting that I should break conventions and make my own choices in life? My heart leapt — if I studied well, I wouldn't have to marry the man of my father's choice! My future could be in my own hands. It was a thought that filled me with power for the first time! My mother, through her foresight in getting me to school, was shaping my future. I had never treated school lightly before but in that moment, school and education became all the more crucial. It was not just about learning about worlds compressed in books, it was also about learning how to have power in your own hands and to wield it! It was about leaving the coconut shell of my existence. Sad as I was about Parvathi's impending fate, I was excited about mine. This I did not share with Parvathi, as it would have been unfair in the circumstances.

Parvathi's father came and went, making arrangements for the wedding. Parvathi was to leave her job the following month. She became more and more morose. I knew she was really upset when her old habit came back. Usually, her long, black hair was sleeked back from her face with coconut oil and tied in a single braid, but whenever she was upset, she would loosen this to twist a strand around her right forefinger, then she would put her thumb into her mouth. It was a most peculiar mannerism, one which I have not seen adopted by anyone else. But I knew it meant she was troubled. When she stopped turning up for her reading lessons, I became really worried. I went to her hut to persuade her to come out but she wouldn't. Her hut was small, dark and dank, and it seemed to suit her mood. She had even stopped going to work and simply sat in the corner, not wanting to bathe, not combing her hair, not eating, a flesh-and-blood human being turned to wood. Broken dreams and sadness hung like a pall in the air.

"*Aiiyah!*" Letchumi grumbled, banging aluminum pots about. "What for behave like this, *one*? At least got chance to get out of this village. Your uncle is better off, give you nice-nice home. You cry too much, eyes go puffy-puffy, then who wants you, *huh*? Where you got chance to get married if like that? When we born as women, we know this our life, why make so bad-bad? That's all we are fit for. Just face it, *lah!*"

That's all we're fit for. Letchumi's words seared my mind. It was the simple philosophy of village women. Paravthi's fate could have been mine. In that instance, I was ever so grateful to my mother for daring to think differently. My mother, who at this moment can no longer think for herself, at that time, was able to realise that I would follow her fate as a woman if I was not educated, the cycle of women being dominated going on-and-on. Where did she derive this wisdom and foresight? I am indebted to her for eternity for making such efforts to create a different future for me. It was no small achievement for her. She had to fight the conventions of her time. And my father.

One morning, some weeks later, a shrill cry woke us. It was coming from Letchumi's hut. The natural thought was that Gopal was suffering another epileptic fit, although Letchumi usually shouted for my mother's help rather than screaming in this manner. My mother and other villagers rushed to Letchumi's hut. Somehow I was certain that it wasn't anything to do with Gopal. I knew. I already knew. My heart had already rolled into a tight ball when my mother came home and told me about it. I was ready for what she was going to say before she even said it. I had already felt it in my bones. Letchumi found Parvathi's cold body when she tried to wake her. Parvathi had taken all of Gopal's sleeping pills. She had escaped her mortal bonds.

However much you believe in the after-life and reincarnation, it doesn't help when someone you love leaves this life. You may believe that their soul is better off but you still miss their physical presence. It was the first death I had to face and I couldn't face it. I refused to go to see her until the day of the funeral. I could not bear the weight of it. I tried to read but Parvathi's face kept flashing in front of the pages. Whatever I did, her sad tearful eyes followed me everywhere. Why hadn't her mother stood up to her father? Why were women so weak? Then with a gasp, it suddenly occurred to me that my mother had just saved me from Parvathi's fate. Because somehow, I know that if I couldn't run away when I was of marriageable age, I, too, would have taken Parvathi's path if my father had forced me to marry a man of his choice.

I could not avoid confronting the situation forever. I wanted to remember her as she had been but I also knew that I had to say my last goodbye. It was the day of her funeral and I knew I had to steel myself to see her for the last time. My dearest childhood friend. I promised myself not to cry. In a way, she helped because when I looked upon her face, it had a stillness and peace that I knew she had longed for. I can still see her face today as she lay there in her cheap, open coffin, her hands clasped at her waist. Her tension and grief had flowed out with the life force and so her face was serene, she looked as if she was only asleep, a kind of Indian Snow White. Colorful petals of myriad flowers were strewn all over her body which was wrapped in a white cotton sari, virginal to the end. On her forehead was a circlet of small flowers, the kind that Indians loved in garlands for the statues of their Gods. Someone had coloured her cheeks with henna, placed the *puttu* which marked her third eye. She looked like a young bride. Her closed eyes were deep in their sockets and she looked really peaceful, no sign of struggle or anguish. In some way, I was glad for her, that she was spared a life with her gross uncle. The women were wailing loudly, hands in the air in gestures of helplessness. Parvathi's father didn't even bother to attend, so angry was he to have the dowry snatched from him. They told me that Parvathi was going to be burned on a pyre, that was why the coffin would not be closed. I pushed the image from my mind, of her body going up in flames, the body that had brushed mine, the arms that had held mine.

Standing there, looking down at her, I thought how beautiful she was. I thought how, in another time and place, some handsome prince would have arrived on his white steed and swept her off her feet. And then they would ride away into the sunset, Parvathi sitting on the horse with the prince, his arms around her as she gazed up at him with a smile, her long, black hair flowing in the wind. Then suddenly, I knew that I wanted to give her a present, send something after her spirit. Chinese people burn paper houses, cars, servants and money so that when the deceased got to the Other Side, they have all the things they would need, sometimes even things they didn't have in their mortal lives, like Rolls Royces and mansions. I knew what Parvathi would have liked. I rushed back to my house and brought out the novel by Barbara Cartland which I had secreted in my mattress roll, so that my father would not find it. I waited for an opportunity. The women were still crying, especially Letchumi. The moment came when Letchumi suddenly fell into a faint. People rushed to help her and during the scuffle, the coffin was unattended. That was when I picked up Parvathi's cold-cold hands and slipped the book into them, then quickly rearranged the flower petals to conceal her favourite love story. Perhaps she'd find her prince, her soulmate, the man of her dreams on the Other Side and he'd kiss her awake.

Twelve

A long time later, when I felt able to talk about it, I brought up the subject of Parvathi's suicide to my mother. Even at that age, I was convinced that Parvathi needn't have died if she was living in another time and place, where women had choices. I was so mad that men seemed to have so much power over women. In writing this, I am also learning more about myself. In my childhood years, I have seen the way women, like my mother, Letchumi and Parvathi were treated and I must have somehow registered this in my mind. It makes me want to prove that a woman is capable of looking after herself without the beneficience of men. It makes me unable to tolerate the bullying nature of men. I had to leave my first husband because he would have made me a product of his whims, shaped me to his limitations, tied me to his insecurities. My mother had invested too much in me for me to allow myself to be a prey to all she had fought to be free from. I fought not just for myself, but for my mother and all oppressed women in the world. All those years, ago, after Parvathi died, I didn't know that something had shifted in me, the something which made me look at men in a different way, made me wary of their power over women. Perhaps it was the time too, when the seeds of frustrations and anger had sprouted inside me and I looked at my father, not just with a daughter's eyes, but with a growing woman's eyes, of some of his unpardonable behaviour towards my mother. I wanted to stand up to my father for my mother, wanted to make him realise that he could not wield his tongue or his fists at his will. But I was brave only in thoughts.

"*Bor eng!* (Useless!)" My father said to me, time and time again. "So fat and dark. *Di tiang ai?* (Who wants you?) How can fetch big dowry?"

Harsh words flung repeatedly at you are like a sculptor's chisel, they chip at your self-esteem, shape you into something you were not in the beginning. Whilst my mother made me believe that I could be somebody in this world, my father showed me the opposite mirror. In it, I saw a fat, ugly little girl, totally unlovable, totally untalented.

That day, when I finally broached my mother about Parvathi's death, she and I were beading *Peranakan* slippers to sell. Fewer and fewer women were wearing the slippers and machines were coming up with imitations far cheaper than what we could make, so our earnings from these were dwindling. At my mention of Parvathi, Mak sighed, then pushed back a stray bit of hair from her yet unlined brow and looked at me with those eyes of hers which never failed to stir me with their beauty.

"Maybe she finished her schooling for spirit already. We are born so that our spirit can speak, *lah* ," she said. "This life is big school for learn-learn. But usually, if take own life, must come back and come back until we complete our lessons."

Her remark wasn't in the least bit Catholic in nature. We went to church on Sunday, confessed our sins and then took Holy Communion. We said the rosary and called on all the saints, the Virgin Mary and Jesus Christ. Yet, in our hearts, the religion of our ancestors had staked its claim. I suspect it was this long-ingrained belief in karma which motivated my mother, making her rise above the squalor she lived in as though she was living the life of a queen. I learnt from my mother that one's attitude is of utmost importance. It is the way you look at things, it is your inner eye which colours your situation.

"It's not just what you eat that shapes your body and your soul; it's what you think and what you feel," she once told me.

Though uneducated, my mother is a great philosopher. Her philosophy is not academic, it's of real life. She had the propensity of seeing something bright even in her darkest hour. Though she tried to pretend otherwise in those days of deprivation, I knew she did worry, mostly because I could pick up her worried vibes. I recall a day when the *chettiar* came to the house to collect the rent, but, of course, she had used the rent money for food. She had just returned from having bathed at the well, her sarong tied across her chest, her hair still wet. You would have thought her enticing. I imagined that she would have looked like a lovely mermaid the night Grandfather found her swimming naked in the sea. Her shoulders were golden-brown and smooth, her neck, slender like a swan's. I am sure that one of the reasons Grandfather gave her a thrashing was to protect her because he could not bear that anyone should see her like that, so beautiful and vulnerable. When Mak opened the door to the Indian *chettiar*, I noticed that his eyes widened. He had a look which I could only guess was what the Malays called *mata keranjang*.

"Where is the money?" He barked out his words in Malay.

"Don't have today. Maybe have, next week, *lah*. You come, next week, okay?" she pleaded. It was the timbre of her voice which told me that she was anxious.

"You said that last week. You think I got so much time to come round every week or *what*?"

"Please," she said, hoping that her soft voice would encourage him to lower his, aware that the neighbours' heads were poking round the corner. "Sure have, next week."

"You better. If you don't have money, I shall personally go to your husband's office to collect, okay?"

"You don't have to. Money ready next week."

He did lower his voice then, adding a knife edge to it which I didn't fully comprehend though I felt from my mother's reaction that it wasn't very nice.

"Perhaps you can find one way or another to pay me," he said tracing a grubby finger on Mak's bare shoulders.

Looking back, I can imagine that she must have squirmed, suffering a feeling of humiliation. I feel the humiliation as if it is my own. Perhaps this is what modern psychologists might call *false memory syndrome*, that I didn't really feel the humiliation. But certainly in remembering the scene, I am humiliated in my mother's place. She and I share a unique twinning of our souls, so that our auric fields overlap, thus our thoughts and feelings flow into each other as naturally as a river flowing towards the sea. That is why when Agatha speaks about our mother as if she's deaf or has an absent mind, I prickle and sit up, poised to react.

"Agatha is like Ah Tetia," Mak often said. "She has the burden of living with ordinary mortals."

Now that the anxiety of my mother's heart attack has dissipated, it would make sense for me to go home, after all I do have a husband back in England. Having two families in different continents is not an easy thing to juggle. You feel torn between one and the other. This has been my heartache for the last 15 years. I was on my own for five years before I decided to marry David and go to England. My ex-husband refused to let the children grow up in a culture foreign to them. As they were very young, the courts agreed. I had a choice of retaining custody of them and continue to live in Singapore or signing over custody to my ex-husband and seeking a new life for myself.

"Your children will grow up," Mak said when I presented the problem to her. "Their stepmother will look after them. They've got all their family here. David has been waiting for five years for you. He might not wait forever. Give yourself a life."

I knew my mother was old-fashioned and that she had hoped my marriage to the children's father would work but she never took sides, never put my ex-husband down, she just gave me permission to live my life the way I wanted to live it. And it was certainly a heroic gesture on her part when she gave me permission to leave my children — she who gave her entire life for the happiness of her children. How selfish I was next to her goodness. Yet, she never judged me. She continued to sustain me in her love. But, despite her support, there was a great deal of indecision, a lot of pain and insurmountable guilt. Happiness with a man beckoned, yet the imminent loss of my children was tearing my guts out. Until today, I cannot say with certainty if I had made the right decision. The price of my new freedom was high and I don't know if I can ever forgive myself. Without telling her, my mother understood my dilemma. If she saw one of my boys, she might say to me, "See how much he looks like you." It was her way of pointing out our connection. Of my siblings, it was Bernadette and Matthew who saw me through difficult times. My separation from my boys was also the beginning of my emotional distance from Jacob. Of all my family, he was the only one in touch with my ex-husband and the boys. Even when my ex-husband was very acrimonious and never gave the boys my letters nor put my telephone calls through, Ah Cob was in touch with them, meeting them regularly. How I was starving for sight of my children, hanging around their school when I was in town, going to places they might go to; how I would have loved to hear their voice, feel their touch. Foolishly, I believed that I was sparing them the pain of a tortured marriage, not wanting them to feel torn in a tug-of-love. I believed that if I told them I loved them, that would be enough. But I didn't reckon on my ex-husband's poisonous nature and worse, his mother's. My brother, Ah Cob, saw the boys, socialised with them because my ex-husband was his friend, yet he would not give them news about me, would not feed me with even one morsel of news about them, not one single photgraph. When I confronted him with it, he said,

"*Aiiyah*, forget them, *lah!*"

Such a cruel, cruel sentence. How could he expect that a mother could forget children she had carried within her body, children who had suckled at her breast? He was actually upset that I should expect him to ruin his friendship with my ex-husband on account of providing me information about my children! It was then that I realised that Ah Cob was very much like my father, so rigid in his thinking, so remote from people's feelings. Like my father, there was only one point of view. His. Fortunately, David and I persisted with the courts until my boys and I were finally reunited.

Matthew said, "There you are. Didn't I tell you, you won't be apart forever?"

Of course, if my father was alive, I would never have been able to go through a divorce. He was an old-fashioned man with old-fashioned ideas. If he had his way, I would have had to marry the man of his choice. I was, to him, a tradeable commodity, to get a good dowry. In some ways, it was fortuitous that he died before I came to be of marriageable age. I had confessed to Parvathi, when we were reading Barbara Cartland, that I would marry a man for love and would run away before I allowed my father to force me into marriage. Pity Parvathi didn't choose to run away and chose instead the course she had taken. Sometimes in my defeatist moments, I wonder if I should have let someone chose my husband for me since I didn't make a good choice myself, anyway.

My father was distant to us emotionally. Though I remembered him taking my sisters and I on outings and bringing home packets of supper, the predominant memory is one of fear, and sometimes loathing. I can never forget the way he behaved the day that I eventually went to the National Library in Stamford Road in the heart of town. A town excursion for us was an event. If my parents took us to the High Street which was *the* place to shop, it was on the Number 18 STC bus. But they were rare occasions. So I was not particularly familiar with town. But there was a place I really loved to visit. My cousin, George, who lived in the same village as us, told me many times about this wonderful place that he visited. It was the National Library, where there were hundreds upon thousands of books, all free to borrow. Since I started learning to read, I devoured every book I could get hold of, from the school library to the mobile van that came around the village. I even read tin cans, the back of packages, government notices and anything else that had words on them. The more I read, the hungrier I became. A whole building full of books that I could borrow for free sounded like an unending gift. Although I read Malay books, too, the English language beguiled me and swept me off my feet.

"I'll take you if you want to come," George said. "But you pay your own bus-fare."

"Oh, yes, please. Of course, I'll pay my own bus-fare."

There didn't seem anything wrong in going out with George, he was a relative, even if he was a distant one. We weren't out on a date or anything. I wasn't particularly interested in George's company but was more thrilled about the fact that I was going to see this place that had thousands and thousands of books, more than anything else and didn't even give a thought to the fact that I was going out somewhere, unchaperoned, with a boy. Surely my father couldn't object. After all, it was already 1964, although my father's values seemed to be anchored in the last century. In anticipation of the trip, I saved up my recess money for my bus-fare.

This was about a few months after Parvathi's death. I was missing her terribly and I felt that the trip would put me in a better mood. It was my first trip anywhere without my parents or my brothers. I had to admit that the whole thing was like some great adventure for a little *kampong* girl. My Aunt came by with George and stayed for coffee and *bubor kachang* with my mother. George and I had a quick bowl each of the mung beans cooked in coconut milk before we left because the fragrance was irresistible. My mother, too, thought that the National Library must have been a wonderful place if they gave away so many books to be read for free. As she read vicariously through me, she too was excited that I would be bringing home lots of books to read. It was our shared pleasure, the first occasion of the mother-child role being reversed. George was only a year older than me but was light-years ahead in street sense. Of my elder brothers, probably only Ah Cob was interested in books, and only those which dealt with Mathematics and Science. When I was 14, he was already married and had left home. Romia was then obsessed with girls and had no time for books, and Matthew was more interested in how his foot flexed in *sepak raga* than in books. I had no one else besides George who would introduce the National Library to me.

We took the bus outside our village, along Upper Serangoon Road. The STC was a trolley bus with overhead cables that met other cables overhead in the air like a huge net. It was a day like any other day in the tropics, hot and clammy. The bodies in the crowded bus smelled of sweat and the food they ate. My fare to the library and back cost 30 cents, which was a considerable amount for me in those days. So I was going to make the most of it. At Macpherson's Third Mile, people came on board having been to the big wet market there, bringing with them the smell of fresh fish, spices and all sorts of food. They carried basket-loads of vegetables and live chickens and ducks whose feet and wings were tied together. Above the loud chattering, the chicken squawked and cackled, and the ducks quacked. I was glad that George had ushered me to the back of the bus. But as the bus made its way towards town, the passengers took turns to disembark, they were not the type of people to live in the expensive part of town. You could see the scenery changing as we approached town, coconut trees and attap houses making way for terraced shophouses with five-foot-ways, then the lovely brick houses with gardens, and finally the office buildings. We passed the Cathay Building, the highest building then at 26 storeys, once the headquarters of the *Kempetai* during the War.

I felt like a grown-up, travelling this far without my parents or my brothers. One day, I would do the journey on my own, without George or anyone to chaperone me. But it was a beginning. We got off the bus at Bras Basah Road, whose name was a corruption of the Malay words, *beras basah* (wet rice), from a Malay folklore about someone stealing rice and escaping with it in a tongkang. But through divine intervention, the amount of rice grew and grew as the tongkang was making its way down the river. Eventually, the thief met his fate when the tongkang capsized and all the rice spilled into the river and got wet. George and I walked a respectful distance apart: he was seven paces ahead, and I walked dutifully behind. As we walked along Stamford Road, my heart began to beat a drumbeat. I was so looking forward to seeing this room that held all these wonderful books which I could take home in turn. Passing some bookshops along the way, we paused to peer at the window displays, the books looked new and grand, especially the picturebook hardbacks, expensive jewels out of our reach. If there was any money at home, food took first priority, storybooks, especially new ones, were not even remotely on the list. Climbing the stairs cut into the small hill leading up to the library was like climbing towards a new planet. For people with a capacity to simply go into a shop to buy a book, this must seem like an exaggeration. But for me, the different worlds upon worlds upon worlds pressed into words, were waiting for my eyes to light them up and bring them to life. Learning to read was such a marvellous skill, I wondered how I had survived before, not being able to read. At the reception, George helped me to register as a member of the library and my hand was shaking when I held the pen. I was signing myself to a new life. Six books! I was allowed to take home six books for three weeks without paying a single cent! It was beyond my wildest dream. If I had not been so conservative, I would have hugged George for making it possible.

We walked through the turnstile and there it was, this enormous Aladdin's cave of books. There were reading tables and rows upon rows of shelves stacked tightly with books. My heart flipped over with excitement. I ran around touching the books to make sure they were palpable and real. People shushed me and George gave me a disapproving look, but he showed me how to use the index to find the type of books I wanted, then he left me. I didn't know where to start. I could learn about England, America or Timbuktu. I could disappear into a world created by Enid Blyton, Lewis Carroll or Louise May Alcott. The entire choice was mine. When you have not had a choice before, this was frightening. How do you make the best use of your time? What should you read? The mind raced ahead of itself and I had to rein it in, forcing myself to stay composed and be selective. Engrossed in my books, it was easy to slip somewhere else and leave my painful world behind and emerge in one where I had lots of food to eat, new clothes to wear. So when George came to collect me, he startled me out of my reverie. I had towers of books on my reading table, unable to decide which to take home.

"You're only allowed six," he reminded me.

In the end, I took *Little Women*, because one of the characters had the same name as myself, *Alice In Wonderland, Robinson Crusoe*, a book on English nursery rhymes, a collection of fairy tales by Hans Christen Andersen with full-colour pictures which I wanted to show my mother and a Malay book on the legendary hero, *Hang Tuah*. None of the books were new, some of the pages yellowed, many of the spines weakened from years of handling. But their sad condition did not matter to me, only their content. On our return journey, George and I did not engage in conversation, so absorbed were we in our newly selected books. The printed words leapt up and down when the bus went over bumpy roads, but I was too immersed to care. My cousin's house was not far from the bus-stop at the entrance to our village. His family was obviously better off than mine because their house stood alone in its small garden which had a mango tree and bougainvillea pots. They had their own bathrooms and *jamban*.

"Thank you so much, George. I can't thank you enough. You don't realise what a world you have introduced me to." It was the last I was to see of George. For a time, it was because my father forbade it, then later because his family moved out of the village and we did not keep in touch. I am still not sure what his connection was to our family, whether he was indeed a real cousin.

I was very proud to be seen walking along the sandy, rutted road with my stack of books. I felt like some great scholar and was showing off that I could *read*. Pride is a sin and I was to pay heavily for it. Most of the village children were like Parvathi, forced into labour at a young age, either at the paper factory or at the rattan factory so they could not read, never held a book in their hands. I was one of the more fortunate ones. That afternoon, I was beaming and smiling as if I had struck gold. I organised all the household chores in my mind so that I could get time to read each evening before lights went out. I was determined to finish reading my allotted books before their due date and go back for more. Mak Ahyee saw me with all the books and she exclaimed, "Aiiyah! *Banyak pandai!* (Very Clever!)" Exactly what I had wanted people to say. I grew a hundred feet tall. But I shrank as suddenly when I saw my father's bicycle leaning against the kitchen wall. What was he doing coming home from work in the middle of the afternoon? When I entered the house, Mak was huddled on the floor, her back against the meat-safe, her hair loosened. My father had obviously unleashed his temper on her again. My blood boiled.

"Oh, Oh, our madam is back, eh? You so brave to go out with a boy!"

So he had found out. Why should he be angry anyway? It was not as if I was compromising myself. He had presumed that my mother had given permission for me to go and had already taken it out on her. The seeds of frustration and anger inisde me were blossoming. Why should he be the only one to decide what to do and when? Why did he always take everything out on my mother? I started by being piqued, then I became mad. Perhaps I inherited a little of my father's temper, too, but it had been latent for so long. Now it pushed me to say something. But still, my upbringing buttoned up my lips, stopped me from reacting. We have to respect our elders. We have to respect our elders, I chanted mentally in my head. Even when they are wrong and behaving badly? A small voice in my head asked. And the voice won. Now, if I had been a man, a much bigger man, I could have socked my father right there and then. It was a blasphemous thought! But my father never gave me a chance. He moved towards me with menace in his eyes. Well, I'm in for it now, I told myself. It's the *rotan* for sure. I gritted myself for the caning. I would let my mind drift so that I would not feel the lashes on my body. The books would be worth the punishment.

"I went to the National Library to borrow books. They're important for my studies. Look!" I thought it wise to explain in case he had the wrong idea why I went out, unchaperoned. I held the books out as proof of my outing. "George took me straight there and then we came home. That's all."

"Don't talk to me about your studies. This is all your mother's fault, encouraging you to think. I said education is bad for women, poison their minds, make them less meek. Before, you wouldn't dare answer back. Now you open your mouth like a chicken backside! You let other people see you walking alone with a boy and you say *'That's all'*? You disgrace me, behave like a slut."

I didn't know what *slut* meant. But I knew he was angry and wasn't listening to reason. His arm shot out and knocked the books out of my hands. I was startled. I had expected him to attack me not my books. My beautiful, precious books. Their pages opened like wings to take flight. But like wounded birds, they flapped uselessly then tumbled to the cement floor. I quickly squatted down to rescue them. In the next instant, I received quite a shock as my father kicked the books out of my hands. The books took second flight and in the process, some of the weakened spines snapped and the books came apart. I was horrified.

"No! No! Stop it! They don't belong to me. I have to return them."

In response, he picked up one book, *Little Women*, I think, and started tearing its pages. The sight of him, so nonchalantly destroying something I love, brought up all the frustration and anger I felt towards him. What had the book done to him that he should hurt it? At the same moment, all the times that he had beaten my mother, my brothers and myself flashed before my eyes. Okay, so he had his reasons. But we were always wrong, never him. *He* was always right. Suddenly, his bad temper and injustice grew to huge proportions in my mind. Now he had committed the greatest atrocity — tearing my precious book. He had done everything possible to thwart my education; and now that I had one through my mother's efforts, he was still not going to let me enjoy my love of books. I saw him as unreasonable and purposely wicked. That was when I lost it, years of upbringing and respect and tradition flew out of my mind. Now all I wanted to do was hurt him in the same way he hurt my mother, my brothers, my books. I did the unthinkable. I raised my fists to my own father. With a cry that rose from the well of disappointments, I lunged at him. Caught off guard, he crashed into the meat-safe, nearly toppling it over.

"Ah Phine, ah!" I heard my mother shout to restrain me, but I was beyond caring. My anger propelled me forward like someone crazed and I hammered my fists on his chest. He recovered very quickly, seized my wrists and kneed me in my belly. He was very strong. All his weight-lifting was not for nothing. Besides, I was still only a young teenager. I fell onto the floor. Then he kicked me hard. Like a football, I rolled over. He kicked me again. I think I heard my mother pulling at him to stop. He pushed her away and she must have fallen down because I heard a soft thud. He took off his belt and began whipping me. I shielded my face with my arms and they took the lashings. I decided to move out of his sphere. I raised myself but he kicked me and I doubled up. Determined to get away, I got up again and he kicked me and I went down. This occurred repeatedly and I knew that somewhere in-between I ceased to be his daughter and he ceased to be a man. My ears were buzzing. I felt blood flooding my mouth. At some stage, I passed out.

Thirteen

$\mathscr{M}$y greatest fear when I came to was that my father would not let me return to school. As long as my father was alive, my entire schooling hung on the thin thread of his approval; if he disapproved, I could not continue school. He knew this, knew that I had to behave, compromise if I wanted to continue school. So I learnt that the way of open aggression was not always the best. There is a Chinese proverb that says, _The river flows gently but can erode mountains._ It is the Yin way, not the Yang. I had to learn to be subtle. I wouldn't let my father see that I was hurting inside more than I hurt outside, though internal wounds are not so easily exposed. Patches of blue turned green around the edges on my skin. Because I was so brown, bruises didn't usually show. Like our dark unfathomable eyes, our complexion does not betray our emotions. Even when the heat rises from my neck to my face, no blush is displayed. So we appear to be deceptively inscrutable. But that altercation with my father was mapped all over my body, the straps of his belt making its mark, the weight of his foot, his fists. In our world, the welts and the bruises were testimony of my disobedience, not necessarily of his character.

"Cannot go to the library anymore!" My father commanded. "If you don't listen to my words, you will not go to school at all!"

Some privileges are better lost to win the war. Matthew returned the books for me and paid the fine for the damages. For the next four years, my feet did not touch the hallowed grounds of the *National Library* again until after my father died.

"Never mind," Mak tried to console me. "You have enough books to read anyway from your school library."

I wonder if she understood that it felt as though I was thrown back into prison, the sunshine of a wider world of knowledge shown then taken from me. Years later, when I read Richard Lovelace's *To Althea From Prison* which said that *"Stone walls do not a prison make"*, I resonated with the words, understanding that a prison could indeed be created without walls. My mother knew what it was like to earn my father's wrath, so she sympathised with me but she would never have said anything against my father, nor allowed any of us to say anything against him.

"He's the one to put food in your mouths,' she said.

She was loyal to him to the end. I had just turned sixteen when he died. All of his working life when I was a child, he had cycled to and from work, between *Potong Pasir* and *Bukit Timah* and around the island. He had strong leg muscles and a superb physique formed by his weight-lifting. The only evidence of his age was his smooth frontal pate. His downfall came eventually from his cigarette-smoking. Thank goodness, our front and back doors were usually left open, otherwise he would have polluted our small house with his fumes. He retired from work at 55, gave up all those miles of daily cycling. In one year, his muscles turned to flab, he developed a duodenal ulcer, which gave him a lot of grief for two years; in the third year, he was dead. I had been at the hospital earlier that evening, sitting by his bedside. His face was bleached of colour, his abdomen bloated.

"Phine," he said. "*Ah Kou* (his mother) is here. Do you see her?"

My grandmother, his mother, was long dead. When he said that, the hairs on my flesh stood on ends and I knew he would not survive the night. My mother and sister-in-law took over from me to stay by his bedside for the night. When Mak came home at three o'clock in the morning, I knew that *Lao Ee* had come for him. They brought him back in a casket, the lid open during the period of the wake. I stared at the corpse, remembered thinking how deeply set his eyes were, though I had not noticed it before. His anger and his life had left him deflated and he looked much smaller than when he was alive. I can still see the day of the funeral as his coffin left our attap hut. My father had come in poverty and left in poverty. I was sure that my mother would sigh with relief that he was gone and she was freed of her tormentor. So I was surprised to hear the anguish in her cries.

"Why are you leaving me alone? Who is going to take care of me and these children?"

How little I knew of human nature. For years, her words rang again and again in my brain, it was as though she has somehow betrayed me by being so loyal to him, that her pain and my pain, which resulted from him was imagined, not real. Little by little, through my own experiences, through being married do I understand that a wife's loyalty to her husband is unique, no matter how he treats her, he is still her husband. Linked and bound through their bodies and emotions, through many of the trials they share in their life together; it's a cleaving that is not like any other even if they don't bring forth any children. What we saw of my father was not all that *she* knew of him. Life is not black and white, it is about light and dark with many flickering shadows.

The real Catherine Koh Soon Neo is in shadow now, eclipsed by a self which robs her of her true light. The doctor and every one else who has experience of the disease tell us it will get worse. It's a sentence with no possible escape except through death. It's hard to know what to wish for, an early death for her so that she doesn't have to suffer anymore or for her to continue in a shadow of a life so that we would not miss her? It is one of love's great dilemmas.

"They're not aware of what they've become, you know," people say.

But I'm not entirely convinced. I believe that the despair and anger she sometimes displays stems from a deep frustration at her decreasing ability to remember. Though I don't want to, I have to leave her. I have another life now, in a place where she cannot follow. It is terrible when you're going away from someone who is ill, you never know if you're going to see them alive again. And it is worse when that someone is ill and also suffers from an increasing loss of memory. Double-edged. You never know if you're going to be recognised when you next come back. That is my concern. I wonder though if it is a selfish worry. Does it matter if I am not recognised? I cogitate upon this. Yes, it does. If she doesn't recognise me, it means that the mother I know will no longer be present. The thought descends upon me like an ice-cold shower.

How much can you do for your loved one? How much is enough? Length and breadths are for measuring static things, things which can be seen and boxed. It is impossible to measure things which hold no shape and is only a space in your heart. I try to think what I can do to please her, my last chance to spark her face with joy before I leave. And then I remember her telling me about the fruits her family used to have for breakfast in the mornings when Grandfather was alive and owned fruit estates. I go out to the wet market not far from where Bernadette lives to buy Mak a selection of fruits. It is a special excursion for me, too, because I really love the sound and the chatter and the laughter that normally permeate the stalls in these markets.

When I was a child, wet markets gave local lives colour and fun.

Even the rich shopped at them, servants trailing to carry the heavy baskets of their employers. If you ever saw a European, he would stand out like a white egg amongst a nest of brown.

Lao Pasar and *Tekka* were renown markets housed under wrought-iron Victorian roofs, with numerous stalls selling a plethora of goods, heaps of fresh vegetables from the farms of Chua Chu Kang or from Malaya, beautiful flowers from Cameron Highlands, spices from India. However, the hanging bloodied carcasses of goats and pigs were not as palatable a sight. Live chickens squawked noisly in their cages until they were selected to be killed; a cauldron of water was kept on the boil to dunk the slaughtered chicken in, so that they could be easily feathered. Fish of all kinds, with giant prawns and squids lay on beds of shaved ice to keep them fresh. Embroidered clothes from Indonesia would compete with local batik and Chinese silks and all sorts of other crafts. And, of course, there were the food stalls, Indian food, Malay food, Chinese food and even fish and chips were temptingly available. The different smells were often delightful, except for those of dead meat and dried blood. Mak favoured *Tekka* which was at Serangoon Road and not too far from home. It was where she went if there was money available and Chinese New Year was around the corner. When I accompanied her, I hung about in the hope that she would buy me one of my favourite treats, a lovely soft-boiled turtle egg. I always tried to manoeuvre her to that stall where the wizened old man would be boiling the eggs. It was delicious straight from the boiling pot, the old man would pierce a hole at its top and hand me the egg. I would stand there and suck out the soft inside of the egg with a slurping sound. If the empty shell was boiled again quickly to give it back its shape and then cooled, it made a suitable ball for playing ping pong, the sound echoing in the hollow shell as it pinged and ponged across the wooden table.

My mother was good at making a little food seem like a lot. It was a necessary skill. A few slices of meat or fish could look plentiful with lots of vegetables. Where greens were not affordable, we got food laced with tubers, normal potatoes, sweet potatoes, tapioca or yam. They were the stuff that filled your belly, made you think you were not hungry. On bad days, we ate boiled rice with soya sauce and nothing else. But Mak always served it with a smile. She shone light into our darkness. Our evening meals were a family ritual, all of us sitting cross-legged on the cement floor, eating out of enamel plates. She would regale us with stories of the life she knew or of traditional folk-tales. After dinner, she became a minstrel playing her guitar and reciting us some *pantun*. Sometimes a neighbour would join her and they would recite a playful *pantun* which was a duet of remark-and-response. On such evenings, my father would watch her face and the way her hands fluttered in the air delicately like some Chinese *wayang* singer. More than not, after such evenings, late in the night, he would scuttle across the room to join her in bed. It was obvious that her beauty and manner had aroused his lust or could it be that he was indeed a man who was much more attuned in emotions that I gave him credit for? Why should I be surprised that he should be so sexual when he was so firm in his body, riding miles on his bicycle and exercising every day? Whatever moved him to action, it could not have been easy for him to show his love or assuage his lust in a small hut where our two beds lay head-to-foot with one another, he and my brothers in one, my mother and sisters in the other. If I had not been awake on my canvas bed beside them, the sound of the wooden bed creaking would wake me, as I am sure, would have awakened my brothers and sisters. There were whispers in the dark which suggested that he wasn't just ruthlessly possessing her without preamble. My father usually wore a singlet and sarong at home and the sarongs probably helped to expedite their love-making because neither of them wore anything underneath their sarongs. They tried to suppress their moans, which in some way intensified their feelings and intensified the feeling of tension in the hut. But more than not, he could not stop himself from calling out her name or her for that ultimate sigh which signalled the end of his short escapade and a return to his bed.

I search for my mother's favourite fruits: mangoes, papaya, pineapples. Oranges, apples and grapes, which had to be imported, were not for the common folk during our youth; they were sold mainly in the posh Cold Storage on Orchard Road, the first supermarket in the country, a place beyond our reach until I worked there many years later, which brought me into contact with my present husband. When my mother came to England all those years ago to eat grapes which were seedless, she thought it was marvellous since the ones with seeds used to get caught under her dentures. Seedless grapes were a novelty then and were quite costly, so they became a special treat to get for Mak. I buy some to remind her of those early days and many of her other favourites. She told me that they didn't have durians for breakfast, so I am not going to get them. Whilst looking round the fruit stalls, buying this and that, I recall how much she loved *jambu ayer,* those small, bell-shaped fruits which were translucent and tinged with pink. They used to be resplendent on trees in our *kampong.* I rarely see these fruits now. When bitten into, their juice would flow like sweet water, hence their name. Mak used to love them sliced and dipped into a saucer of soya sauce with fresh chillies and salt. But I can't find them in the wet market near Bernadette's place. So I take a taxi to Geylang Serai where they are more likely to be available.

There is a made-up Malay village near Geylang Serai now which purports to display life as it was in the *kampong.* But the sheaves of attap on the roofs look too new, the huts too regulated and pristine. Our village,

Potong Pasir, like many other *kampongs* of that time, were a tangle of *lorongs* or sandy passage-ways which fed into huts made from unpolished planks washed with *kapor*, and sheets of corrugated asbestos or zinc patching broken walls or roofs. Bathrooms were open to the sky. Voyeurs would climb the surrounding coconut trees to peep out from in-between its fronds when the village beauties go there to bathe, while the really desperate would even watch old ladies strip. Village life had its own unique amusements.

I buy the bryani and other foods which Mak like. I know she can't eat them all, her appetite is small, like a sparrow's. But I buy them anyway. Still, I can't find the *jambu ayer*, the search for them now becoming like a search for the Holy Grail. At last, when I am about to give up, I see a small bunch at one of the stalls.

"*Manis, tak?*" I ask to ascertain its sweetness.

"*Tolong chuba,*" the woman gives me permission to taste one. I bite into it and the juice of the fruit flows down my chin and I am happy because it will make Mak happy. It's the small things now which delights her heart; she is past huge incidents and events. Her life is strung around small beads of daily happenings, whether she has been fed or whether someone has sat down to talk to her that day. It is life trimmed down to the minimum. Her world is now the coconut shell of her reduced mind.

When I arrive at Bernadette's place in the taxi, Mak is sitting on the settee looking out the French windows. Left alone with Dolores all day, she finds excitement in the activities on the street outside the house. She hastily gets up to open the front door to see better and walks with her painful gait down the short drive to the gate.

"Oh, it's Ah Phine. Dolores! Dolores! My daughter has come from England," she cries out as though she has not seen me around for the last few weeks. Then to me, she says with genuine surprise, "So you have arrived!"

All these weeks spent with her and she doesn't even remember I have been here. This is our personal tragedy because it robs her as much as it does me. I pay the taxi driver and start to unload. Always quick to respond, the angelic Dolores opens the electric gates and comes out to help with the shopping. Mak doesn't know how to operate these modern things. In the initial years of her move from the *kampong* to Bernadette's HDB flat, she didn't even know how to use the gas hob. Nor wanted to. In a beautifully fitted kitchen with running water and all modern amenities, we would find her squatting at one corner of the kitchen fanning the coals in her clay stove. Although Bernadette had a washing machine, Mak washed her clothes by hand and hung them to dry on bamboo poles outside the eighth floor flat. She was in a time-warp then, she's in a time warp now. But for different reasons.

"*Aiiyah!*" Mak exclaims. "Why buy so many things? Cannot eat finish, *lah.*"

My mother still lives in the days of want, so excessive expenditure is anathema to her. I want to surprise her the next morning with her buffet of fruits so I just say that I've bought things that I am taking back to England, which is partly true as I always take spices and other ingredients home.

"You mean you're going back so soon? But you only just got here!"

Sometimes it seems futile to do something for someone whose memory is already in shreds. They can't remember what you have done and you are left with a feeling that perhaps it was not worth the effort after all. I am saddened to think like this but I have left my husband and son for six weeks and my mother can't even remember that I've been around for that long. So I can imagine what it must be like for Bernadette, who has to do things for her day after day only to hear Mak say, "If Ah

Phine was here, she would take care of me."

Surely, there is a karmic debt between the two of them. There must be some lessons that they need to learn together. All the same, it can't be pleasant for Bernadette to have her efforts canceled by Mak's remarks.

Potong Pasir was razed to the ground in 1976, bulldozers coming round like cattle on stampede, kicking up a flurry of dust. The seeds were sown for the skyscraper buildings that would sprout from its soil. Mak went to live with Matthew and his wife in a flat, looking after their baby daughter when my sister-in-law returned to work. When Agatha married and had children, she went to live with them to look after my nieces. Her life, in her youth, had been one of slaving, rearing and nurturing, and her life in her old age, was still one of rearing and nurturing. My own children were taken care of by my mother-in-law whilst I worked. When Agatha had a maid, Mak went to live with Bernadette who was still unmarried and needed to get a HDB flat. Under Singapore law, an unmarried person under forty was not entitled to a flat unless she had an aged parent living with her. So that was how our mother came to live with Bernadette. My sister has had more physical years with Mak than I have had with our mother, yet Mak still harks back to the times she and I had with each other. I try to salve Bernadette's pain by explaining that our mother is not being deliberately hurtful, that she is unaware of the things she says, that she is somehow steeped in the past where I was the one who was there for her.

"It's all right for you, you're always the goodie and I'm the baddie."

I am neither the goodie nor the baddie. Some roles in life seem chosen for us, without our consent. Perhaps in the wisdom of our soul state, we ourselves made the choice, but why don't we know? What I do know is that I'm not just my mother's daughter. I am her hope and dreams.

When I separated from her at birth, she passed her baton to me to complete *her* race. The handing over of the baton didn't happen in one quick changeover, it has taken years, years of subtle learning through which she feeds me her desires, her hopes, her dreams, her life which has not been. When I divorced, I felt that I had failed her as well as my sons and husband. Only in retrospect have I learnt that if I had stayed in that marriage, I would have thrown my life away — and my mother's. So I lived life to the full because I was like a pregnant woman, carrying another life within me, eating and living for two. When I used to relate to her my activities, learning to drive, swim, ski, sky-dive, her eyes would glow and her face brightened, the corners of her mouth lifting. She lived on a borrowing of my life, licked with pleasure off my plate. And I must honour her.

"Look, it's Ah Phine, jumping off aeroplane," she would show my pictures to the neighbours or anyone who called on her. "Look, this is book Ah Phine has written."

Even after she left *Potong Pasir*, there were many who called on her, those who had known her in the *kampong*, known the woman who had put others before herself, the one who had delivered babies in the middle of the night and attended to calls for help. But the visitors are getting fewer, nobody feels like making a journey to call on someone who can't remember anything about it afterwards. Of my brothers, only Matthew continues with his weekly Sunday visits, bringing Mak's favourite *nonya kueh* for her to eat. Today, if I tell her about things I do, she would not be able to grasp their significance. The world beyond the coconut shell is irrelevant to her. And that is how I know that our joint race is over, I have taken our baton to the finishing line. From now on, the race is my own and I must now run for myself. A twin soul pulled asunder. There is a kind of grief that comes from this tearing, like a Siamese from its twin. I am a gosling on uncertain feet.

When you know of someone who is ill, you do not know what the morning would bring. You live by the hour, by the day, thankful that there is yet another respite from that final reckoning. When each of my sons was a baby, I used to spend many nights awake, watching for the rise and fall of their tiny chests, terrified of cot-death, a fear that every mother would know. When it became too dark to see, I put my finger to his nostrils so that I could feel the faint spray of air onto my finger. I breast-fed both of them throughout their first year to give their immune systems an added boost. Each day that they continued to live and grow was a small miracle to me. There is nothing anymore which would give my mother's immune system a further boost. So each day she lives is a small miracle.

I rise early but Dolores is earlier. I know she is preparing breakfast for Bernadette and her husband before they go to work. Some days when I feel lazy in England, I think of how nice it would be to come downstairs and have breakfast already prepared; and after a day's work, to have dinner on the table like my sisters. David has suggested that we bring a Filipino maid over to England, but I don't want her to feel alone in a vast country. Where we are in the countryside, a distance away from cosmopolitan London and Birmingham, there are very few Asians. In Singapore, the maid can mix with other maids at church or Lucky Plaza each Sunday, speak her own language, and meet her own kind. I know the loneliness of being a foreigner in an alien country, I can't inflict that on another. As I descend the stairs, I can smell the aroma of coffee percolating. It's a lovely smell which reminds me of *Potong Pasir*. I am surprised how the trail of thought leads me to my father. So many incidents of his foul temper have occupied my mind that there has been no space left for his acts of kindness, but now it appears that these memories are squeezing through, demanding to be remembered. The picture of my father's face in my mind's eye is one which is always distorted with wrath, but there is another emerging now, a softer face, smiling as he served breakfast. He did not do it all the time so when he did allow Mak to lie in, it was a weather-vane to indicate his good mood. It was a particular treat when he visited his mother the previous evening to return with minced meat patties which he would save for our breakfast. He'd make *moey*, a Teochew rice porridge cooked in water until it is soft, to go with the minced meat patties. Whilst the *moey* was cooking on the clay stove, he would brew the coffee in an enamel pot and if the aroma didn't wake me, he would come and tickle the soles of my feet till I awakened. He was a different father to the one who haunted me. Why had I not allowed myself to remember this before? And why am I retrieving the memory now? Did I really hate my father or was I just very angry and wounded by him? Probably hate is too strong a word — there must be a word that describes this filial feeling I have for him but which is still coupled with this strong aversion to his behaviour. But I don't know the word.

Dolores helps me with skinning the fruits, slicing them and laying them out onto platters. When my mother had told me about her family buffet, she said something that made the image of the rainbow stick in my mind, so I try to fan out the sliced fruits to create a suitable effect with its rich colours: red pomegranates, orange papaya, pink *jambu ayer*, yellow pineapple and mangoes, green honeydew and seedless grapes, dark purple mangosteens.

"What's all this?" Bernadette asks when she comes down for her toast and coffee. Unlike myself, Bernadette loves her toast in the mornings, whereas I never eat bread if I can help it, preferring the huge variety of Asian breakfasts: *nasi lemak, roti prata, thosai, ta mee, kway chap* and many others. I learnt to reproduce them in England and David is always amazed that I can eat curry and chillies for breakfast, that I wouldn't eat bread for breakfast even when he ran a bakery business. Bernadette is dressed in a very smart red suit which contrasts beautifully with her cream-white complexion, a complexion that is much favoured by the Chinese, unlike mine. She is meticulous over her make-up and her choice of accessories is rather becoming. When she sweeps down the stairs that morning, she reminds me of my schoolfriend, Elizabeth, when she had invited me to her house, looking like a queen, or a grand lady with impeccable taste and wealth.

"Mak used to tell me that when Grandfather was alive, they had a selection of fruits for breakfast, so I thought I'd surprise her."

"She never told me anything like that."

Her voice trembles with the knowledge of having been excluded from a shared confidence. It is difficult for Bernadette. She is nearly five years my junior and, therefore, further from our mother. I was there first and had staked a strong claim in the relationship with Mak. Perhaps Agatha feels this sometimes, which would account for her reactions as well. But there are responsibilities that a first daughter has which subsequent siblings may not have. Before I was 12, I was already involved in housework, helping to wash the clothes of a family of nine by hand and had to empty the smelly chamber pot. Because of Robert's illness, Mak had to go to hospital with him often, so I had to do all the cooking and cleaning, fetching water from the well or the standpipe, clear the drains of slimey, green water, and bathe and feed my younger siblings. I was the one who had to help Mak in the sale of her cakes and *nasi lemak*. Because Mak had set the precedence by having me educated, schooling for my two sisters was a natural progression and not the traumatic issue which had been mine. Though they had the hand-me-downs of my school uniforms, at least they were of the right colour. Therefore, it is inevitable that what I remember of our childhood may not be what Bernadette remembers. Our perceptions cannot be the same. By the time she was of an age to understand things, Jacob, Romia and Matthew were already contributing financially to the home, so food was not as scarce as it had once been. Better drainage and hygiene facilities provided around the village by the government meant that rats weren't scuttling around the houses at night. When Bernadette was six in 1963, things were already changing: Singapore had just shed its colonial cloak to merge with Malaysia; in August 1965, when she was eight, Singapore broke off from Malaysia and became an independent country. Electricity was fed to villages like ours. Our father even bought a black-and-white TV, the first in our part of the village and every evening, we would invite all our neighbours in to sit on our cement floor to watch television. We even had a small refrigerator! Matthew and I filled the ice trays with syrup water and we called these blocks *ayer batu Malaysia* (Malaysian ice cubes) and sold three squares for 5 cents to the village children. It was very popular and gave us the money for our exercise books. Bernadette had been too young to know all this; she had been too young to worry.

In the old days, Mak was always up with the sun. She was up before us and went to bed last, a typical, slaving homemaker. When she came to England in the summer David and I had our garden party to celebrate our wedding, she did the same, waking up when the sun lit up the sky to cook breakfast for everyone. Until we explained to her that we did not have equal days and equal nights as in the Equatorial regions. It was hard for her to comprehend. How do you explain the concept of the earth revolving around the sun or of solstices to an uneducated person? These days, time for her is measured by when she is fed or when Bernadette or Andy comes home. She cannot remember what day it is even if you had told her earlier, her days running into one another like spilled paint merging. When she wakes is dependent on the kind of night she has had, like all ill people, whether she has had a bad night or a good one, whether she slept at all.

I hear soft shuffling sounds in her room, not the sure, confident steps of her youth but fumbling, uncertain steps. Limbs needing to be uncoiled and stretched before they allow movement. She goes to her ensuite bathroom and a little later, I hear the tap water running, the toilet flushing. I am glad she no longer has such distance to walk to the well to wash herself or to the *jamban* or to have to share it with the other village folks. She has no difficulty in squatting but will not be able to raise herself from a squat position, her bones weakened and depleted by osteoporosis, her muscles having lost their tone. Somewhere along the way, the clear skin and eyes and full head of hair have deserted her. Her door is ajar and I push it open slowly. She is sitting on the bed, loosening her pathetic, little bun.

"Shall I help you comb your hair?"

When I was a child, it was one of my greatest pleasures when she would let me brush her hair. Unfurled, her hair would spill down her back right up to the waist, a rich cascade of beautiful, black silk threads. I would stand behind her and run the comb through again and again, the ends of the comb massaging her scalp and she would close her eyes as if in bliss. I have watched that head of hair as it took on silver streaks which turned to pure white, witnessed its autumn as the strands of hair fell away. They are near winter on her head now, sparse white hair remaining on a barren landscape.

"No!" She says too abruptly. "I can do it myself."

She is still spirited, momentarily jarring me by her tone. But I realise that it is her last stand at independence, her final claim to self-hood. She hates being dependent. Often, she used to tell me how terrible she would feel if she was an invalid, her body an object to be ministered by someone else. If she could, she would walk to her death. Sometime ago, I saw a play at the West End in London, where a daughter smothered her sick mother with a pillow. The audience laughed, albeit a nervous laughter and I walked out on the play. The scene disturbed me for a very long time. Now faced with a mother who is suffering, I can empathise with the daughter, understand that she was helping her mother to leave the world in a dignified way. So many children dealing with aged parents who are terminally ill or severely incapacitated are often caught in a dilemma of indecision about whether to prolong their parents' lives artificially or otherwise. I am praying I will be spared such a decision.

"Come out here. I have a surprise for you."

"*Aiiyah!*" She exclaims when she sees the spread of fruits and her favourite foods. After Bernadette and her husband had finished their breakfast, Dolores has placed a crochet-tablecloth over the wooden dining table and the platters are arranged in the order of the tiers of rainbow colours. It is impressive.

"So much food, so much food," Mak says as though in disbelief, the joy in her voice lighting up her wrinkled face, her almost-opaque fish eyes. She claps her hands childishly. "And all these lovely, lovely fruits! It's been a long time since I have seen something like this. Grandfather used to own fruit estates that spanned the whole of Malaya, you know. Did I ever tell you that when I was a child, we used to have a buffet of fruits for breakfast? Just like a rainbow. Just like a rainbow."

Fourteen

Though I enjoy being in Singapore, I also like the thought of leaving it. When I first felt that way, I felt guilty, as if I was being unfaithful to my family and my fellow Singaporeans. Although I love the hawker food here, enjoy the lack of formality and the ability to slip into my old tongue, it is no longer home. I find it hard to cope with the constant battering of traffic sounds, the claustrophobia of buildings and the mass of people. This is not just peculiar to Singapore but to every big city I know, and both David and I avoid them like the plague, accustomed as we are to country ways and country peace. During the past six weeks, when I had found myself being hemmed in, I took drives to the East Coast so that I could look out to a long vista of trees, beach and sea. There is something healing about an open sky, raw countryside and a huge body of water. Here, at the East Coast I was still blighted by noise, by the huge freighters that plied the international waters that is so close to shore. Both Bernadette and Agatha's families belong to a private club which is by the sea and they have very kindly taken me there, but the club looks out onto land where trees are being up-rooted for more buildings, exposing red earth as though its heart is bleeding. A short distance away, across the waterway, on the shores of Johore Baru in West Malaysia, oil refineries are spewing out acrid smoke. I miss my regular walks down Ludshott Common, right behind my house, with hundreds and hundreds of acres of rolling hills belonging to the National Trust. I miss my meditation seat, a sawn off tree trunk by the side of the lake at Waggoners Wells, where I can watch the wild ducks paddle and then fly off as quickly as they had landed, the branches of trees dipping into the water. Nearby, under the wooden bridge, there is the sound of a small waterfall cascading into the lower lakes, the chirping of the birds, the call of the visiting cuckoo. I could lose myself in the sounds of nature, all mechanical noise outside my perception. I love being there in autumn when the leaves turn into gold and red, detach themselves from the branches and eddy softly down from the trees like red and gold feathers. Or when the trees are bare, poised to yield new life. Or when tight buds slowly uncurl to show two small, green leaves. Above all, I miss that freshness in the air, clean and sharp, sometimes smelling of wood-smoke, gorst or heather. But I don't say this to my family. Like many people here, they have the propensity to misinterpret liking other things, another life and another place as criticising Singapore and Singaporeans. Preferences and opinions should comply with the general norm. It's the way they have been taught to think. Country before self. You don't find this mass devotion anywhere else, this moving as one united body, one brain.

"Why don't you come round for dinner before Christmas?" Agatha says. "I'll go to the market myself to search for *nangka* to make the *lemak*."

Agatha knows this is one of my favourite foods, impossible to reproduce in England because the *nangka* fruit is not readily available in either the local supermarkets or the Asian ones in London. Besides, the dish makes use of the fruit when still young and tender and is really only good with freshly squeezed coconut milk. I am touched that my sister is going to such great trouble for me. It's our mother's specialty and, fortunately, Agatha had learnt how to cook it from my mother before

Mak's mind had let loose the recipe. In some ways, our mother's incapacity has triggered off some good. Bernadette used not to have to cook because Mak was always there to do it for her. When she tried to cook rice, she always put in the wrong measure of water and it became *moey*. When she made chunky potato soup with pork pieces, she put in such a ladleful of sugar that it became syrup water! But she learnt very quickly and is now quite good and able to teach her maid. Grandmother was right after all. Many years ago she had told my mother and my aunts, "Must know how to cook or run household, *huh*, if not, cannot handle your servants, you know."

If Bernadette had not learnt how to cook from my mother, she would not know how to teach Dolores to cook the food she liked. And it is the same with Agatha, who is now an excellent cook, with the same high standard of cooking skill as our mother, so I look forward to the dinner.

"Aunty Phine, how come you still know Singapore roads?" Andy asks.

Bernadette's husband is busy so I drive her and Andy to Agatha's home. My youngest sister will only drive when absolutely necessary. I feel sad that Mak is unable to join us. She used to love getting out of the house and seeing places but now she doesn't enjoy it anymore because she gets car-sick and places are no longer familiar. Lights and noise confuse her. Dolores stays behind to look after her. Agatha's place is in Changi, only fifteen minutes away from Bernadette's. Where they live is the vestigial remains of Singapore's countryside, a few Acacia and plane trees providing testament. Unlike housing estates where HDB apartment blocks dominate the skyline, this particular area is prime land, not far from the coast, graced with stylishly designed private apartment blocks, condominiums with swimming pools and sports complexes, and grand terraced houses. We pass *Tanah Merah*, the name borrowed by Noel Barber for his eponymous novel. I have fond memories of this place because when I was a teenager, there used to be government-run bungalows by the sea which we could rent. My group of friends and I had wonderful weekends there. But it's all so different now. Agatha's house is larger than Bernadette's, is semi-detached and therefore much more exclusive, with a back and front garden and an outside drive for guests' parking. Bernadette's place overlooks other houses; Agatha's is across the road from Changi Prison.

It is difficult not to notice Agatha's and her husband's wealth. A Mercedes and BMW sit in the driveway, Italian sculptures in the living room, Van Gogh's print of *The Sunflowers* on the wall. The room is so large that there are two matching suites of settees and armchairs standing on the gleaming marble floor. A flight of stairs lead up to two more storeys with all rooms being ensuite. Another flight of stairs descend into the dining room with its own patio and waterfall, kitchen and maid's room. We are emotional miles from *Potong Pasir*. Mak has often likened this place to an *istana*, a palace. Once I had thought that my friend Elizabeth's house was a palace, but compared to Agatha's, Elizabeth's was a hovel. Our success is Mak's success because without her, we would not have grown up in the right soil and would not have flourished, would not have become the upright trees that we are. So I am glad at Agatha's success, glad that she had the wealth to return our mother to a grandeur she once knew. I remembered my own promise to my mother on the day she found me a place in school.

"You know, Mak, I will study very hard and when I finish school, I will earn a lot of money and I shall take you to Malacca to see the place where you used to live and anywhere you want to go."

After I left my first husband, I took Mak to Japan, Korea, Hongkong and Taiwan. We also went to Indonesia and, of course, Malacca. Second Aunt was still alive then, and I took her along, too. Grand Aunt had already died. My mother still had all her wits about her then, but we never found the site of the bungalow which Grandfather had built. Perhaps Mak and Second Aunt never really did want to find it, to rake up painful memories. We went up and down the coast but everything was so different and they could not identify the place where their home had been. So, we had a lovely holiday instead, visiting all the markets and shops, buying her the voile material that she loved for her kebayas, the gula melaka for making her desserts.

"We must live for tomorrow, not be sad-sad for the past," she said on the way back.

And Mak's tomorrow is in her granddaughter, Agatha's beautiful elder daughter, who looks so like Mak in her younger days that it is uncanny. You can put her face next to Mak's on her wedding day and you wouldn't be able to separate the two. Joanna, at 20, is tall, slender and dark-skinned, her face the same shape as Mak's when her jaw line had been taut, her skin firm. She even walks with the same grace, the same fluidity of movement. And best of all, she has my mother's nature, gentle and caring. To see her is to wish I had a daughter. To see her is to see my mother young again. Recently, someone saw her on the street on Orchard Road and approached her to take part in a television commercial, which she did. Through her, my mother has become immortal. Joanna and her younger sister, Gloria, greet us with smiles as we come in. Gloria is naturally fair-complexioned like her mother, but is tanned from her running as a school athelete. She has also brains besides speed and is one of Singapore's top scholars. Perhaps it is she who has inherited my mother's healing skills because Gloria intends to be a doctor. If only her grandmother could understand, she would be proud. Andy dashes upstairs to play with Agatha's youngest who is also a boy and close to Andy's age. Agatha is dressed in a lemon-yellow suit trimmed with black, with diamond studs on her earlobes and an enormous diamond choker round her throat. Like Bernadette, her complexion is creamy-white, the kind favoured by traditional Chinese.

"Do you like my Escada outfit?"

"When you get fed up of it, you can give it to me," Bernadette says, although she's much smaller.

The television is on and is telecasting CNN News, perhaps for the benefit of their guest from Texas, who is my brother-in-law's business associate. My brother-in-law runs a successful soft-furnishings business. We are introduced to Don, who is in an open-necked shirt, the colourful and patterned kind that some Americans think is compulsory casual wear. His belly stretches the shirt and the buttons look as if they are about to pop. He is in keeping with the present environment, with a gold necklace looping down onto his hairy chest, gold bracelets on his wrists. Despite the cool air-conditioning, Don has a ruddy face and is sweating profusely, his brow and the hair on his chest glistening.

"This is my sister from England."

"What part of England are you from?" Don asks with a predictable drawl, but not waiting for an answer. "I've been to London. Have you been to London? How do you put up with all that damn traffic? They should take down those decrepit old buildings and widen the roads."

The evening is going to be hard work, my cheeks are already straining from the practised smile. I'd rather be discussing books with Gloria but like Joanna, both are dutiful and have gone ahead to help the maid set the table for dinner. I let the man's chatter float pass me. Bernadette is better at talking to him, her face animated as her American accent becomes more pronounced. She used to work as a secretary in an

American firm in town and has emulated the rhythm of their speech. It gives me the chance to drift into the background. I pick up one of Agatha's old albums to browse through. She is extremely organised and all the photos have dates assigned to them and even the occasions on which they were taken. I am pleased to see pictures of our village, precious since the village is no longer around; and more precious still are photos of me as a youngster. Photos are testimony to one's life and I have lost mine in my acrimonious divorce. When I left home, my ex-husband had burnt all my albums, those that held my image, from birth to adulthood, perhaps in an effort to erase me from his life. When the decree nisi came through, he sent me my part of the photograph which had contained an image of our family in happier times. He had scissored himself and our children away from the photo and sent me the remainder twisted round his wedding ring. The act was so much in his character.

In Agatha's well-organised album, there's a black-and-white picture of Matthew standing with us three sisters taken in all our Chinese New Year finery. We are wearing identical dresses that Mak sewed with can-can underneath. Imagine the stiff and scratchy can-cans in the tropical heat! Especially when it was probably the cheap variety. Bernadette, at six or seven, is cute with her dimpled smile and has always remained the prettiest, Agatha is willowy and elegant. Regrettably, I look like a stuffed dumpling with a weird hairdo. Mak had taken us to the hairdresser in a bid to make us more modern. It had been a painful exercise, my hair wound tight round metal curlers with wires protruding from them which made my head look like an electrical Medusa. I felt as though I was being fried. Both Agatha and Bernadette had pliable hair so their curls came out soft and gentle, sweetly framing their faces. But mine, released from the rods sprung, out in a fright like a shocked porcupine. The tops of our heads showed our staircase of heights, Matthew being the tallest, followed by myself, although Agatha soon overtook me in subsequent years. We are posing by the banana tree, its broad leaves acting as backdrop. When the photo was developed, one of the old village ladies had pointed to my picture and made a prediction.

"This one has legs that will carry her far. She is born to travel and will move away from this country."

Strange how I did not remember that until recently. There I was in the wilderness of Alaska and I suddenly remembered the old lady's prediction. David and I had started a travel company taking retired British people on holiday in motorhomes to North America and we began with a journey to the Gold Rush region of Alaska and the Yukon. We were comtemplating the beautiful Emerald Lake with its waters glittering in the sun like the jewel it was named after. Apparently, the deposits of marl, a type of shell at the bottom of the lake, is the reason for its glorious colours. David had a bakery business when we got married. When I was invovled in it, his family was afraid that I might inherit it. So we gave it to his children and started our own business so that we could start afresh, with no shadows from his past marriage. I wasn't prepared to work for him as an employee, so we went into it as partners. As he has the business brain which I am entirely without, he runs the business and handles all the finances, whilst I handle the marketing and wrote all the brochure and sales literature. It was the kind of partnership my mother would have been proud of, if she had understood it. It was the kind of opportunity she bought me with her hard work and sacrifices. That day when we were sitting by the lake, outside our forty-foot motorhome, having a cup of coffee, David waxed lyrical about the beauty of the region. Emerald Lake is halfway between Whitehorse, Yukon and Skagway, Alaska. And I suddenly remembered the *nenek*'s prediction from all those years ago.

"Do you know," I said to David, "once when we were still living in

Kampong Potong Pasir, an old lady predicted that I, of all my brothers and sisters, would travel far. How would she have known that?"

It is funny about memories. A memory isn't recovered in a complete package from the past — it is excerpts spotlighted by the mind. Certain incidents and situations beome highlighted and they become triggers for us to explore the entire picture. Memory is about remembering, but is it usually about what we *think* we remember? This particular photo, for instance, pulls me back to our kampong, to a specific memory of my sisters and I playing marbles. I can see clearly the spot where we stood in the photo, in front of the banana trees, in our sandy yard. This was where we played our games: *hantam bola*, *teng-teng*, also called balloon or hopscotch, *keledek* and *chaptey*. *Keledek* was actually tapioca and it had given its name to the game because the stones used were normally flat like slices of tapioca that were dipped in batter and deep-fried. Two opposing lines about ten feet apart were drawn in the sand and the idea was to get your stone as close to one of the lines as possible. The winner was the one whose stone was the nearest. The loser had to piggyback the winner back-and-forth the two lines, according to the number of times that had been negotiated. I used to be welcomed in this game but then when I got fat and heavy after the ministrations of the WHO medical team, I became unpopular. I was only asked when the kids were short of players. And when I won, everyone groaned. *Chaptey* was okay because it was an individual competing with another to flex the sole of their foot to kick the *chaptey*, made with a circle of rubber pieces for its base and three or four feathers stuck to it. Generally the same badminton court which was used for film screening was also where my brothers would play *sepak raga* with his friends, a game I have never been allowed to join in. The *raga* was a rattan ball and it was similar to volley ball, played over a net but using the foot.

But there were some games which we had to play to make money. Even before I was 12, I had to find sources for extra money, to buy exercise books for school or the occasional treat. Mak and Ah Cob were already working so hard for the money to keep me in school, it wouldn't have been fair to ask them for more. Now that I could read and write, I decided to write very short stories to sell to the other village children. (In retrospect, it was odd that I chose to write my first books in English rather than Malay.) I could draw reasonably well, so I combined the two skills and made a ten-page comic book complete with story and illustration and sold it for five cents a piece.

Matthew, four years older than myself, has always been my favourite brother. He is small in stature and has a very gentle personality, just like my mother. He and I would buy boxes of sweets or crackers, split them up to sell them individually at a lesser price than the shops, so that the village children would buy from us. We organised a Sports Day, with several events and collected a small fee for entry. Part of the collection was used for prizes for the top three winners and we'd keep the rest. Our other source of income was from colorful, glass marbles. We would find out the number of marbles the village shop was selling for 10 cents and we'd sell ours for the same price with an extra five. The village kids couldn't resist the bargain and they seemed unaware that the marbles were theirs to begin with anyway. We won them first and then sold the marbles back to them. One of the variations of playing with marbles was an arrow drawn in the sand in the compound and the marbles were be lined along the stem of the arrow. Three or four feet away would be a *stay line*, from which the last person could toss his marble. The person furthest away would toss the first marble. The aim was to shift a marble from the arrow and what was beyond the marble which was dislodged from the line became yours to keep. As Bernadette was the littlest, I always put her on the *stay line*; Agatha got to go somewhere in the middle and I would attempt to get a place far beyond all the other village children so that I got first whack at sweeping up the marbles. It was hard to make Agatha understand why this strategy of placing us in intervals to the village children was vital to our winning the most marbles.

"How come you always get to go first?" Agatha used to complain.

But she has no cause to complain now, she has it all, success with a capital "S". She is a high-powered executive in an international firm commanding a five-figure salary, has a long-term successful marriage and three beautiful children. She travels to exotic places, has a lovely home in Singapore, kept in splendid condition by a full-time maid, and has apartments in Kuala Lumpur and the Gold Coast in Australia. And she is a wonderful cook, as good as Mak had been. In the middle of the rosewood dining table is a line of hot-plates on which there is a row of dishes with a variety of mouth-watering dishes, from stewed pork to beef *rendang,* spicy chicken, sambal, mackeral, soya sauce tofu, long beans and many others. Of course, there is also the promised dish : *nangka lemak.* Agatha must have slaved in the kitchen all day, the selection of *Peranakan* dishes is widespread. Our mother has taught us the importance of cutting and slicing a vegetable or meat in just the right way to suit the recipe and every single dish of Agatha's is perfectly cooked and presented. She could open a restaurant and it would have a roaring trade. We all tuck in.

"This is absolutely delicious," I say, meaning every word.

"I love Chinese food," says Don, and I cringe.

I get a bit cross when Westerners can't differentiate Chinese food from Southeast Asian food, when Singaporean/Malaysian food use spices and ingredients not found in the usual Chinese food. I can understand when people don't know that Peranakan cuisine is unique, and is the haut cuisine of Asian food, but I am irritated by this generalisation. People in the West think that all Chinese are the same. I often asked people if all Caucasians speak the same language and eat the same food. I am sure that the Italians would not like to be put in the same category as the Germans, nor the French, the English. Yet they are all Europeans. So why should all Chinese be the same? But Agatha does not seem to mind.

"Thank you," she says, preening at the compliment. "If I may say so myself, my food is really excellent. You see, even though I haven't published a book, I've got all my recipes on computer. I wrote them down as our mother recited them to me. Phine's book is only good for England, with ingredients that she can find there. But mine is more authentic."

Fifteen

"*C*hristmas is only around the corner," Agatha says. "Who knows whether this is Mak's last Christmas. Why don't you stay for a while more?"

She is right. It would make sense. It could be the last Christmas I spend with our mother. Or it could be the last Christmas which she *remembers*. I call David and though he is not keen on my continued stay, he thinks it makes sense, too. I ask David to come over to Singapore, but he says that he has a lot on. He always says that. Fortunately, my elder son has worked it out with his long-term girlfriend in Singapore that she'd chip in for his flight out here after term breaks up, so that they can spend Christmas together. And as his younger brother is in Singapore, waiting to go into national service, it will mean having the two of them together for Christmas here. All in all, Agatha's idea is a timely one. Although I shall miss David terribly, he'll have his mother, children and grandchildren around him, so he will be well-entertained. In any case, he's on the phone to me everyday, sometimes twice a day, for at least half an hour or a whole hour. Like our courting days.

Christmas trees and tinsels feel strange in a hot climate. It is interesting how my perceptions have changed, because I never saw it like that when I was living in Singapore. But now that I am used to the bleak Christmases of England, and the snow-clad ones of Europe and the USA, I can't think of the heat as Christmas-time. But Christmas is more celebrated here than anywhere I know, in the churches and in the commercial districts. You can't escape its commercial trappings, with carols blasting from every conceivable speaker, from early November. You couldn't go to the shops without seeing advertisements to buy this or that and smiling Santas on every window. Every break in a programme on the radio and television trys to entice you to buy something for your loved one or yourself. Hotels, particularly along Scotts Road and Orchard Road, bring in genuine, giant Christmas trees, decked with fake snow and twinkling lights to bring customers to their premises. To draw customers away from the hot humid streets into the hotels, the air-conditioning is turned to high to simulate a temperate climate. It gives people a chance to wear their jackets, waistcoats and leather boots. Patisserie chefs concoct gingerbread houses, yule logs and Christmas cakes with white icing, sprigs of holly with blood red berries. Figures of skaters skim the surface of these cakes or on ice sculptures, ladies dressed in mini Santarina outfits. All the Northern winter objects of snow, reindeer, holly, mistletoe, Christmas trees seemed displaced in equatorial Singapore, just as my mother had seemed displaced when she visited England in her flimsy sarong kebaya and open-toed sandals or Ghandi when he wore his dhoti to rainy Liverpool. Orchard Road looks more Christmassy than any place I know, with each hotel or department store competing to display the best Christmas facade and decoration. Reindeers drawing Santas on sledges are depicted in numerous designs. The whole street is festooned with coloured bulbs, both along and across the walkways, stretched from building to building. It is a hundred times more festive than the lights on Oxford Street in London. Mak has always loved a drive through Orchard Road when the Christmas lights are all up. So I decide to take her out. It requires a bit of persuading, because she complains of feeling tired, but she eventually relents. Andy and Bernadette come along for the ride, too.

"*Aiiyah*, so nice!" She exclaims as we see coloured bulb nativity scenes, angels, Santas and reindeer. Lighted snowflakes drift down from the tropical sky; aerosol snow cap the tops of giant presents in colourful wrappings and bows in shop windows.

I nudge the car slowly along the crowded street. Not that I have a choice since there are cars on the left and right of me, cars in front, and cars behind. Obviously, others have the same idea to come out to see the lights as well. On either side of the road are pedestrian malls, filled to capacity with moving bodies of people. Young people form such a huge percentage of the population that the crowd is nearly all made up of teenagers or those in their 20s and 30s, all of them so very slim, with such leggy arms and legs that you wonder how all the food centres in Singapore make money. Their bean-pole figures are beginning to give me a complex. When I am in the UK, or even in Canada and the USA, I feel quite young and fit, but here, I feel old, overweight and sometimes downright ugly. Whenever I have the opportunity to go to the shopping malls to get something, I am inevitably stopped by an anoreixic-looking young lady selling cosmetics, asking if I wanted to try their brand of whitening cream. Somehow this innuendo that I shouldn't be so dark reminds me of my father, so it puts me in an ill-temper.

"I'm happy with my colour," I say crossly. "I don't want to be white."

Perhaps I should have said that to my father, too. But my words don't have the desired effect on the salesgirls, they only make them look at me with such pity in their eyes. To them, I must seem ridiculous when I have the choice of having a fair complexion but choose to be as dark as the maids trawling behind the Marms and Sirs, carrying the babies or taking care of pushchairs and parcels whilst their employers shop around the malls and eat at food courts. Not only is my complexion not in fashion for the Chinese, it tells everybody I am not in the right class. To accentuate the problem, there is no Chinese or Malay word for *tanned*, so everybody will say I am *black*. From thinking that I look all right in the West, I am suddenly made to feel out of place. Amazing how such a transformation can occur when you cross continents.

"If one more person asks me if I want to buy a whitening cream, I'll scream," I complained to David.

"Don't you change anything. I love you just the way you are. I think you're the most beautiful woman I've ever seen."

I'm sure he was laying it on a bit to give me back my confidence. I guess that is what love is all about. But I was too grateful to protest. So now I look at all the youngsters and say to myself I don't mind what they think of me. After all, ugly as I appear to be to people here, I am so lucky in love. What more could I ask?

"*Aiiyoh!* So many people *one, huh*. Give me a headache. My head is spinning round and round," Mak says.

The coloured lights now dazzle and confuse her. Things outside herself and her comprehension tire her easily. I had hoped to treat her to supper somewhere, but she wants to get back. She is uncomfortable in unfamiliar surroundings. People with Alzheimer's seek routines and familiar places. So we have to shorten the outing. She is certainly not like she used to be. At the rate of her deterioration, it is prudent to spend Christmas with Mak because I don't know how many more Christmases she is going to see. When someone is ill, every single day is a hurdle to be gotten over.

Mak used to love going to church for Midnight Mass on Christmas Eve, because she loved listening to the carols although she can't sing them. But now she doesn't feel up to going. So I go with Bernadette, Andy and my boys, although I'm not a church-goer. It is the one time in the year when people really dress up for church. Bernadette wears a red, embroidered knitted top with a matching mid-calf skirt and a pair of ankle-length leather boots. She explains that the church is air-conditioned and is cold. Andy is cute in long trousers, white shirt, bow-tie and waistcoat. The boys wear silk shirts with their fashionable trousers. I am desperately trying to find something that looks dressy without feeling warm, so I choose a lemon trouser-suit, with embroidered lapels. It's like a fashion parade in church, with some men in jackets and some women in evening wear. It adds to the festive ambience. Compared to the poor attendance of Mass in English churches even on Christmas Eve, the church was packed, with people having to stand at the back of the pews. Unlike the high percentage of old people at Mass in England, a great number of the congregation here are young people and young families. I thought how proud the missionaries who came here to convert our people would be to see such a turnout.

Like Chinese New Year, Christmas in Singapore is a continuous round of eating. Bernadette has first go for Christmas lunch so that everybody can come and wish Mak a Merry Christmas. Dinner will be at Agatha's and on subsequent evenings at Matthew's, then Romia's, then Jacob's. This is not counting friends who have invited me. I help Bernadette and her maid to chop, cut, slice, pound spices, fry and cook. We arrange platters and decorations on the trestle table covered with a festive tablecloth. Bernadette sets out a buffet spread of the traditional turkey and ham, baked by Cold Storage, alongside Peranakan specialty dishes like *Itek Tim, Ayam Buah Kerluak*, etc. I had organised with my sisters to wear our *sarong kebayas* to take a photo with Mak whilst she is still standing upright and has reasonable recognition. Matthew's wife, who is Chinese but not Peranakan, decides to wear the outfit as well, so too her daughter and Joanna. Agatha's daughter looks stunning in her *sarong kebaya* and more and more like my mother in looks. Beside her slim figure and that of Matthew's daughter, we three sisters look like overweight mothers-in-law!

My two elder brothers have three children, and Agatha has three, Bernadette has one and Matthew has one. Jacob's son is married with one child, whilst Romia has two married children. Altogether, my mother has thirteen grandchildren, one great-grandchild, with one on the way. My elder son will be coming with his girlfriend, so there will be 26 people for lunch. And that's only our immediate family. Except for Matthew and his family, I haven't seen my other elder brothers and their families since my last visit. Mak sits on the settee, dressed in her best *kebaya*, ready to receive the guests. She had put on her favourite earrings, a five-petalled flower studded with diamond with Chinese gold surround. The pierced holes of her earlobes have extended over years of wearing heavy earrings, and now her earrings drag them downwards. Once, on festive occasions, she would insert the yellow *chempaka* flowers into her bun or twist the *bunga melor* chain around it. But now her bun is so small and pathetic that it cannot support either. The lighted Christmas tree, with all its tinsel, helps to remind her that it is Christmas Day. She loved Bing Crosby's carols so Bernadette had bought a CD, and Bing's *I'm Dreaming of a White Christmas* is now playing. Every now and again, Mak would bring her hands together to clap like a gleeful child.

"People are coming already. People are coming already," she says excitedly as she peers out the French windows. Soon the front doorstep is littered with footwear of all colours and sizes. Asians never wear footwear indoors.

"*Aiiyah*, Ah Phine, ah," Romia says, "How come you put on weight?"

His wife, whose skin has never been exposed to the sun because she wears long sleeves when she goes out and carries an umbrella to shield herself from the sun, takes one look at me and says, "Eh, Phine, ah. You're so black!"

When Jacob turns up, he says, "Wow, you're almost as black as me."

Perhaps I need the whitening cream after all. Or I need to introduce a new word to the Chinese and Malay dictionaries. Up until then, I had thought I looked rather becoming in my *sarong kebaya*, suddenly I am not so sure. I try to make conversation with Romia's and Jacob's children, but like many successful young Singaporeans, they are so full of themselves, telling me about their professions and where they go on holiday, and not once did they ask about my life in England. They had not bothered to keep in touch with me and when I learnt that they had been in UK and Europe without contacting me or bothering to ask if I needed any spices or ingredient from Singapore, I decide that I did not want to give them more of my time and move to talk to my sisters-in-law. My boys turn up and I give each of them a kiss, including the girlfriend. Both boys are taller than me, so I have to tip-toe to reach them. It's a not a custom in this country, so the younger shyly offers his cheek.

"*Aiiyah*, no need, *lah*," says the elder.

I pick a few of Mak's favourite dishes from the buffet table and take it to her, still sitting on the settee. She is talking with animation to my sisters-in-law. I address her and she looks up with such sheer wonderment as if she has only eyes for me and my heart turns over. "See, it's Ah Phine," she announces. "She's come from England to visit me."

After lunch, we stand and pose for the photographs. Mak stands in the middle, first with only her daughters, then her daughters and granddaughters. She looks small amongst us, like a tiny sparrow. Then we take a picture of her with all her children and their spouses and their children and grandchildren. My throat catches as I think that this might be the last gathering that we have would with all of us together. My mother has held the family together for such a long time, not in a matriarchal manner but by her love and her ability to cook. When she was able, she used to cook every single Sunday so that we could all come and visit her. Every single Sunday for years, she would cater to more than ten of us for lunch. Until she could no longer cope. We see each other because of her. If she goes, what will happen to the family? I have no doubt that I will see my brothers and sisters, but perhaps not so much of their families. It's too large to grasp, too large to try to continue holding everyone together. Bernadette says that every year, she is getting more exhausted in having to cater to them all. If the younger generation has any sense, it is them who would have to pick up the reins now, to keep the family together.

I am pleased that I suggested that the girls should wear the *kebaya* because Mak is pleased. She says, "Good-good. Nice to see young people wearing *sarong kebaya*. It keeps tradition alive. It won't be long before our Peranakan culture is dead." She expresses my sentiments entirely. Pernakans are marrying non-Peranakans. Our children, because they are classed as Chinese, study Mandarin in school. They won't speak Malay nor our patois. Many Singaporean children, particularly the Chinese-Singaporean, are not taught the old Asian customs. Like Andy, many are not taught to call the elder before eating, not taught to bend low when passing in front of an elder and many other forms of respect that we, as children, used to be taught. Though they think of themselves as Chinese, I don't see much of any Chinese-ness in them. They look Chinese, but don't act Chinese in that they lack Chinese graciousness and good manners. With their western clothes, mobile phones and loudness, they appear like Westerners, but without western graces. Mak would have said that they weren't brought up properly.

"You know," I say to my nephews and nieces, "you are the next generation of Peranakans now. You have to practice our customs to keep our tradition alive for your children so that they can keep it alive for theirs. Otherwise, the knowledge about us Peranakans will soon die off and we will pass into history."

"What's the big deal about being a Peranakan?" Romia's elder son, Brad, says. "It's only Chinese people dressed up as Malays, *what*."

It is hard to say goodbye to someone who is ill, you never know if you're going to see them alive again. Death is a burglar who robs in stealth. And it has no respect for age or time. My mother is too poorly to come to the airport. For someone used to exerting herself and not the type to give in to physical exhaustion, this lethargy is so out of character. It tells me that she is truly unwell. Although Alzheimer's is a disease of the brain, it seems to have a toll on her body in a round-about way. Her failing memory makes her unfit for the usual things that she does, so she can no longer keep as active as she used to be. Her heart condition has stabilised but it's her overall physical health that is also deteriorating. It is getting hard to separate one from the other now, the physical and the mental are twinned in their destruction, stripping her of the power to be who she wants to be. I have to tear myself away. Life is about moving on after all. Despite my telling her that I am leaving, she seems to have no comprehension of the idea until she sees my packed cases on the marble floor.

"Going home already?" She says as though it is the first time the subject is being broached. There is a kind of simplicity in her question, almost as if she's existing in a void, with no past and no future to colour her perception. All you see is what you get, no memory left between the lines. Once she was an ice berg, the submerged part of her being providing stability and informing her social personality; now she is just a cork, floating on the surface of the water, bobbing up and down as the waves take her.

I feel at a loss. I cannot mouth the words, *I love you* or *I shall miss you*. Our culture and upbringing do not encourage such a rendering. In some things we are forthright, in this we are not. We show love by giving food, doing things, by our actions and our respect. We do not normally hug and kiss. We do not articulate our feelings. My sons still blush when I say to them in English, *I love you*. They are the words of lovers, not parent to grown-up child or vice versa, nor of siblings. It is our handicap. I move forward to take Mak into my arms but she keeps me at bay, deny me the solace.

"No need," she says. "I don't feel well."

"Okay, Mak, I'm going," I say.

I feel inadequate, unfulfilled. When words or touch are not permitted, it puts a stopper to the transferring of emotions. There is no poetry in sorrow. Especially sorrow which is left unleashed. And so that is it. Deflated, I walk out the front door. She follows on my heels on uncertain steps. A little bit lost, a little unsure what is really happening. Bernadette's husband picks up my cases to put them in the boot of the car. I give Dolores a quick hug, press a thank you note in an envelope with some cash into her palm. Andy tugs at my hand, reluctant to have me leave. When I was packing my cases, he said to me,

"Aunty Phine, I will transform into your suitcase so that you will carry me to England. Then when we get there, I will transform back into me!"

"What about school?"

"I want to go to school in England! Study at British Aerospace!"

And he could, too, with his brains. Bernadette goes to the passenger seat in front. I sit at the back, Andy on my lap. I close the car door, give Mak a final wave. She waves back. She looks small and frail, her attention already elsewhere. I know I have slipped into her past, our days together in the last eight weeks will soon be out of her knowing, written on a piece of paper whose glue will not stick to her mind. This certainty comes to me with a stab in my heart. In her terms, we have ceased to create memories together. I have to hold on to mine for the two of us. It is not so much for me that I want her to remember, but for herself so that she knows she is loved, that she is not neglected. My brother-in-law eases the car out of the driveway and I play a word-game with Andy so that I do not have time to listen to the tune played by my emotional heartstrings.

In real life, there are no neat beginnings nor endings. Events are sometimes held in suspension for an extraordinarily long period. It is the same with my mother's illness. At first when I arrive back in England, I fear a sudden phone call that will summon me back to Singapore. But as time lapses, I relax, picking up the threads of my life with my own family, a business, new writing. Obligations to fulfill. One isn't an island unto oneself. It is seven o'clock in the morning and the phone rings. Both David and I wake up with a start. Such an early call suggests an urgency, and is probably made by someone from a different time zone. I am seized with fear. But it's only my stepdaughter Sadie. She believes that because she is up, others have to be too. Someone should teach her that it's not sociable to call at this sort of time in the morning unless it's an emergency. Consideration has never been her strong point.

"Where have you guys been? We don't see enough of you. The children don't get a chance to know their grandfather."

Her voice is like the persistent whine of a mosquito. I put David on the telephone to his daughter. I have enough in life to deal with.

Telephones transmits a voice but not a face nor a heart. Every week, I would call Mak. She used to remember that I always call her on a Monday afternoon and would eagerly await my call. When her days became blurred, she only knew what day it was when I called or whether Bernadette was working that day; daily events becoming her calendar, her way of measuring days and time. Her life is reduced to this, a notching of each small thing that takes place in her day which has become the entire sum of her coconut shell. The weeks and months pass. Each time I pick up the telephone to call her, I am apprehensive that she may not know who I am or that she will not recognise my voice. It's a kind of gamble. Deterioration plays roulette with her memory, some days she remembers, other days, she is vague, unsure of where I am. But she has not forgotten me yet. I have to be grateful for these things.

"How are you, Mak? It's Ah Phine"

"Ah Phine, *ah*! Are you coming round for dinner? I can cook some *rasum*."

It is touching that although she has forgotten so much and can't remember where I live, yet she can remember my favourite foods. It is instinctive for her to be caring, concerned about others. Alzheimer's scalps her memory and parts of her personality, but her true nature is still hanging on. There is an intrinsic part of her which she hasn't lost. Is there a continual struggle within her to hang on to bits of herself? Is she aware that her personality is splintering, disintegrating? I hate to think of her being aware of this. I am in a cleft stick. If I don't remind her that I am in England, she will expect me for dinner; if I do, it will wake her to the fact that she has forgotten. I feel a need to try to make her remember because otherwise she might slip more quickly into a vacant mind.

"I live in England, Mak."

"Oh, ya? When did you go there? If you're free, come and see me some time. I don't feel so good you know. My eyes are watering a lot and I get very dizzy. Especially when there's so much to do. You know, all that cooking. People coming and going. I get really tired nowadays, not like I used to be. I have to watch that Andy you know, it's Deepavali and I don't want him to get under the cow's hooves."

For a few seconds, she has lost me. I cannot follow her train of thought. But the word association of *cow* and *Deepavali,* the Indian Festival of Lights, sparks an image in my mind, of a cow, beautifully decked out with floral garlands, tributes from its Hindu devotees. Then I remember it. She's talking about the religious procession that used to wind through our village in the evenings during the Indian Festival. The cow, which is a holy animal in Hindu scriptures, was garlanded by the villagers on its journey along the rutted road, carrying a small statue of a deity on its harness. The priests in their dhotis walked bared-footed along the sacred cow, drumming and playing their cymbals. The villagers would join their singing and chanting. And though we were not Hindus, we all turned up to watch and to benefit from the fruits of the occasion. Every now and again, the procession would stop and the priests handed out sweets and roasted chickpeas to the people lining the sandy road. As a child, I did not understand the significance of the procession. In fact, I had quite forgotten about it, if Mak had not reminded me. But her words triggers my own memory and I can see the bright lights of the shrine, the statue of Krishna smiling, his neck wreathed with several garlands. The music was cheerful and dancers danced bare-footed along our mud-packed road. Every now and again, the procession stopped for devotees to come forward to slam fresh coconuts on the ground. The husked coconuts would break, sending shattered pieces across the ground, its water pouring out to wet the thirsty earth. Then children like myself would rush forward to pick up the jagged pieces, white kernel on hard brown shell, jostling and pushing to get at them. I never knew then why the coconuts were smashed so violently, but now I do. Like the process of Raja Yoga, Hindus believe that to attain spiritual enlightenment, the ego has to be eradicated or as one of my gurus laughingly called it, *"an ego-dectomy."* The coconut is supposed to represent the ego and smashing it is symbolic of the intention to do away with the ego. Hindus still practise this at the entrance of their temples before they go in to worship.

Mak must have the festivities in her mind's eye when she speaks to me about it. She sees the crowd and the noise and fear that Andy might get under the cow's hoofs. Of course, in reality Andy would not have witnessed such a procession since they don't hold them anymore in the same way. I was always pleased when I could collect enough coconut pieces for my mother to clean the sand off them, scrape the kernel off the shells so that they could be grated and used for cooking. We depended upon such gifts for our treats. It would be interesting to find out what had triggered these memories for Mak. Nonetheless, I am grateful to her for reminding me of some of *my* happier days in the village. There *were* happy days. Though we were deprived materially, there was such a camaraderie in the village that living elsewhere didn't generate. Our doors were always open in the day, unlike in the blocks of flats when they remain shut. Everybody knew everybody else, not stuck in their own flats, oblivious to their neighbours.

"Mak Ahyee! *Sudah makan belum? Mari, lah, saya ada masak bubor kachang!*"

When she had finished the day's work of washing and cooking, Mak would take a rest, sitting on the threshold of the kitchen and she would invite our Indian neighbour to sample her *bubur kachang*, a sweet dessert made from mung beans and coconut milk. They sat cross-legged on the floor and would occasionally share a *sireh* together. Preparing the betel nut leaf and its condiments was carried out like a ritual and they would chew and talk and spit out its reddish juice. (When I became a dental nurse after I finished my Senior Cambridge, I learnt that chewing *sireh* caused cancer of the buccal cheeks, so I made her stop.) But she had never chewed it regularly like my Aunts anyway, so it was not difficult for her to give it up.

While the mothers sat on the threshold of the houses, talking to each other across the *lorong*, the children would thrash each other in *hantam bola*, using the hard tennis balls for the game. It was really a boy's game but up until I was 12 when I was made to wear a dress, I was allowed to play only because I looked and acted like a boy, climbing trees, playing marbles, my bare chest as flat as our sandy yard. My sisters preferred *teng-teng,* hopping and skipping over the rectangles. *Hatam bola* required an ability to run. Each player was allotted a hole the size of the tennis ball. One person would roll the ball into the hole whilst the others crowded around the holes which were dug side by side to each other. The moment the ball entered a hole, whoever the owner was had to retrieve it, whilst the others ran away. Then he would have one throw at us. The person who was hit got to roll the ball next. The rule was that we should only hit the legs but more often than not, the rule got broken and it could turn out to be quite painful.

"If you don't fancy having *rasum* today, I can make you some *asam pedas.*"

Mak is going through a list of my favourite foods. The she talks about Mak Ahyee although they haven't seen each other in years. But I let my mother talk even when I know that the talk is not about actual things happening to her right now. It is good to hear her voice because some days when she is really unwell, our conversation is brief. Sometimes when I telephone, she seems to have difficulty speaking to a disembodied voice. It is far better that she continues to extract memories from her past and to thread them to the present than for her to have no memories at all. I am told that at some stage, she will eventually lose the capacity to extract old memories. Then she will retreat into a cave of silence with no echoes of a lived life to bounce off its empty walls.

I wonder if people like my mother or other mentally handicapped people, like those who suffer from autism or Down Syndrome, are already journeying between the earth and the etheric plane. They are not understandable to us only because their body is in this plane but their mind isn't. Perhaps they are freer than us. A while back, I used to work with the mentally handicapped for a few years in Guildford, Surrey, using yoga as a therapy. My main task was to help them and their carers cope with mood swings by encouraging them to breathe longer breaths rather than the short, sharp ones they take when agitated. Except for the outbursts that threw them off-centre, most of them exhibited a child-like capacity for joy, their faces almost angelic and free from earthly stress. I often used to wonder if it meant they could disconnect with our earth plane by choice. Therefore, should I be unhappy when my mother reached that stage of disconnection?

We are all connected to other human beings in so many different ways. If we see each connection as a ray of light, then each person radiates a multitudinous array of lines to people they interact with at all levels, some connections stronger than others. It is a light network that links the spirit. The ray of light between my mother and myself is bright, keeping the two of us within sight of each other although we may be thousands of miles apart. We don't just see with our physical eyes. She and I share the same soul space. Spiritual twins. Of course I am aware that ours is not the only connection, she is obviously connected to my brothers and sisters and to the people she tended in *Kampong Potong Pasir*, but the intensity of their light is different. Sometimes, I suspect that she and I are spiritual Siamese twins, attached to each other by our spiritual hearts, our *anahata chakras*. But even Siamese twins have to be separated to live a fulfilling life, and develop their own personalities.

Sixteen

Mak has made it to the new millennium. Amidst the world's celebrations and fears of the Y2K Bug, I too celebrate my mother's will to survive, yet fear the bug that will end her life. Is it instinct which causes a person to continue to fight to stay alive or something more, an unfulfilled task that the soul has to finish? What guides our life to fruition? There is a Chinese superstition which says that if the ill survives the Chinese New Year, they will survive the whole of the new year. Thankfully, my mother sees the Dragon Year in. So it's not surprising that she also manages to notch another birthday on 3 March. Amongst the many things that she and I share, we share the same astrological sign in the English calendar. Is it her 85th or 86th? No one knows for sure. What does it matter now? Her mind is already arrested in its growth, no matter what her chronological age is. How long can the ship of the body last without its captain, the mind, to provide the directions? Will it rock amongst the tempest of her illness, and ram into ice bergs?

Winter has come and gone, the bare branches beginning to show life, tight buds poised to unfurl. I feel lucky that I have the opportunity to walk through the Common with its expanse of land and sky. In between the shivery showers, the sun steps out with great daring, the sky so blue and the clouds so fluffy and still that it looks devised by human hand. Earlier, as I crossed our drive to get to the Common, I was touched by cold water. The garden hose had been left on to fill the swimming pool in the optimistic hope that we will have a lovely spring and a warm summer. As I pass, a break in the hose sends a delicate spray of water to wet my ankles. Standing at a particular angle, I could see a rainbow arc into the air in brilliant colours from the small hole in the tubing. Ever since I kicked rainbows out of puddles with my bare feet in the *kampong*, I have loved rainbows. I look for them in the glint of cut-glass, on any shiny surface, on water. It gives me such a thrill to see a rainbow whatever its size, whatever it falls on. I consider it a gift! The kind of gift I would like to take to my mother because she, too, looked for these small things in her daily life with her watchful eyes. Tired as it may sound, money and success do not bring happiness. True wealth is the ability to appreciate the throbbing vibrance of living things around you. Sometimes when I see David chained to his principles and his desk, with hardly a moment to relax, especially when the sun is shining brightly outside, I feel sad for him. He is stuck in his office, glued by obligations and needs. He lives and works in a beautiful house with a beautiful garden surrounded by beautiful countryside and yet he has no time to see our cherry tree in bloom, fat pink clusters of blossoms along its branches. With so much space outside, all he breathes is the stale, confining air of his office. He might as well be in prison.

"But I have to earn a living," he says.

It is what he believes. I keep asking him to cut down, sell up our big house, have a smaller garden, fewer cars. But I think work is an excuse for him to fill his emptiness. I want to love him by taking him on my walk so that he can smell the sweet scent of the gorse bushes, feel the grass under his feet, hear the twittering of the birds. But he rejects my offering. Nature is a healer and I am convinced she can slow down the carousel of his frenzied thoughts, untense the muscles that pull his mouth tight. He hunchs at his desk, weighed by his view of responsibility, his need to see his children in comfort and luxury. Perhaps, like me, he fears having to return to the poverty of his youth. He does not understand how wealthy he already is.

Though I walk alone, I am never lonely on these walks. I save the treasures that I see to present them to my mother. I feast my eyes on the bright yellow flowers on the gorse bushes, leaves looking silver when they turn on the wind, new growth on firs standing upright like brown candles on a Christmas tree. I thank the One above for plucking me from the confines of a small congested city to release me into this green and lovely countryside where flowers and trees are left to grow wild and straggly, where animals run unhampered. My mother comes with me on these walks, her spirit and mine sharing a love of nature. She was so connected with the earth before, she loved to dig into the dark loam soil with her bare hands, birthing chillies, green beans, tomatoes, coriander, curry leaves, papaya, rose and jasmine bushes. She reared chickens and ducks for their eggs, clucked and quacked with them as if she spoke their language. Only when they were old did we slaughter them for their meat. Mak respected life in all forms. In our village in *Potong Pasir*, our garden was no more than a small bed in the sandy compound, yet my mother treated it like royal grounds. When she came to England and saw our large garden, totally without fruit trees and vegetables, she said in a sad, disbelieving voice, "*Aiiyah!* All this land and no fruits, no vegetables. What a waste, *lah*."

Once I was be able to describe what I experience on the Common and she would drink in the scene, her face lighting up with joy. She would be able to see what I see, pinch the landscape from my mental frame and our sharing would be complete. But these days, it's impossible to tell her what I see. It's as if the palette of her mind has run out of hues to paint pictures that are not before her eyes. A blindness of her inner senses. What she can just about grasp these days are the shadows of reruns from old films, images of her life that had been captured in her mind. But even then, they are not smooth running, they fuzz, snap and crackle. She cannot remember today but she can recall yesterday.

It is late May and Bernadette calls to say that Uncle Kanchil is ill. For me, he is a name from the past, the uncle who fled to California to start his own history. One of his daughters went out to live in Singapore and has been in touch with my brothers and sisters in Singapore but I missed out. I had not seen him for more than 30 years. He's my mother's youngest brother and thus her only living sibling since Fourth Aunt, then Great Aunt and Second Aunt died. Now only *he* can tell me if what my mother had told me about their shared life are facts and not the fantasies of her mind. Uncle Kanchil had continued to make annual visits to see Mak and once Romia took her to see him in San Francisco. But lately, he has had several heart attacks and is living on knife edge, continually linked up to an oxygen tank.

"I'd like to take Mak to see him before it's too late."

Did Bernadette mean it would be too late in the sense that Uncle Kanchil might be dead before Mak could make the trip or too late in the sense that our mother will not be able to recognise her own brother? Some things are better left unsaid, words can make real what is still in the future. There isn't any point in tasting the bitterness before biting into the fruit. I can sense that it is necessary for Bernadette to make this trip with Mak; away from home and the ever attentive Dolores, it is her opportunity to mother our mother all by herself, create a stronger light connection.

"Yes, if Mak is able to travel, why don't you go? You haven't been to America. It will be a good holiday for you as well. I'll pick up the tab for her fare."

"No, it's all right. She has enough in the bank."

Bernadette never ever takes advantage.

I don't know if my mother remembers how much she has told me about her brother. And I don't even know how much she has told my sisters and brothers about that part of her life. Did they know that our mother arrived in Singapore with her mother who was in shock over the loss of her husband and fortune? Was I the only one whom Mak shared her confidence with? Or was I the only one to commit her words into my memory? When we are dots *within* a pattern, we cannot see the whole pattern. Do we have the capacity to step outside the pattern and see our own place in it? Looking back at my mother's life, it seems as if she is somehow aware, on a different level, of the pattern she is to weave. When she told me her story, was she already acting according to a divine blueprint that was already drawn out, telling me her story so that when she stopped remembering, I could regurgitate it and authenticate her life?

"I will not marry unless my mother and brother come with me," Soon Neo had said all those years ago when the Old Aunt came with a proposal of marriage.

Grandmother, only in her 40s, suddenly widowed, suddenly plunged from riches to rags never recovered from her loss. There was the loss of her husband, and then the loss of all material comfort. It was up to Soon Neo to take charge. My father was really generous because he took a bride, mother-in-law and brother-in-law into his home. Uncle Kanchil was only 12, he was my grandparents' last attempt at getting a male heir. When they first arrived in Singapore, starting their new life in a small hut, Kanchil had sat with thumb in mouth, eyes wide as if the shift from an opulent house to this basic existence was a nightmare he was struggling to wake up from.

"Eat, eat," Soon Neo said to him gently. "You are the only male in our family."

"Third sister, I'm so scared," he said in a shivery voice.

"You don't have to be. I'll take care of you, *what*."

She was five years older than him, third youngest of the four sisters. Yet Soon Neo took care of her little brother and her sisters until they were married off, the youngest one, Fourth Aunt, to die so soon after giving birth to two children. Grandmother caused few problems, she simply sat and stared at the wall. But Yong Tong paid for Kanchil to go to school to continue his education. Soon Neo was so grateful to her husband that she did everything possible to make him happy. Perhaps that is one of the reasons why in later years my mother will not tolerate anyone speaking ill of my father.

So, of all his sisters, Kanchil was closest to my mother. She became *his* mother. Brought up to be served by servants, he did not know how to fetch water from the well to bathe himself, nor did he know how to get his meal or how to comb his hair. When Soon Neo tried to do these things for him, Yong Tong would bellow, "Let him do it for himself! He's not a child anymore."

Kanchil would shrink at the sound of Yong Tong's voice, unused to being shouted at. He had been the only heir back in Grandfather's household in Malacca and had been treated rather preciously. It was quite a shock to be told to find kindling to start the clay stove or to blanco his own school shoes. Often, Soon Neo would find him sitting on the cement floor, legs drawn up, one arm around his knees, sucking his thumb, forelock over his face.

"You don't have to cry, *lah*, she said to him. "But he is right, you know. We don't have servants to do things for us anymore and you must learn to take care of yourself. One day, you're going to be a man and you must take care of your family. Meanwhile, study hard and you can get a good job. Maybe someday, you will earn enough to have servants of your own."

"Why don't you run away with me? He's not very nice to you."

"Shhh! Don't say things like that. We'd still be in that small hut if not for him. It's just that he has a lot of worries. He's got his mother and three brothers to look after, too. So he has to work very hard, *what*, and he gets tired a lot of the time and loses his temper. Take no notice of it, *lah*."

From that day on, the young boy never uttered a word against his benefactor.

I remember distinctly one of Uncle Kanchil's visit to *Potong Pasir* because he came in a uniform which made him look so handsome. He was quite tall and had the same delicate features as my mother. He was very smart, quite incongruous in our surroundings of shanty huts and outside bathrooms. I used to wonder why he came only in the daytime when Ah Tetia was at work. He never used to say much, not the kind of uncle to bounce nieces on his knees nor regale us with his adventures. He was actually a rather shy person, his presence the only way he knew of telling his sister how much he cared for her. At one stage he probably did write to her. But then Mak could not read so could not reply. The only thing my mother could read was her name, and that probably from recognition rather than knowing the letters which made up the words. Perhaps one of my brothers helped read Uncle Kanchil's letters or maybe not. So the letters stopped coming and soon, even he stopped coming.

When he married, his wife wrote the occasional letter and the annual Chinese New Year and Christmas cards. For a time, I used to read them to Mak and after I left home, Bernadette would read them to her. Her link with her brother was through us. She was dependent on our translations of his words and his meaning, unable to read between the lines herself. I think it is terrible to be unable to read, so much knowledge, so many worlds would be beyond one's reach. When you walk on the street, you can't understand road signs, shop signs or notices, a foreigner in your own country. Though she was illiterate, my mother understood the power of education, the power that comes from the simple ability to read. I am in awe that she should have had the great foresight to give me this precious gift which enables me to continually scale frontiers that are new to me. For this and everything else, I shall be eternally grateful.

"Look at Great Aunt and Second Aunt's children. Look at the lives they are leading."

It was Mak's way of reminding my siblings and myself of her endeavours that had kept us in school. She fed on our acknowledgments that she had done right. Both Great Aunt and Second Aunt did not place as much value and emphasis on education for their children. Unlike my mother, they did not understand what education could do. Or perhaps they did but were not prepared to forego their own pleasures to scrape and save for book-learning which didn't mean much to them. And so their children became janitors, factory workers, drivers and rubbish collectors and they in turn married janitors, factory workers, drivers and rubbish collectors. (Fortunately for my cousins, in the 1960s, the Singapore government set up *Lembaga*, adult education centres to educate adults who had left school early or had no schooling at all. It was this which pulled them out of illiteracy and so some of them moved up a rung on society's ladder.) We knew very little of our cousins by Fourth

Aunt because when she died, her husband refused to let them communicate with my mother and her sisters, so they lost contact. I cannot describe the feeling of enormous fortune that I feel every time I think how my life could have been different if my mother had lacked the determination to put me through school. Little do we realise as children how much the landscape of our future is going to be shaped by our parents' decisions. I am much aggrieved at my mother's loss of herself, that she who has given so much, now in her ailing years has to wait to be given. It seems unfair that having put others before herself throughout her life, she is sentenced to this continuing nightmare that is now her existence.

"Why don't you meet up with Mak and Bernadette in LA?" David suggests. "It will only be three weeks earlier than our trip to Vegas. And I'm sure you will find plenty to do whilst waiting for me in Vegas."

My fondness for a few hands on the Blackjack table has become a source of his lighthearted digs at me. He can afford to jest because he knows that I will never spend more than US$100.00 in gambling. We are due to be in Vegas because one of our guided tours for our travel company begins in Las Vegas and ends in Seattle. He and I were scheduled to fly out at the beginning of July, which is the start of our summer season in the USA and Canada. David and I own a forty-foot luxury motorhome for our travels around North America. It is our home away from home complete with modern conveniences, renovated to accommodate a desk that serves as our computer stations. It has a queen-sized bed in the rear, a hip-bath with a shower, a separate toilet, a very practical kitchenette and even a washing machine. It is certainly more luxurious than our *attap* hut in *Potong Pasir* had been! And the hut had not been that much longer either, only a little bit wider. At least this motorhome has running water and our own private loo. It is our home and workplace for more than four months a year.

Although we have two Wagon Masters with each group, we like to personally supervise the tours. We pride ourselves on providing a unique holiday, taking older people on a soft adventure holiday, where they drive themselves in motorhomes away from cities into the wilderness. We are the first travel company to provide this service. This particular tour will take us through nine National Parks, which include the Grand Canyon and Yosemite. My cousins in Los Angeles have decided to give Uncle Kanchil a big celebration for his 81st birthday, in case he doesn't make it to the next. It would be a chance for me to see Uncle Kanchil again after all these years and get to know my cousins. Also with our tours not ending until October, it will mean that I won't see Mak till Christmas, a whole year since I last saw her. So David's suggestion makes sense. He alters my flight ticket and I tell Bernadette my plan. She is coming out of Singapore with Mak and Andy. I have to pick up one of our company vehicle in Seattle and drive more than a thousand miles on my own to LA to meet them at Uncle Kanchil's, before I meet David in Vegas. So I would have to start out a few days earlier than them. Just before I leave, Bernadette calls to say that Mak has been agitated and is in total confusion. She fears that Mak will be unable to handle a long flight and trip. We have visions of her panicking whilst on board the plane and creating a fracas. So Bernadette decides against taking her. I am disappointed because I was so looking forward to seeing her but have to go by my sister's judgment. After all, she is the main carer. She also reminds me that though I thought of our uncle as Kanchil, he himself wished to be called Uncle Joe. But I don't pay too much attention to this.

One of my cousins is picking Bernadette and Andy at LAX Airport whilst I make my own way towards Uncle Kanchil's home. He is like the last piece to the jigsaw that was my mother's earlier life. I want to hear from him, his views about the exodus from Malacca and how they coped when they arrived in Singapore. Surely, Uncle Kanchil must have a great deal to tell. His son, Barry, whom I have not met, emails me a long list of Do's and Don'ts for my journey. He worries that I might fall asleep at the wheel, that I am not aware of the distance and vast country I am covering and the lonely nature of the drive. I email him back to thank him for his concern and assure him that I will be all right as I have driven all the way to Alaska and the Yukon, though I didn't mention that it was with David. He is sweet really and I am touched that he can be so caring about someone he doesn't even know. It rains all the way on my drive from Washington State through Oregon. But as soon as I cross the Cascade Mountains into California, the rains cease as if someone has turned off the giant tap. The sun comes out with a tenacity that equals its tropical brother. The journey from Sacramento to LA is boring, with a flat desert landscape that stretches for miles. Throughout my long drive, David keeps in touch with me on the mobile telephone.

"Don't talk to strangers," he says.

But at one of the rest stops, a stranger is the one who comes to talk to me. I have been to the restrooms and is getting into my car when he comes right up to the open window of my *GMC Jimmy*. He is a big, white American. I am instantly on my guard, I lock the door quickly and start the engine, ready to back the vehicle up and run over his toes if necessary.

"Do you have ten dollars to spare?" He says. "I've run out of petrol and I've left my credit card behind."

I am aware that it is likely to be a con and I want to get rid of him. Keeping my eyes on him, I reach out for my handbag, take out my wallet and hand him a ten dollar bill. He thanks me profusely but not with any indication as to how he is going to pay me back. Not that it matters. I am just eager to get away as quickly as I can, grateful that there has been no trouble. Apart from that, I cover the 1,600 miles in two days without mishap, stopping at a motel each night. I choose one that is not too quiet nor isolated and looks safe. I indulge in a little self-pride about my own daring, about this *kampong* girl who has come a long way from her days in the shanty village. I can't help thinking that if my mother hadn't given me the courage to grab life by the horns, I, at middle age, like many of my contemporaries in Singapore, would be swopping menopausal symptoms and talking about bad backs. I could have lived a safe life without ever breaking out of my routines and predictability. Because of how my mother had nurtured me and had given me a firm foundation and a zest for living, I am capable of notching university degrees and of handling an exciting career; capable of skiing down snow-clad mountains and climbing the treacherous Chilkoot Trail in the Gold Rush Mountains; capable of being an active companion to a 62-year-old foreign husband who is still fit, vibrant and adventurous enough to canoe 500 miles up the Yukon River at his age. My achievements are her achievements, because of what she has slaved and done for me. I don't know how my brothers and sisters see her role in their lives but there is no doubt in my mind of her immeasurable gift to me. So I blow her a kiss of thanks as I drive up the mountains on my last leg towards LA. Still in the mountains, I can see a canopy of dense pollution hovering over the town. I have flown in to LA before but not driven into it from this direction.

From a double lane that is almost as straight as a ruler through the desert, I am surprised when the road suddenly wraps around the mountain tops and multiplies into four. I am startled by the immediate change of pace, cars zip pass me at maddening speed and recklessness. At each entrance to the freeway, more cars join the flow until every bit of space between cars is totally taken up, so much so that movement of traffic is reduced dramatically. It is late afternoon and it costs me two hours of my life just to cross the town of LA. At one point, I am very conscious of my car being poised under several concrete archways of flyovers and I recall the carnage I saw on television during the San Francisco earthquake when one freeway had collapsed to fall on another. I can't wait to get out of the congestion! With relief, I leave LA behind, following my cousin's written instructions and directions to the suburbs. I get to the house without further problems. At last, I am at my destination's end. Because of my mother, and particularly because of her deteriorating mind, this meeting with Uncle Kanchil means so much to me. Uncle Kanchil and his wife, Angeline, have a typical suburban Californian house. My cousins' Mercedes Benzes are parked in the driveway, so different from the capacity of my Aunts' children. Bernadette and Andy have already arrived. My nephew throws his arms about my waist at the sight of me. For a moment, I am non-plussed to see him and my sister out of context in a different environment. For them, the LA evening is cool and they have sweaters on. Cousin Barry introduces himself and says, "So you are here safe and sound!"

It is nice to put a face to the emails that zipped into my computer. There is no necessity for introductions to Uncle Kanchil. He is sitting on the settee with oxygen tubes coming out of his nostrils that lead to an oxygen tank. He is very thin and frail. Although I am already aware that he and my mother look alike, I am still struck by how similar they are in features, even to the spread of their age-spots. He also reminds me of Matthew, in the curve of his head and the line of his jaw. He is very pleased to see us and asks after Third Sister. His wife, Aunty Angeline, and cousin Barry have prepared a sumptuous meal of chicken rice, steamed chicken and roast duck, which is so typical of Asian hospitality. With all that unexpected spread which they must have slaved hours over, it seems hateful to confess that I am a vegetarian. But I had not eaten meat for nearly 20 years and my digestive tract would not be able to tolerate it.

"No problem!" cousin Barry says.

He has a very cheerful disposition and is the size of someone who loves his food but not exercise. Totally unflustered, he whips up a chilli omelette in minutes, fry some tofu and *dao miao*. He is so unlike my stepdaughter, Sadie, who invited me for dinner, *knowing* I am a vegetarian and yet did not prepare anything I could eat. Barry and I are six months apart and we get off to a great start the moment we meet. When I tell him that Asian, particularly Singaporean hawker food, is hard to get in England, especially in Surrey, he says he'll take me for *laksa* the following day. Later, whilst Bernadette is regaling everybody about her the ups and downs of running a business, I have a chance to get Uncle Joe on my own. I sit beside him and I say,

"My mother always speaks so well of you. She always says Kanchil this, Kanchil that …"

Up until then, he had spoken quietly, his demeanour laid-back. Suddenly, his nostrils flare and his rheumy eyes flash, as if I had mentioned the unspeakable. In a tone that seems rather sharp and one that bears no comment, he says. "He's that other guy. My name is Joseph! I am Joe."

Seventeen

"*Makan! Makan!*"

True to his word, cousin Barry takes me out for *laksa, thosai* and all the foods I had missed, even though it is only six months ago that I was in Singapore. He feeds me like I'm a refugee who hasn't seen food for a long while. Of course I protest about his taking time off from work to feed me, but not with great enthusiasm. It is great to find someone who enjoys food as much as I do. My sons, like my nieces and nephews, do not look for Singaporean food when they go abroad. They're just as happy to eat pizzas, burgers and steaks. They think it's because they are adaptable. Actually, it's because they have already been exposed to western food from an early age. For older folks like myself, whose families were not in the income group to frequent restaurants when we were growing up, western food was very much out of our reach, except for the occasional fish and chips wrapped in newspaper. And that constituted a special treat. What you eat when you're growing up is a decisive factor in what you look for in your diet in subsequent years. Cousin Barry understands my needs perfectly. We drop Bernadette and Andy off at LA's tourist attractions: Disneyland, MGM and Knotts Berry Farm, places that I have been to before, whilst Barry and I eat our way around LA County. He is fun to be with and his knowledge of where all the best foods are is typically

Singaporean, although he has lived in California for many years. Although he speaks grammatically correct English and not *Singlish*, his accent is still Singaporean, unlike his daughter's, nieces' and nephews'. Apparently, they had lived in Singapore for a time and then returned to California. His sister, Jennifer, takes me out to an Asian hypermarket so that I can stock up my motorhome fridge and freezer for when I get to Vegas. She buys me spices, *sambals*, durians and mangoes. LA, like San Francisco, Vancouver and Toronto, has a huge Asian community, much more collossal in population size to London, so all imaginable Asian food and ingredients can be found in these cities. Jennifer still maintains Singaporean mores, she drives around with sleeves-envelopes, cut off from a blouse so that her arms would not be darkened by the sun. I am quite sure that she regards Bernadette as the more wealthy, more refined sister because Bernadette is so fair whereas I am the colour of the Mexican girl who comes in to help her with the housework.

The birthday party for our uncle is a great success though he sits observing it all from his seat, still attached to his oxygen tank, clapping his hands. It is held at cousin Jennifer's ranch-type home around her swimming pool in the Californian evening, with a cast of talented relatives who sing, dance and play the piano, trumpet and guitar. Barry plays the saxophone with verve. All of Uncle's children and grandchildren are there, and of course his friends too. It is strange to see so many Asians in one party here that it is almost possible to forget that I am in the United States, except that the majority of guests speak in American accented English. Bernadette is in her element. Someone asks her, "Have you lived abroad?" And when she says, "No," he asks why she speaks with an Australian accent, she replies, "Not everyone in Singapore speaks *Singlish* you know." She and I decide to wear our *sarong kebayas*, especially for Uncle Joe and he is indeed very pleased.

"Like your mother," he says.

Because of his inability to breathe unaided, his words are sparing. So I am not sure if he means our dressing or our looks. However, his remark touches a chord in me, anything that reminds me of my mother has the capacity to move me. Although he doesn't say much, I can gauge that his feelings for my mother are intense whenever he mentions her. His and my private exchange is not brought up again. He is frail and I do not wish to contribute to his distress although I feel a little cheated that I cannot verify the facts of my mother's story about their exodus and their new life in Singapore. I had so looked forward to completing the family jigsaw puzzle because Uncle Joe is of sound mind and can easily set the record straight. For some unfathomable reason, he is reluctant to air the family closet. Then I thought, perhaps he doesn't want to discuss things with me because he doesn't know me well, or that he's in ill health and therefore doesn't want to recollect a painful past. But surely, he must have told his family; after all, his beginnings are their beginnings, too; surely he won't deprive them of their roots and history. So, just before I drive Bernadette and Andy to Las Vegas for their short holiday, I take my cousin, Jennifer, his eldest daughter, aside and ask her, "Do you know if your father ever used the name 'Kanchil'? Does your mother or any of you know about his family's flight from Malacca?"

"No, *lah*. Dad has always been very secretive. We have often puzzled over this. We know he is very fond of your mother and used to visit her. He told us that when he's better, he wants to visit her. But he has never spoken about your father. It's as though there was something between them that he doesn't want to remember. We have heard from the grapevine that something did happen in Malacca that caused them to leave the town. But we don't know what. It's weird, but no matter how we begged him, Dad will not tell us about his life before he was 17."

Cousin Jennifer stresses this several times, "We don't know anything about his life before he was 17."

So now I, too, will never know.

Bernadette and Andy have only four days in Las Vegas. She calls home every day and on one of the calls, learns that Dolores has to rush back to the Philippines for a court case because her husband has threatened to wrest custody of their children from her. Agatha has to send her maid over to look after Mak. Matthew drops in at his lunch hour to make sure that our mother gets on with the maid-on-loan. I take my sister and nephew to the Hoover dam and other Vegas attractions. Andy is delighted to ride the gondola down the replica of the Grand Canal at The Venetian, one of the many themed hotels on The Strip. Then Bernadette receives a call from Romia to say that Dolores is not returning. Of course, this is a catastrophe. Bernadette works full-time and so does Agatha and all my brothers. There won't be anyone to look after Mak.

"Agatha says that maybe it's time we consider putting Mother in a nursing home," Bernadette says.

I am silenced by the prospect. Of course I am thinking that she should be in a place that she is familiar with but then I am not the one who has to care for her, what can I say? I have to bow to Bernadette's decision. Fortunately, in the next breath, she says, "I'd rather stay at home than put Mak in a nursing home."

Telephone calls bat back and forth between Bernadette and Romia. My brother has decided to start interviewing potential maids. Meanwhile, I take Bernadette and Andy to see the volcanic eruption and White Tigers at The Mirage, the battle between the French and the English at Treasure Island, the flower conservatory at Bellagio. We receive another call from

Romia to say that he has found an excellent replacement, a 30-something Filipina who had trained as a nurse and has requested the maid agency to transfer from her present employer in Singapore because they are mistreating her. What a marvellous coincidence to have a trained nurse! Maria had not qualified as a nurse because she could not afford to pay the fees for the Final Examinations and came out to Singapore to work because she is paid three times more as a maid what she would be paid in the Philippines as a nurse. One Singapore dollar is equal to 24 Philippine pesos. As a qualified nurse, she would earn 2,800 pesos a month which is approximately S$115.00. As a maid, all her meals and accommodation is completely free and she takes home S$350.00 a month which is about 9,200 pesos. It sounds a lot but it is about £225 a month! (However, the maid's employer has to pay a levy of about the same amount to the government.) The maid herself has to repay the employment agency their fee and her airfare in instalments. It seems tough.

The fact that Maria is already working in Singapore means that she can start getting used to Mak immediately. Apparently, according to the employment agency's contract, she would get a day off after working for three whole months. I am astonished that nobody thinks this is unacceptable, including the maid herself. When Romia asked her if she was willing to take care of an old lady suffering from Alzheimer's and could be difficult, Maria said that she was willing. We express our gratitude to whoever has engineered her availability to us.

The day comes when I have to take Bernadette and Andy to MacCarran Airport for their flight back to LA and then a connection to Singapore. Though I feel sad at our parting, I have to get things ready for David's and our clients' arrival. In one of our summer seasons on these holidays for retired people, we could eat away at least 10,000 miles, approximately the distance of Singapore from England. Every time I return to Singapore, Andy will say, "Aunty Phine, why don't you adopt me?"

"Why do you want me to adopt you when you have your own parents?"

"So that I can see bears and moose. So that I can go to California, Nevada, Nova Scotia and up to Alaska and the Yukon."

He is very practical, my eight-year-old nephew, who will be turning nine in August. Wisely, he didn't miss a chance to remind me about his coming birthday whilst we are in Las Vegas and persuaded me to buy him an advance birthday present, a toy of the huge American trucks which fascinates him.

One of the problems of life on the road is that communication with family is a challenge. Although I carry a three-band mobile telephone, the areas that we go to are so remote that there are no telephone masts. The only times we can be in touch is when we are near towns, where we can get access to a landline or a public telephone. Although there are satellite telephones, the cost is too horrendous for us at the moment. Most of the time I keep in touch with my boys and Bernadette via emails which we get access to in public libraries and cyber cafes. But as we travel hundreds of miles away from towns with libraries and cyber cafes, we can only keep in touch occasionally. This causes me the greatest worry when David and I are on the road. I hate to find out things about our families when it is too late. Bernadette knows that she can contact our office in England if there is an emergency because David is in touch with his office manager every day. The 16-hour difference between Singapore and certain parts of Canada and the USA is another obstacle to my communication with Bernadette.

By August, we have finished with our Las Vegas to Seattle tour and in September, we begin our Nova Scotia route. So far, of all the places I have seen, Nova Scotia is my favourite place with endless coastlines that curves and dips so that as you come around the bends, you are greeted with the fabulous sight of sea and sky and little fishing coves. Scottish culture thrives in these places, with many people still wearing kilts and playing the bagpipes. We are now 11 hours behind Singapore. My mobile doesn't work here at all because the country is still on the analogue system. So I use the public telephone when I want to get any news. Mak seems to be almost always sleeping when I call, so I don't get to hear her voice. Every now and then, Bernadette sends an email about how troublesome Mak has been, shouting at them or throwing things around. I am always saddened when I receive such news, not willing to admit that this woman that she is talking about is actually my mother. You read books on Alzheimer's and understand that this sort of behaviour is all part of the disease, but when it is happening to someone you love, you still find it hard to come to terms with it. You keep on hoping and praying that the doctors might be wrong and that Mak is only suffering a severe case of senile dementia. You will not accept a verdict that is similar to a life sentence. If I only knew then, that there is worse to come.

To call Bernadette at 10am on a Sunday, I have to stay up until 11pm of my Saturday. At Halifax, I take the opportunity to play a few hands of Blackjack at the Nova Scotia Casino, which is right on the waterfront so that I can use their telephone. David says I will find any excuse to pop into casinos. He would rather sit in the bar-lounge nursing his gin and tonic. At exactly 11pm, I get off the table and call Bernadette. I am always apprehensive when I do so because I never know what to expect. But when Bernadette takes my call without bursting into tears, I know that I can relax a little.

"How's Mak?" I ask.

"Oh, it's terrible," she says. "Today she went to the bathroom to pass motion and didn't know how to do it on the toilet. She squatted on the bathroom floor and did it there! Maria discovered the mess."

So the terrible thing has begun. As the books foretold — the awful moment when normal everyday things are outside the comprehension of the Alzheimer's sufferer. The disease is a tragedy of monumental proportion, robs the sufferer of her dignity, reduces her to a mindless child in a wizened body. For my mother who had pride herself on cleanliness and personal hygiene, this is an even greater insult. Even when we had been so poor with no indoor bathroom and toilet, she made sure that our home was clean, our clothes washed and ironed. All her aluminium pots gleamed and shone, the aluminium that is supposed to have contributed to her disease. She washed the chamber pot with her own hands everyday until I took over the task. During the hot seasons when the water in the village well receded, she would put out pails and containers to catch any rainfall or dew so that she could continue cleaning. She used leftover water from the washing of clothes to scrub the floor, clean our *char kiak* or wooden clogs, and our canvas school shoes.

"As long as you have water," she often told me, "you are not that poor that you have to be dirty."

I am scourged by Bernadette's news, my heart bleeding afresh. This woman who appeared to have lost her senses is the same woman who educated us to the proper use of precious water in *Potong Pasir*. When the reservoirs in the country ran to a dangerously low level and more water had to be bought from the Malay Peninsular (now West Malaysia), the village standpipe where we got our supply of drinking water would be turned off, too. And Mak would queue patiently with all the villagers for the municipal lorry to come with its load of rationed water. This is the same woman who had the fortitude to send me to school, the same woman who acted as mid-wife to many of the village births, healer to the sick. This same woman who gave away her own food to the *kampong* folks who were in greater need, a gentle quiet heroine who brought joy to lives which she brush-stroked with her smile and tenderness. Who is there to restore her to that former glory? Who is there to heal her now?

Eighteen

"*I* think I ought to go back to see Mak after our season is over," I say to David. "From the sound of her deterioration, Christmas is too far away."

"Yes, that sounds like a good idea. I shall see if I can go across, too. But I do hate those damn flights. It's agony for my gout."

Our last tour for our travel business is from Montreal to New England to see the fall colours. But we had a couple of weeks' break before it begins. We need that time anyway to drive from Nova Scotia to Montreal. But we can squeeze in a few days of leisure. So we decide to take in a whirlwind view of Prince Edward Island, which is outside our tour route. From New Brunswick, we use the Confederation Bridge to get to Prince Edward Island. The bridge is a feat of modern engineering at 12.5 kilometres long. It spans the Northumberland Straits, which completely freezes over in winter. The island, called PEI for short, is incredibly rustic and unspoilt, with soft undulating hills very much like England, with many towns named after those in the United Kingdom. Our campground that evening is in a place called Stratford. But we have a long journey to Montreal, so we can only stay a couple of days. We zip through New Brunswick and go into Shediac, lobster capital of the world, to try some lobsters and are disappointed that they are nothing special.

Then signs begin to change from English into French and that surprises me, since the majority of Canadians don't speak French or Quebcois, the variety of French that they speak here. We go into a tourist centre to ask for a map of the area and is handed a map totally in French. The first thing I discover is the Quebecian's arrogance.

"Do you have the map in English?" I ask the young girl.

"What is the point? The place names are all in French anyway."

Throughout my months of travelling, seeing lovely areas of wilderness and beautiful places, I never forget that without my mother, I would not be here. If I had not gone to school, I would not have gone to University and would not have worked as a marketing executive and David and I would not have met, would not have been able to communicate even if we had met. My destiny would have run on a different track. I keep casting my mind back because I still can't get over how lucky I am that my mother forced a change in the couplings that re-directed my train. I owe her so much.

David and I stop at a campground in Quebec City and are charmed by the old part of town which is very European in character compared to the rest of Canada, with its narrow cobbled streets and town square. David and I have a meal and a couple of games of chess. Then we stand and watch the fireeater demonstarting his skill in the square to a cheering crowd. It is eleven o'clock in the evening, which is a good time to call Singapore. I call Bernadette and she starts to cry when she hears my voice, and my heart plunges a few fathoms.

"Mak is in hospital. She had a fall and broke her hip. I emailed you."

But of course I had not been able to get online for a few days. This is the kind of news I had feared, another setback to an already ailing body. I am so distressed, I pass the phone to David. It seems that Mak is in a very bad way. The doctors are not sure if they can do a hip-replacement because they don't think she'll survive the operation. Hasn't my mother gone through enough? If I still believe in a God to rail to, I would. But I don't, believing now that it is all karmic. But why does Mak need all these experiences? What is she supposed to be learning still? Philosophy is easier to digest in print, but when it is a part of real life, it feels like one is trying to swallow dry paper.

"Shall I come out?" I ask Bernaedtte when I get on the phone again.

"It's hard to say. She's been in there four days. And she doesn't look good. She's confused about where she is, so she's screaming and shouting at the nurses. She's on traction at the moment, in a straitjacket and strapped to the bed to stop her from moving. One of us needs to be with her 24 hours."

I am stabbed by her words, visions of our mother straitjacketed like an inmate in an asylum, fearful and confused, struggling with everybody who tries to help her. When I was a nurse, I worked in Woodbridge Hospital, a mental institution, located in what used to be Singapore's countryside in Yio Chu Kang. The staff of the dental unit had to go to the hospital one day a week. I was sent out there, every Tuesday for two years, to assist the dental surgeon. The place was dismal, resembling a prison more than it did a hospital. I was only 17 and it was quite a traumatic experience the first time I went there: people sauntering around with that dazed look, their hospital garments looking like sack cloths. The more serious cases were in straitjackets or tied up, some locked in personal cells, their dentures taken away from them. Is my mother reduced to this? Has she crossed some invisble line between disease and sanity? What is the difference between the two when an Alzheimer's patient starts to lose sight of her days and weeks, her own memories, and worse, the workings of her own body?

"I'll come out. I'll find out if there are flights available when we get to Montreal."

We set off from Quebec City the next morning. Instead of the leisurely run to Montreal that we had anticipated, our drive there is a race. We take Highway 20 West, following the beautiful St Lawrence River on our right, though we have no time to stop at the shoreline towns. With our motorhome and the tow vehicle behind, our rig is nearly 60 feet long, so it must look odd to other motorists that we are zipping along like a wagon-train on fire. David and I take turns to drive so we cover the 155 miles in just under three hours, ever watchful for the blue lights of the Highway Police. The Highway Police ought to be busy because I have never witnessed such lunacy on the roads as I do here. The design of the highways and freeways exacerbate the problem, with entrances and exits at random coming onto the highway and departing sometimes on the right, sometimes on the left. The signage is typically French and are not consistent or well posted in advance, so you can be caught unawares as to where you are supposed to exit or join another freeway. Cars zip in front of us so abruptly that David is reduced to using swear words. Thank God he's driving and not me. A sixty-foot rig with two tons of metal, kitchen, bathroom and bedroom in the back, plus a car in tow, is not easy to brake when some lunatic changes lanes to come into yours without much preamble. Montreal is the most nightmarish city I have ever driven in, even worse than Bangkok or Singapore where, though chaotic, the madness is minimised by the lower speed limit.

We park the motorhome in a campground outisde the city and make our way to the airport to find a direct flight to Singapore. But there isn't any. I would have to fly West to Vancouver, Vancouver to Hongkong or Taipei, then to Singapore. We come away despondent, then David remembers that I have a flight home to London. If I can get an earlier flight back than the scheduled return flight after our tours, I could pick up a direct flight from London to Singapore. With his usual efficiency, he arranges it with his office manager in England. David says he is sorry he can't come with me because he has an important meeting in London later in the week and he decides to fly out the same day with me, then return to Montreal after the meeting to meet up with our next group as they begin the tour to New England. Just before we leave, we hear that David's former general manager, Dave, who had worked for more than 25 years in the bakery with David has had a heart attack and is in a London hospital. On, 14 September, David and I fly out of Montreal and arrive in London the next day, only to be told that Dave had died minutes before we arrived. It must be sad for David, but all I am thinking is please don't let me be too late to see my mother alive. David goes to the hospital whilst I have a rest in a day room at an airport hotel. My flight to Singapore is at 10pm the same evening. By the time, I arrive at Changi Airport on the 16th, I am a walking zombie.

Through the glass walls from where the baggage carousels are, I see Andy jumping up and down with glee when he sees me. He and my ten-year-old nephew, Agatha's son, are waving frantically to catch my attention. When I see them, I wave back and blow them a kiss. Bernadette sees me and smiles and my heart slips into a restful gear, like on my last visit. Knowing Bernadette, she would most likely dissolve into tears when she sees me if Mak's situation had changed for the worse. After gathering my luggage, I push the trolley out and see that Agatha is there, too. For a moment, I hold my breath in suspense, wondering if there is bad news to tell because Agatha has not picked me up from the airport before. I hug everybody and still, there's no news forthcoming.

"How's Mak?" I venture to ask, then.

"She's calmed down a little. They've taken her off the traction but she's still in a straitjacket," Agatha says.

Her voice is mellower and she has lost tremendous weight. Bernadette, too, has lost weight and both of them look tired. They are the real victims of our mother's illness, they are the ones who have to look after Mak and be witness to her day-to-day deterioration. Their emotional trauma must be great, as it must be for my brothers. Our mother's illness has taken a toll on all of them. I know I am the fortunate one to be spared all the daily problems and the continual heartache. It must be far, far more difficult for them than it is for me. Bernadette pushes my trolley whilst the two boys grab each of my hands in an open display of joy that I am home.

"What happened to your car?" I ask Bernadette when we climb in to Agatha's people mover, a seven-seater vehicle.

"It's past its ten years. Had to be scrapped. But the economy has been hit by the depression, and the COE has gone up, so we can't afford the licence."

"COE? What's that?"

"It stands for 'Certificate of Entitlement'. It's a licence to own a car. All cars have to be scrapped when they reach ten-years-old. Then there is an open bidding system to get a licence to own a new car. This is called the COE. If we don't possess a COE, we are not allowed to purchase another car."

"And how much does a COE cost?"

"It all depends on the bidding. Last month it was $60,000. It could get up to $100,000 or more."

"What? To buy a licence to buy a car?"

"Uh huh," both Bernadette and Agatha echo.

As if there are not enough rules in Singapore. I understand that it makes sense to restrict car ownership on such a tiny island which is no bigger than the Isle of Wight, but with three million people on it. But having just travelled the length and breadth of Canada and the United States, I hate the thought of not having a car and not being able to drive. Yet, there is a truly wonderful public transport system here with the buses and MRT being so frequent and efficient. The maximum cost of an MRT ticket is $1.80, which is only 60 pence to travel from the east to the west of the island or from the north to the south, so it's affordable to everybody. But I wouldn't like to live here. It might be all right when I am older but not when I've still got the wanderlust. I like the idea of getting into my car and being able to drive for hundreds and thousands of miles without jettisoning into the sea.

"After dropping your luggage at Bernadette's, I thought it might be nice to take you for some dinner at a hawker centre. You can have your favourite *Chye Tow Kway*. After that, do you want to rest or go to the hospital? I know you've been travelling for two days."

I am astonished at the change in Agatha. She speaks mildly and is so considerate.

"Dinner sounds good. I'll see Mother after that. By the time I get to Bernadette's, I should be ready to crash out."

I am home again. Here, food is the subject of a greeting, a topic of conversation, an exhibition of welcome, hospitality and love. Action expresses more than words do in this culture. If you think in a fixed mindset when you cross cultures and expect things to be done in a certain way, you are destined for disappointment or frustration. You would be far wiser to float freely, to observe but withhold judgment. Now that I am straddled over two cultures, I too have to leave my English persona behind, slip back into being a Singaporean. So Agatha drives us to a food centre by the sea on the East Coast and in the balmy evening air, with the sound of surf washing the shore, we sit and eat our meal. It's much nicer to eat with people who enjoy their food rather than sitting and eating with people who worry about their figures, careful about how much calories they are consuming, how much fat there is in the food and other such concerns. It is more than 40 hours since I have left Montreal so I am tired, and my sisters' and my nephews' voices sound like they are coming from a distance, but the delicious food fuels my energy level a fraction. I need the energy to confront my mother's deterioration.

The moment I walk into the private room, Mak's eyes light up momentraily and she says in a voice that is hardly above a whisper, "Ah Phine, ah, you come already."

"Ahh, Ah Mak still recognises her! That's good," says Romia.

Everybody smiles at Mak's success at recognition, spurring encouragement. It's the praise given to a child for learning a new word or learning to do something new. This is what my mother has become, a child in an old woman's body. It is one of life's ironies, that one can grow older and regress at the same time. Romia, who has grown hugely rotund, is sitting with her and has been there all afternoon. He greets me with great cheer as if we are friends bumping into each other accidentally. He rises from his seat to give me a hug and it's like being hugged by a bear. I can't get close enough to him for his belly. Bernadette is to relieve his watch for a few hours, then Matthew is coming in to look after Mak throughout the night. Apparently, Ah Cob does the occasional day watch and one of their wives does part of the afternoons. Now it's time for me to do my share. It does Mak credit that her family has rallied around to look after her. She has been the centre of our lives and we are the spokes. When the centre goes, how will the wheel hold up?

Mak was already thin when I last saw her ten months ago, but now she looks thinner still. Her face is drawn, her few strands of hair loose around her shoulders. She looks like a small craft in a huge ocean on the hospital bed, her upper body wrapped in its straitjacket, her legs strapped to the bed. Fortunately, I had steeled myself for this moment, aware of how she might appear, otherwise I might have stumbled onto loose emotions. She looks so frail and weary that I know that whatever happens, I must exhibit joy and optmism in front of her, otherwise she might pick up the negative vibes. I bend down to hug her and kiss her.

"You're okay, Mak?"

"Better now," she says.

Romia goes off with a promise to get his Indonesian maid to cook *Titek Papaya* and *Ikan Pari Masak Asam Pedas* for me before I leave. Like Jacob, he never writes or phones but he has made effort to meet up with me when I was in the States or when he visited London. It is really sweet that he thinks of these foods for me because they are Mak's recipes and the ingredients for them are not easy to find in England.

Whatever spark there has been in Mak has definitely fizzled off, her spirit is now flat. She tires easily, dozing even as we are talking to her. My sisters are talking about their boys whilst they play in the patient's lounge and watch TV. At first I am mildly surprised that they can be so chatty around Mak's bedside, then I realise that it is probably their way of coping. They are on the flip side of pain and sadness — and it's a good ploy to keep talking, to keep busy. So I follow suit.

Agatha and her son go off at nine, and at ten, Matthew arrives. Hugging him is the direct oposite to hugging Romia. Matthew is so thin it seems possible that you might crack him in half if you hugged too tightly. Only 54, he's already collapsing into his rib-cage and his lower back has a soft outward curve. His features resemble Uncle Kanchil's so much that it's startling. But I am getting tired, the sounds in my ears are getting louder and I am losing my orientation.

"I'd better go now, catch up on my sleep. Soon as I get over the jet-lag, I'll do the night-shift," I say.

"Take your time," he says. "Take your time."

The nurse has been in to give Mak her valium, so she's already drowsy. I give her a quick peck on her cheek which feels dry and papery. As I walk out of the ward with Bernadette and her son, something occurs to me. My mother has never failed to ask after David when she has seen me or when I come on the telephone. Now, for the first time, she has completely not remembered David at all. It is not a good sign.

My head is till fuzzy when I wake up at mid-day, my body unsure whether it should be acting on Montreal time, London time or Singapore time. The house is unusually quiet, it's rare for it to be empty; even when the family is out, either Mak would be at home with the maid or the maid would be in on her own. This gives the sense that things are not normal. But I guess Andy is away at school, Bernadette and her husband are at work and Maria has gone to do the day-watch at the hospital since Romia has a meeting. When I had got home the previous evening, I was introduced to Maria, who is small and slight like Dolores but is unmarried. She told me that she and her sister are working as maids in Singapore to pay their mother's medical bills. It seems ironic that she is here taking care of my mother when her own is ill in the Philippines. I pass my mother's room on the way to the kitchen to fix something to eat. Her vacant room and bed stare at me dolefully. She keeps it fairly spare, a single bed against the wall nearest the windows, a small wardrobe for her clothes and things. There is a bedside cabinet with drawers and an easy chair next to her bed. There is something sad about an empty room, particularly when its owner is ill in hospital. Suddenly, I feel too dispirited to cook anything, so I walk out in my shorts and T-shirt to a hawker centre nearby and eat *lontong* at the Malay stall. The steamed rice cakes in a savoury coconut sauce with vegetables and tofu cost only S$2.00, which is less than £1.00. I can't get over how inexpensive this is compared to what I would have to pay in London, at least £5.50, which is nearly S$15.00! With my expanding waistline, I shouldn't order another bowl, but I do and make a pig of myself. You can tell I am easily tempted. The same stall sells some *kueh dada*, which is one of Mak's favourite, a thin crepe, made green from the fragrant pandan leaf, wrapped around finely grated fresh coconut cooked in palm sugar. In a restaurant in London, one of these would cost £2.40; here at the hawker centre, they cost 50 cents each, which is about 20 pence! I buy the whole tray.

A short five-minute walk has made my t-shirt all sweaty, so I go back to change and then find my way to the hospital. It is strange that every time I return to Singapore, I revert to a mindset as if I am still in the clutches of poverty and am still living in the kampong, so I wouldn't spend money on a taxi. From one end of Singapore to the other, the taxi would be no more than £7, to the hospital it will probably be £1.50, but I still take the bus. Changi Hospital is very modern, with a lovely atrium, fountain and decorative ponds on the ground level. There is also an air-conditioned food court. Even sick people don't give up their food in this country! There are patients in their blue hospital garments, sitting in wheelchairs, enjoying hawker food rather than ward meals. I take the lift up to the ninth floor. When I hear voices coming from Mak's room, I am surprised, expecting only Maria to be there. Romia, Agatha and Bernadette are in the room and my heart starts to drum. Something must have happened for them to rush down here on a working day. They turn to face me when I walk in, their faces tight with despair.

"Mak has taken a turn for the worse. Maria called us. We've called a priest to come and give her Extreme Unction."

A thought races through my mind. I am thinking that perhaps she has been waiting for me to arrive before she gives up her spirit. Our mother is propped up on the bed, her face looking like a skull with flesh, her closed eyes sinking into their sockets. She looks as if she's being strangled by the straitjacket and all the straps, her breath coming out in small sips. She gives no indication that she is aware that her children are around her bedside. My younger son arrives, but our meeting is tinged with the pall of death. He is so tall now that he has to bend down for me to reach his cheek. Matthew and Jacob turn up with their wives. We talk in soft whispers, the kind of talk that goes around a deathbed, meaningless talk that is geared towards keeping sorrow at bay. Then the priest arrives, in his white frock, bible and stock-in-trade paraphernalia. He's from the parish where Mak had last gone to church, when they were living in the HDB flat, where I went to for Midnight Mass last Christmas Eve. Mak opens her eyes and when she sees Father Tay, she asks, "Ehh? What are you doing here?"

We all laugh, although somewhat nervously. Father Tay talks to her in Teochew, asks her how she is, holds her hand and let her babble on for a bit. Then he turns to us and says in English, "Your mother is not ready to go yet. I've been to many deathbeds and know when death is imminent. She looks okay, a little tired maybe. I won't need to give her Extreme Unction."

"You may be right, father," Agatha says. "But since you are here, you might as well give it to her."

"Trust me. She doesn't need it. I'll give her Holy Communion if you like."

And so, for some reason, just as she seems to be ebbing and loosening her mortal bonds, she revives dramatically. Perhaps the drugs the doctors were using to help her over her fall had affected her and made her worse than she really is. We don't know, but are relieved and surprised. She even accepts the *kueh dada* I had bought, eating it slowly. My mother who has always loved her independence now has to be fed. Firstly, it's because she is tied down to the bed, and secondly, it's as if she has forgotten how. It's as if the concussion to her hip had concussed her mind, too. She no longer drinks or eats without help. It's a huge regression from when I last saw her. At first, I thought that it was because my brothers and sisters started the habit of feeding her whilst she was tied down, but when the nurse finds her more docile, they remove the straps but she still needs to be fed. I am there, alone with her one evening when her dinner arrives. I push the trolley-tray towards her, prop her up and ask her to feed herself. I scoop up the food for her and put the spoon in her hand. She holds the spoon, picks up some food but directs the food to her cheeks. I'm thinking it's a natural mistake, that she's not in quite an upright position, or perhaps her aim isn't good. But she tries again and still she can't manage to get the food into her mouth.

"I'm not hungry," she says, pushing the tray away.

"Come on, let me help."

"I'm so useless now, so useless," she says as the tears flow down unchecked and her body shakes like the earth building up to explode the boiling magma underneath.

I could have cried. Day by day as I sit with her, I am learning how much of her has flaked away, as though she is made of papier mache and she has dried out and bits of her are flaking off. Where she could make conversation before, she now strings words together that are not connected, a lot of gobbledygook which to her seems to make sense. Some days, she can't even remember who I am, mistaking me for Bernadette or Agatha or even a friend. It's pot-luck whether she recalls who her sons are, although she seems calm when Matthew or Romia minister to her needs. And when visitors come, children of my dead aunts, she doesn't know them, although she talks to them as if she recognises them. I am not sure if this is a reasoned thing or if it's accidental. If it is all an act, it's a good one but it's impossible that she can still have the capacity to fake it. To be able to act or fake requires a sound mind. And she's beyond this.

"I must go to the toilet," she says. "I want to move my bowels."

So there is some bodily sensitivity left. There are parts of her body which are still communicating with her mind. It won't be long before even this fragile link is broken and her mind will be adrift, flung into the open, raging sea where nothing, absolutely nothing, can save her anymore.

"You can go right where you are. You have a new kind of chamber pot under you. It's so modern these days. Just go and it will be all right," I say, using an analogy my brothers and sisters use, trying to keep the tears out of my voice.

"Is that right? You mean I can go right here?"

"That's right."

"Okay, *lah,*" she says, too quick to acquiesce, as if there's no more fight in her.

When the two nurses come in to change her diaper, I stay to watch so that I can be her nurse when she goes home. It's a witnessing that will be imprinted on my soul forever, a witnessing that tears me apart. It seems to me the final insult to her. There must be some spirit left in my mother because I am sure I can see the precise moment when she flees from this gross indignity which she has to submit to. She allows her body to go limp, as though she is not at home, so that she herself does not have to witness others taking charge of her body, invading crevices and private flesh whose textures were so far only known to herself and her husband. The young, foreign nurses are not privy to this, unsuspecting that they are gladiators in an emotional arena. Imported from China and the Philippines, they prattle incessantly to her in English as they go about their task, like mothers do when changing their babies, cooing and prattling, talking baby-talk, expecting no reply. This is what my mother has become. How easy we become how others see us, or treat us. She has re-entered her childhood, folded into herself. A long time ago, she passed the baton to me to finish the race. Now she is moving backwards to the starting line and I can feel the space between us getting wider as I move forward, and she back.

As the weeks in the hospital trundle along on leaden feet, I watch with anguish as this fault in the ground widens and widens, a yawning chasm that is caused by the turbulence underfoot. That is when I know that her geography has altered beyond repair. There are more features of this new landscape that are unfamiliar than familiar. But we still take her home when the hospital needs the bed, when nothing else can be done for her there. The hip has to heal on its own, the X-rays show a clear fracture that can only be healed if she's completely immobilised.

"She mustn't walk for another month or so," the orthopaedist says. "However, in her case, because she is suffering from Alzheimer's, it is possible that after that period is over, she may not remember how to walk again."

The prognosis is another tremor on top of the quake. How long more can her foundations last? But they say in the Yukon, that fireweed, a beautiful red-blooded flower, can germinate from poor quality soil that has been in a fire; and fossils and long-buried treasures can be unearthed during a quake. So too my mother's condition bring out the hidden qualities in my brothers and sisters, all of them rallying around trying their best to make Mak comfortable and happy. There is a unity in the family again, like different peoples in a nation going to war. When Mak was able and had us around for lunch every Sunday, we had been very close, even going to play squash together in the late afternoon, brothers and sisters, and some of our children. But when Mak stopped cooking, each of the families, particularly Jacob's and Romia's, stopped meeting frequently. But now, we come together again, to fight this battle together. Matthew is endearingly tender when he attends to our mother, feeding her, coaxing her to eat, wiping her mouth, tucking her into bed, soothing her when she gets agitated. For a man, he is unbelievably sensitive and nurturing. Romia tries to hide his core of softness by talking loudly and laughing, and he looks somewhat displaced with his large body and his huge hands spoon-feeding our mother. Only Jacob seems to retain his manly persona. Although he visits often, he can't bring himself to cross into uncharted territory where he has to play mother to his own mother. He finds it difficult to feed her. But I notice that he is not as cool and calm as he appears to be. He is hurting badly inside, hurting because his mother lies in the bed having been battered by his father and battered by life, yet he cannot say the things he would have liked to say to her. His tears are often close to the surface but he talks in a brusque manner to pretend otherwise. Perhaps, he, like Agatha, feels he has to disguise his soft-centre with a loud voice and strong opinions to throw off the real scent.

Bernadette is rapidly wilting. Never one to be energetic before, this constant to-and-froing from office to hospital has taken a great toll and she complains of backache and vertigo and all sorts of otther ailments. It is interesting that whenever she visits, Mak would revert to her pidgin English when talking to her, prefixing her name with *Marm* in the way that Maria would address her as if somewhere along the way, she has become Bernadette's servant. Agatha's commitment to some new religious sect is manifesting itself in her mellower manner and more thoughtful ways. She had phoned around to cousins and a former *kampong* resident so that they can come and bid Mak their farewells. Agatha is supremely efficient, getting all the supplies we need to take care of a bedridden person at home. She even manages to locate a hospital bed for homeusers and even paid for it in its entirety. Because Mak cannot understand what is happening to her, she needs to have a cot to ensure that she doesn't try to get out of bed. Also she requires a bed that can be cranked up and down to feed and change her. By the time Mak is discharged, the bed has arrived and is installed in place of the old single bed in the room. But the person who returns is not the same one who went.

Nineteen

*N*ow it is down to Maria and myself to attend to Mak's daily needs as everybody returns to their jobs and their normal way of life. I sit by my mother whilst Maria carries out her household duties. Mak's sleeping pattern has changed and though aided by Valium, can only sleep in the morning and is up all night.

"She's afraid to sleep," my cousin, Rose, says.

She's the elder of Great Aunt's two daughters and is a janitor at the local swimming pool complex. She has been very frequent in her visits to the hospital and always brings my mother and myself something to eat. Although she speaks a kind of pidgin English picked up from her years of working, I was astonished to discover that she couldn't read a simple message. I had called her one day and her 20-something-year-old son answered the phone and he said she was out. I told him to write a message to tell her to call me because he was going out before Rose got back.

He said, "There's no point in writing a message. My mother cannot read."

The impact of his words was like a thunderbolt. So this was how I would have ended up if my mother had not perservered and got me into school. I would be middle-aged like Rose, and in this modern thriving metropolis, with signs everywhere — on taxis, buses, noticeboards, government letters and junk-mail coming through the post, newspapers, copy on advertisements, labels on bottles, packages — I would not be able to read. When I put the phone down, I had to catch my breath, as though I had been teetering on the edge of a dangerous precipice. This is what my mother has rescued me from, pulled me back from a huge crevasse even before she knew I had to be rescued. Of course, it's not just the ability to read that is of importance, it's the world she has opened to me, the opportunities, the pleasures and the capacity to be challenged. I think of all the wonderful mothers in the world who have given so much of themselves to their children, and I pray that children everywhere are grateful for the gifts their mothers have given them, even if it looks as if there had been no apparent gifts. Pause, think and remember.

"What's there to be afraid of," I ask my cousin.

"You know. The other world," Rose says, in her simple manner. "My mother was like that before she died. I was the one who watched over her. They start seeing things."

I'm not sure I concur with her view that Mak is afraid but she certainly has started to talk to people I cannot see. It's disconcerting to be there when she's talking to a blank space in the wall. It's as if a door to the other world has opened for her.

"Who are you talking to, Mak?"

"Second Sister," she says. "She wants to take me with her."

In our culture, when people start talking like that, it's a sure sign that their own end is not far away. I was at the hospital the day that my father died. He was in great pain, only the morphine stopping him from going mad. He kept on looking at his hands and asking me the time. Then he said, "Ah Kou (his late mother) is here. Ah Kou is calling me. Ah Kou is calling me." He died that same evening.

"Do you want to go?"

"I'm thinking about it. Look, Elder Sister is calling, too."

So I pass the information on to the family and they all come to see her, sons, daughters, grandchildren, great-grandchildren (the second great-grandchild had arrived a few months before). And for the first time, I am wishing her to go, too. It's a terrible thing to wish for your mother's own demise, someone you love beyond words. You feel like a traitor to have this thought, are raked with guilt. I am torn between wanting her to get better and wanting her to go when there is still shreds of her dignity left. There are days when I hold her hand and watch her trying to catch her breath, struggling and struggling; and I think, if only I have the courage to help her end it all. It would be simple, nobody needs to know, a pillow over her face and she will be released. It is then that I recall the play that David and I saw so many years ago when a daughter had smothered her mother with a pillow as the mother sat in the wheelchair, a complete vegetable. I had wondered why a daughter would want to do that to her mother. It seems so wicked, so evil, to want to hasten the death of someone. But up until this moment, I have never thought like this. Up until this moment, when I have never known what it is like to suffer as you watch the one you love, fighting for a few scraps of breath, knowing that pain is torching her arthritic body, her broken hip, her mind torn asunder, I have never known what it's like to want to terminate a life, but now I do. Watching her in so much agony, I can only hope that her soul knows what it is doing. Her words from long ago came back to me, "Work that calls is guided by soul to express spirit. It is work that will bring you greatest happiness."

Perhaps this is the work she came for, who is to know? Her words stirred something in me, reminded me of my own quest. I have always wanted to be a full-time writer. It will bring me the greatest hapiness, I know. So what am I doing still struggling in a business that doesn't fulfill me? Yes, there are the bills and mortgage to pay, but I can always find new excuses. If I want to follow my dream, I just have to do it, not allow other people's opinions and circumstances to inhibit me. I may not make any headway, may never get published. But at least I would have given it my best shot. I owe it to my mother, too. She had prepared the grounds for me, gave me the education I needed to be a writer. Now I just have to do it. I promise myself that when I get back to England, I shall tell David of my plans, get him to find someone else to handle the marketing for the holiday business. It is time for me to live my dream.

In Holland, they have just legalised euthanasia. Yes, there are moral implications to this. But until you have watched a loved one struggling with such pain, you would not dream that you could wish for their demise. I would never, never judge those who might make that final step for their loved ones. Because now I know the knife-edge that they walk on. Yet, I believe in karma, believe in the ways of the spirit, believe that in her soul-knowledge, my mother has her purpose and reason for clinging on to mortal life, so we must not take away her choice. I believe that a debilitating brain does not override the wisdom of the soul. But I cannot say that I am always strong in my beliefs, I am mortal, too. Agatha, who is well into spiritual energies and entities, say what I dare not say to everybody, "Let her go. We must all let her go, otherwise we are holding back her spirit and she'll be earthbound."

Of all people, it is Jacob who wouldn't let her go. And Bernadette.

"You're so hard," my sister says to us, bursting into tears.

Matthew tries to soothe her. "I know it's painful for you, Dette. But think of how Mak's suffering. Think of how, if she is capable of knowing, how she wouldn't like to be what she is today. She used to be so independent."

Each day finds my mother dwindling a little bit more, the change so perceptible that you can't imagine that there is any life left. A former neighbour from Potong Pasir turns up when she hears of Mak's situation. Sylvia is a middle-aged Eurasian lady who had lived in the room in front of 52B. Although her place was called a house, it was no more than a small room with a living area cum kitchen, though it included a bathroom but no toilet. Their jamban was more posh than ours, though this term is relative; they had a key to theirs and it was only shared by two homes. When she moved in, she had a little boy, Leonard, aged four. Her Indian husband, a schoolteacher, had affairs all the time she lived there and there was little money left over for food, and herself and Lenny. Every time he came home, there would be a fight and my mother would pick Lenny out of the crossfire of their battles. Sylvia was so frustrated and lonely that poor Lenny got the brunt of her temper. Always, it was my mother who rescued Lenny, pulling him out from under her rotan, soothing him as he screamed in fear.

"Your mother used to scrimp amd save some food for me each day," she says tearfully after coming out of Mak's room. "Sometimes an egg, sometimes some rice. I'll never forget it until the day I die. She was so hard-up herself and yet she would never see me go hungry. And without her, Lenny won't be alive. And now, look, he's a father with a daughter of his own."

I am so glad that Sylvia has come to remind me of the woman who has disappeared. It is so easy to forget. Every 60 seconds grow into an hour, then into a day, then a week, months, years, the distance between us and that memory widening. Within each of those minutes and hours, something else happens to us and each incident is piled upon another until the incident furthest away in time gets buried amongst the rest. Unless we remember to retrieve some memories from the mud, it is easy to forget. It is the same with someone you know. If the person is no longer in your sphere of interaction, it is easy to forget them. If the person with you is not at all like the person they were, it is as though the person in the past is gone. It's the same with my mother, she is no longer what she used to be and our current perception of her is how we see her today. It takes someone like Sylvia to exhume the mother we know, breathe back life into the essence of the woman who was Catherine Koh Soon Neo, the *nonya* and *bibik* of *Kampong Potong Pasir*. We have to keep on reminding ourselves that we must learn to look beyond present appearances and behaviour to uncover what is real. There is a Buddhist lesson here somewhere.

But what is reality? Is it only something we can perceive? Does it mean that that which we can't see with our mortal eyes, hear with our physical ears, feel with our senses is not real? My mother behaves as if there is another world which is now open to her, a world still shuttered to us ordinary folks. She is visited by people long dead, she converses with them as if they are as solid as Maria and myself. It is uncanny that she would turn her head to face the door as if someone is actually walking through, cork her ears in a certain angle and direction as if to hear better, expresses emotion as if what the other person is saying is either funny or sad. She often laughs, sometimes argue. We learn to get used to this. But this morning, when I return from my swim, she is crying in agitation, with Maria trying to comfort her. Maria doesn't understand either Malay or Teochew and so is not privy to the things that bothers Mak sometimes.

"What's the matter?" I ask her.

"Ah Tetia is here," she says. "He wants me to go with him. But I don't want to, I don't want to."

At last, her true feelings about him is revealed. When he was alive, she voiced no dissent, allowed no blackwash against his character. Perhaps she felt that if us children were mutinous to our father, the captain, the ship that was the family would sink. She walked seven paces behind him, served him before herself, nodded meekly in agreement, except when he opposed her endeavours to help the village folks and her endeavour to send me to school. Once or twice, after his death, she had confessed, "Life with Ah Tetia was not easy." But she has never been so vehement before, never mouthing this absolute refusal to go with him, even if it is to the spirit world.

"Mak," I say. "You don't have to go with him. Robert has visited you, hasn't he? Remember he asked you to go with him, too."

At the mention of my brother who had been crippled all his mortal life, she smiles. He was her youngest and her favourite, the one who brought so much joy to the family whilst imprisoned in the coconut shell of his body. Every dream I had of him since his passing, was that of a handsome young man, very close in looks to Matthew, standing tall in a prefect body and perfect legs, walking as he had never walked in his lifetime on earth. And I know that Mak has dreamed of him, too, and recently, had mentioned his coming through the door, offering his hand to walk her through the next journey of her life.

"*Ya juga*," she agrees. "He has asked me. Do you know he can walk now?"

"I know."

"I'll go with him," she says, then she pauses. "When it's time."

And I know then that the time is not now. She is not ready, her task in this world is not complete. Whatever that may be. And true enough, she begins to get better. She is sitting up in bed more often. And when I cajole her, allows herself to be put into a wheelchair for her meals. The doctor had advised us to get her sitting as soon as she is able because lying down all day, her chest would cave in and might give rise to pneumonia. But she had refused every effort we made before to get her out of bed, and suddenly she became willing. What has caused this change? The few minutes turn into half an hour and the half-hour turns into an hour. The day we wheel her out of the sick-room is a triumph and I thought, maybe Bernadette is right to hang on. Agatha reinstates a holiday which she had cancelled on account of Mak's poor condition. Our mother's revival, in some way, does not bring the joy I thought it would bring. It seems to me that the longer she lives, the longer she has to suffer the humility of being taken cared of, because the damage and corrosion to her mind, to her perception of things, is permanent. Nothing can reverse it. And I wonder if there is any point in her living to face it all. But none of us can play God, none of us can decide for her the moment or the way she has to go.

Some months earlier, Bernadette had bought an electronic piano whose keys have the capacity to light up to assist Andy in his learning. The computerised piano also has another function which allows the piano to play on its own. You select a tune, throw the switch and it plays by itself. We put Mak in front of the piano and turn on this switch, select one of her favourite tunes which she used to play, a song called *Rasa Sayang*. So she sits in her wheelchair all animated as she depresses the keys and she thinks she's playing the tune. But her face lights up and she smiles, sometimes even laugh as she tosses her head as if her hair is still long and glossy. She even stretches up perceptibly so that she is not as slumped in the wheelchair as she had been. I see her too as she must be seeing herself, in her teens, sitting on her piano-stool in my grandparents' bungalow by the sea, when there was serenity and security in her life, when all she had to do was play the piano.

Now that her body is healing, there is not a great deal I can do by staying on. It is already the end of October and I have been away from England since June. Besides, my husband and elder son are already back home. I have to share myself with them, too. After showing her the technique, Maria is quite capable of putting Mak in her wheelchair by herself. She washes her, changes her diapers and cleans her without complaint. We are truly fortunate to have Maria sent to us. I pray that somewhere in the Philippines, someone is taking care of her mother as she is taking care of mine. Once a week, Bernadette and I have to shampoo our mother's remaining head of hair in a special basin and Maria can assist Bernadette in doing so. Andy tries to persuade me to stay on until Christmas, but it will be too long away from my own family. So I make plans for my younger son to come to England and I book my flight.

Except for her check-up at the hospital, Mak has not been out of the house since her return. Now that she feels comfortable enough to sit in the wheelchair for an hour, I decide that I would wheel her to the path along the canal in the late afternoon so that it is not hot but yet light enough for her to enjoy the view. At first she's unsure of my intention and is a bit apprehensive. But I prattle on and give her assurances. In case of any emergency since it's our first time out, I take Maria with me. Andy has a day off from school so he comes along on his push-bike. We manouvre the wheelchair up and down concrete pavements, across the tarmac-estate roads and arrive at the park which leads to the canal. It's like taking a child out for the first time on a pushchair. We point things out to her and talk incessantly so that she doesn't get frightened. We travel along the cemented path right by the tidal canal and she starts to relax. Across the canal is a golf course and across the expressway is the beach and then the sea. So she can look out to water, some grass and trees.

"Look, Mak," I say. "Look at that colourful bird!"

It's a lovely omen. At my voice, the kingfisher takes flight from its perch on the bank to display its beautiful feathers. I am especially thrilled because this city is walled in by so many buildings and strictures that it is hard to think of it as having anything wild and free.

They say that Alzheimer's patients need a routine to provide stability in their lives, so I make the trip out as part of her routine. I establish a particular route, too, so that she can come to see some kind of pattern, I hope. If Andy does not come with me, my mother is entirely mine for that hour and it grows into our special time together. I would walk her down the path and she would chat to me, although sometimes, her talk doesn't make any sense. And that is when it occurs to me that people can have words coming out of their mouths without them creating any meaning. But in my mother's case, it doesn't really matter now.

"Hello, *ada baik*? How are you?" she asks astonished people as we travel along the canal. And worse, when she talks as if she knows their relatives. "How's your mother? Is she any better?"

But I am no longer embarrassed. She seems happy enough and that is all that counts. I take her to where the tracks of the MRT run overhead and will wait until she sees at least two trains before we leave. She has a fascination for trains because in her time, there was only one train that ran out of Singapore to the Malay Peninsula. And Alzheimer's had already attacked her brain when the MRT started running. But she loves the colours painted along the sleek trains and the speed at which they run. I make sure that at this rest-point, I give her a drink from the water bottle Maria has filled with ice water for us. Then I wheel her along to the other end of the canal to watch the aeroplanes as they take off from Changi Airport. If she is still in the mood, I would sit at a stone bench so that she can enjoy the breeze and tell me tales from her old days and hear more news of the dead people who come to talk to her. I point out the flowers to her and before we leave will always pluck a few for her to take home.

"So beautiful," she says, holding the flowers like a bouquet in her hands. "So beautiful. I love flowers. I have always loved flowers."

The hibiscus and bougainvillea are prolific and are public property in the park. But when she starts admiring flowers that are cascading down from someone's garden-walls, I have to practise more stealth in stealing them for her. But it doesn't matter now. Nothing matters now but that I can bring a smile to her lips, brighten her face for a fraction of a second. That is all that matters now. One afternoon, Gloria, Agatha's younger daughter, who has just turned 18, comes with me on our walk. She exhibits a real keeness to learn the routine I had set for Mak. Her elder sister, Joanna, who so looks much like Mak and is devoted to her, is away at University in New Zealand and keeps in touch with her grandmother's progress via email.

"Don't worry, Aunty Phine," Gloria says. "When I finish school early, I can take Mama out too, when you're not here. But do I have to steal flowers for her, too?"

My niece is a lovely girl and I am touched by her thoughtfulness. Members of my family have shown such camaraderie that I am so proud that they are my brothers and sisters, my nieces and nephews. Last Christmas, I had been a bit disappointed by the behaviour of two of my nieces and a couple of my nephews, but their respect for my mother is still evident, the Confucian ethics of family still lingering. I am glad, too, that the younger generation is here to provide the continuity when the older one has moved on. After all, this is truly the way of the world, as in nature, that one generation must go to make way for the next, that all creatures live and then must die, so that the soul can be propelled to the next stage of its learning.

"Your mother is so lucky," Syliva says on another visit, this time dragging Lenny along; Lenny who has grown as tall as he is wide. "It's because of what she has given of herself that so many people love her. She is a special lady and she is blessed, indeed."

Twenty

The damp, English cold is a shock to the system when you have been in warm and sunny places for months. But the visual impact of Autumn with its beautiful colours scattered in the trees make up for the loss of warmth. My mother has always shown me that you need to colour your life with an attitiude of joy, so that in most situations you can find something positive, something beautiful. She lived her life by example, not by mouthing platitudes, and for her, doing the most banal or unpleasant chore like clearing the chamber pot, became a meaningful action for the spirit. That was when she was in control. Is her spirit in control now or has her damaged brain overruled its influence? To us who lead ordinary lives, living in this mortal world, it appears that her mind has mutated to something that we don't recognise. It's the same with the English weather, when the clocks move back at the end of British summer time. England is deluged with heavy rainfall and unexpected floods. The rivers run riot and overflow their banks. And so I return to scenes of chaos, of stalled vehicles, flooded high-streets and dispirited people. It is like the 1950s flood in Singapore all over again, but on a much larger scale. People blame the greenhouse effect caused by pollutants and carbon dioxide, some scientists agree and some don't, attributing other factors. Is this a mutation or is it a pattern that has repeated itself with hundreds of years in between so that we can't recognise its warp and woof?

Emotional climate can change, too, by the pollutants of anger, a negative thought, a wrong word. Or it can change with a sunny smile, a jewel of praise, the treasure of confidence. A mistral must have swept through the hearts of my stepfamily when we have been away from them all these months, causing a change to the dry landscape. Perhaps the wind sighs and says it's better to tolerate a stepmother than not seeing their own father at all. We have a call from James, the elder twin, inviting us to lunch. Of all the stepchildren, he has been the least judgmental, the least troublesome. Whatever problems we had encountered with him were the normal ones of parents with a teenaged son flexing his emotional muscles. A keen cook, he promises me a delicious vegetarian meal.

"The kids missed you guys," he says of his son and stepdaughter.

Laden with presents, we drive up to his home in Buckinghamshire, where the atmosphere is lovely, his partner very warm and welcoming. Lunch is a beautifully baked aubergine stuffed with cubed vegetables served on a bed of rice. When I hug the grandchildren, they smile and call me Grandma, although shyly. For the first time in years, I have a sense of family here in England. And the tsunami of it all is when Sadie rings up a few days afterwards on my home telephone. Usually, she only calls her father's office telephone which is in the annexe to our house, so that she never has to speak to me. Her voice is light and cheery, her tone unmistakeably friendly.

"Hi! How about coming to lunch next Sunday? By the way, how's your mother?"

I am so stunned, I am at a loss for words for a few moments. She has never asked after my sons or my family. I was treated as if I didn't have a life beyond her father. For three years, while my elder son was in

England at college, she had neither asked after him nor invited her stepbrother even once to her place for a meal. She complained when she thought I had forgotten a birthday present for her younger son one year, yet she has never bought any of my sons either a Christmas or birthday present. So this tide of change is overwhelming. A year ago, I had treated her to the Body and Mind Spirit Festival in London, which impressed her a lot, after which she had taken up Reiki, learning to be a Master over a weekend. Perhaps in finding herself, she has let go of her fears and prejudices. But so many harsh words have been spoken, so many deplorable acts have been perpetrated against me that I dare not allow my heart to melt so easily. Together with her mother and the younger twin, she has shot me with nearly 20 years of pain and loneliness. When your flesh has been flayed, it takes a while to heal. Yet I cannot rebuff a proffered hand. This is my mother in me, her gift of the spirit.

"Sunday lunch would be nice. I've already wrapped the Christmas presents so I'll bring them. And one for Alex's birthday in January."

"Phine, it's only November."

"I know. But I'm going into hospital in a fortnight for my right hand and it might be out of action for a while."

And so we take that first faltering step towards a new kind of relationship. But David insists on calling Sadie and reminding her that the last time she invited us for a meal, there was nothing for me to eat, and would she make sure that there is food for his wife, who doesn't eat meat. For David, too, this is a change, to stand up to his family about their treatment of his wife. But that is another story.

Life is about change, about movement. It is when we stay rooted to old habits, old thoughts and old prejudices that we are stunted in our spiritual growth. It is the security of familiar things, familiar environment, which chains us to our past. When we move on, we move to a different viewpoint, like further up the hill so that we can see our past as if in the valley below us — and things look different from that perspective. It is time for me to walk up the hill myself to look at where my life and my father's crossed, to try seeing him with an adult eye from this new vantage point.

I had a grotesque view of my father. He was a spectre that used to loom huge and dark over my childhood figure like the oversized shadow of an evil cartoon character splashed across the wall. For years, I only remembered the worse of him, denied his spirit my smile, afraid to allow him access into my heart. I was to him what my mother dared not be. I argued, disobeyed and rebelled. I would not allow him to shape me, twist me into form the way he shaped and twisted my mother. I defied him for her. When he caned or belted me, I was not submissive but kicked back, bit into his arm. He would hit me senseless, my ears ringing. I was angry with him for what he did to my mother, for the honour he denied her. I don't know if the anger I used to feel against him amounted to hate. But I know that as much as I love my mother for giving me the ability to read, I hated my father for his continually destructive attitude over my education. I cannot forget the way he punished me for going to the National Library, making me feel so wrong, as if I had been doing something nasty or wicked. When I read books, he would snatch them away from me, telling me that the words contained in them were poisonous and would corrupt me. I cannot imagine my prospects now if my father had succeeded in taking me out of school — he would have denied me all the pleasures of the written word, all the mind-training of education, all the freedom to think. I still have nightmares of a parallel world where I am an ignoramus, unable to read, unable to write, unable to express the thoughts that swim around in my head.

"Education is bad for women," he often said. "Poisons their minds.

Makes them less meek."

My father died when I had just turned 16. George had been the only boy I had been out with and I had paid severely for my small excursion. Ah Tetia made sure that no boys came near me or I, them. He impressed upon me that I had to keep myself pure for my husband, that any contact or relationship between a boy and a girl before marriage was wrong. Not only was I not allowed to date, I was not even permitted to go out in a group that included the opposite sex. It was straight to school and back. I was a frog under a coconut shell that my father had created. But now I force myself to remember that my father was a product of his time as we each are of our own. Many parents in the *kampong* did not approve of dating. Although it made good moral sense to keep oneself pure, it also meant that I had very little experience of men. Or as the Bible puts it, I do not *know* men. My ex-husband was my first boyfriend, my present was my second. I was too scared and insecure to date even after my father had died and released me from his dictatorial ways; his influence extended beyond his grave. Though Ah Tetia disapproved of me being educated, eventually he came to recognise its value as a bargaining tool.

"You will certainly fetch more money now," he said, as though I was cattle. "I can marry you off to a rich man."

If he had lived, I would have met my husband only on our wedding night. Like Parvathi would have, if she had lived if she had not been betrothed to her uncle. As far as my father was concerned, a daughter was less like a wife, to fetch and carry, to cook and clean, a liability that he had to feed and clothe until she came to be of marriageable age when she would be bartered off. From then on, she is assumed to belong to her husband's family as if she no longer has any blood ties with her own parents. He had no idea that our genetic blueprints matched, that even if he had sold me off, I could always be linked back to him. During my fits of rebelliousness, he denied and disowned me. And the memory of that near sale when I was six months old kept returning, making me feel hurt and insecure. He would sell me at any excuse. And that made me harden my heart towards him. But it is wrong to carry hatred in your heart. Hate is putrefied love and oozes black in your blood stream, contaminating all the other tissues and organs. Hate shapes your mind and shadows your views. It does not allow you to be free, but forms a curtain between yourself and the real circumstances. But time and maturity does take the edge off anger and I know now that it was not my father I hated but his deeds, unthinking and violent. His words about my worthlessness and my pursuit of an education are less hurtful now. I have proven myself to *me*. I am *not* worthless. *Black* and *ugly*, I can't do anything about the way I look, but I can try to look good by being fit and looking fit. That should make me passable. Though I don't believe it to be true, I am grateful that David keeps on telling me that I am beautiful. So my father's words begin to weigh less on my mind now as they recede into the background of my life.

David and I live in a small English village on the borders of Surrey and Hampshire. Between our kitchen and the stable block of our 100-year-old house is an area of uneven ground where rainwater collects, making the place muddy. With the help of a good local builder, we decide to make something of this area and decide to turn it into a cobbled patio with a fountain, which can be seen from the kitchen. The builder works well and before long, the patio is finished, transforming the area. We add a wrought-iron bench, where you can sit to catch the afternoon sun, a couple of planters with flowers, and water plants trailing down from the fountain. The 30-something builder and I are chatting, admiring his handiwork when out of the blue, he asks, "Have you heard of that actor-chap who is famous for his old horror films in them black and white days?"

"Which one?" I ask. "Vincent Price? Christopher Lee?"

"No, no. Short guy. Wrinkly and horrible looking."

"Oh, you mean Boris Karloff?"

"Yes, that's the one. His real name is Henry Pratt, actually, and he lived near here, not far from Passfield. I did some work in his house once. There's a blue plaque by his front door."

"Really?" I say. "My father used to love him. He took me to all the Boris Karloff films, frightened the life out of me, but I loved them anyway. He must be quite old if he's alive."

"I think he's dead. But his garden is shaped like a coffin. You can drive all the way around it. I'll take you to see it if you like."

And so the builder takes my elder son and me down the road to see Boris Karloff's house and garden. Of course, my son is too young to know about Boris Karloff but, like all youngsters, he's into horror and action films like Stephen King's, where guts are spilled and heads decapitated, so he's truly fascinated to see a coffin-shaped garden. I think the garden is interesting, but what is more intriguing to me is the fact that this tenuous link with my father should emerge at this very juncture when I am re-thinking my thoughts about my father. Perhaps his spirit has returned to remind me of some of the lovely things that he and I had shared.

"You're making too much of a co-incidence," David says, the perpetual sceptic.

But I believe that there is no such thing as a coincidence, that everything happens because they are meant to do so — and it happens at the right time, whether we recognise it or not. My father's two favourite actors were Boris Karloff and Edward G Robinson. I don't recall much of the latter but can never forget Boris Karloff's face, which always looked terribly evil. Going to the real cinema was a very special treat, so I never minded what type of films we saw. Most of the time, we only got to see films that the film-man brought and we had to see it outdoors on the cemented badminton court. So it felt really grand to be sitting in an enclosed auditorium on proper seats and not on boards straddling kerosene tins. The cinemas my father took my siblings and myself to were the Alhambra, Cathay and Lido. Unlike the Alhambra, the other two were really posh and had air-conditioning which was a new thing. Downstairs from the Lido was a Magnolia cafe and ice cream parlour. I used to peer through its glass walls and watched all the grand people in there eating and laughing and I promised myself that I would eat in there one day. (I actually worked briefly as a marketing executive for the firm that produced *Magnolia ice cream* after I graduated from the University Of Singapore and had eaten all the ice cream I wanted until I was sick!)

Agatha would often scream with uncontrollable fear when she went to horror films, so our father stopped taking her. Bernadette was too little to understand, so she got left at home, too. Ah Tetia usually took Matthew and myself. So it was my father who sowed the love of films in both my brother and myself. He took us to English epic films like *The Ten Commandments, Spartacus* and period Chinese films, like *Madam White Snake* and *The Water Margin*. Every now and again, when P Ramlee or Saloma were starring, he would take our mother and us to a Malay film, Mak's favourite being *Ibu Mertua-ku*. It is interesting that I should recall this now because when I reviewed my mother's married life and remembered how few her outings had been, it was easy to let these trips to the cinemas slip past my memory, too. So she did have some days of frivolity with my father, acting like the young lovers they must have been.

When she went out, she used to thread the small *bunga melor* around her single bun and she would wear her best *kebaya*, her face powedered with *bedak sejok*. Although she walked several paces behind Ah Tetia, he would hold his head proudly to have such a beautiful wife trailing behind him.

Once when they were out, I was left in Matthew's charge. He decided to take me to the playing field at the bottom of the hill where the rich people lived to teach me to fly a kite. I was about five or six. I held the spool of string that was attached to the kite. Matthew held the kite and hoisted it up and I was supposed to keep the kite in the air. It was fun when eventually the kite started to fly. I kept my eyes on the kite and moved about on the field. At one point, I moved backward and suddenly fell into the monsoon drain, screaming as I went down. Matthew rushed to get me out but I was already bleeding and grazed. Mak and Ah Tetia arrived home to find me in this state and Ah Tetia gave Matthew a whipping. It was the one time I remembered my mother holding me so close. Our people do not openly hug and kiss like in the west, so a physical display of love is unusual. But on that day, Mak held me close to comfort me and I remember thinking how beautiful she looked and how lovely her fragrance was.

So, the picture of my father that is now emerging from the deep recesses of my mind is less of a hateful person. It was he who generously took my grandmother and Uncle Kanchil in with him when he married my mother. This is not the deed of a cruel or hateful man. Perhaps I have allowed the pain he inflicted on me to colour my perception of him. Now that the sluices are open, I permit myself another memory, of my father taking me to see the fireworks that sprang from the ships at sea. My sisters and I stood at the Victorian balustrade of Queen Elizabeth's promenade, and clapped our hands in glee as we watched the colourful sparkles that flew into the sky. I think it was a celebration of the Queen's Coronation or something. Although Ah Tetia went to the cabarets without my mother, he would return home bringing her a peace offering: a packet of *Hokkien Mee, Char Kway Teow, Chicken Rice, Char Siew Rice* or *Satay*. And she, in turn, would wake us up to share in her largess. I cannot tell you how wonderful it was to wake up to the smell of food when there were days when we would wake up not knowing if we were to be fed at all. If my father had been as evil as I tended to remember him, he would not have had the kind of heart to show such concern. So I learn that memories can be shaded by pain. My mother's recent reluctance to go with my father, even to the spirit world, showed me that my memory with regard to my father, though shaded, is not flawed. But I am ready to forgive him now because I can see that he was as much a victim and product of his circumstances as each of us can be in our own time. I am sure that his soul was giving him lessons, too, and all our lessons differ, depending on what we have incarnated to learn. Now, I am more willing to resurrect that soft side of him, a man whose face was occasionally lit by a smile. Now with an adult eye, I can see that he, too, lived within the limitations of his own education and social status. He was also constrained by the strictures of society. He was not alone in his views of wives and daughters and the way to treat them. He believed sincerely that education was not for women. Sure, he had a hot temper and was prone to wield his strength on his wife and children, but it must have been a result of his own despair. After all, he started his working life as a clerk and he had so many children to feed, three brothers to put through school and he was supporting a mother whose husband was lost somewhere in China or enroute. When my mother lost her babies, he must have felt some guilt and perhaps some pain, too, though he would never admit or talk about it. The pressure on him must have been phenomenal.

It has taken me all these years for me to see my father as he really was. I was blinded to his true nature by the physical and mental pain he inflicted on my mother, my siblings and myself. He had marked my life, marked me in the way I related to men. I have been weary of depending on either of my husbands for sustenance, secure only when I am working and in control of my own finances and fate. Perhaps in my subconscious mind I put them, as men, in the same ilk as my father, willing to trade me for a price. So I had to keep guard, be vigilant. One of the reasons my first marriage failed was because my ex-husband tried to be what my father was to my mother, he refused to let me be free. He'd drive me everywhere, dropped me off and picked me up even if I was out for a girl's lunch, examined my dressing when I go out to check that the hem was not above my knees, nor the neckline too low. Even though I wore little make-up, simply a lipstick and an eye-liner, that was forbidden to me, too. This was in the 1970s! He was so insecure that he even stopped me singing pop songs which might have suggested that I had feelings for another. Eventually, the straw that broke this camel's back was that he became like my father, using his muscles when words failed him. When I left, he said, "So the bird has broken out of its cage." Yet he did not see or understand the irony of his own words.

The Boris Karloff reminder is the key that has set me free from my father. I am beginning to see that if my father's circumstances had been different, he could have been a much nicer man. He had only been human, with human failings and weaknesses. I realise now that to hate him is to tether him to my psyche, to poison my own insides. Besides, everyone who comes into our sphere in life teaches us something, whether that person is good or bad, gives us joy or pain. It is not what they do to us that teaches us, it is how we respond to them that is the teacher. And, we can only keep growing if we keep on learning. It's when we stop learning that we stagnate. At last, in middle age, I dare to look at myself and see what I had inherited from him. When I was younger, I wanted so much to cleanse myself of my father's influence that I had refused to accept that some parts of his being might linger in me. I wanted to believe that I was all of my mother and nothing of my father. In this respect, I was as naive as my father had been, not comprehending that once the genetic codes have been written, they cannot be erased. Once or twice, when I was a child, when my mother was cross with me, she had flung the words, "You got a temper just like your father!" I would shrivel up inside and run away somewhere to cry. How could I be like the man I hated? I worked really hard to rid myself of this taint, tried to scrub myself clean. Now I know, not all of my father's characteristics had been bad, there were some aspects of him that could be lovable. He had shared with me his love for the cinema, and in so doing he had helped me to expand my horizons, helped me to focus on my visual sense. He had always been one to care about fitness, cycling everywhere and carrying weights every evening after work. Without my realising it, he had bequested this to me, for I am into yoga and go to the gym regularly and love walking. How can I hate what is so intrinsically a part of myself? So what I thought had been a dark relationship with my father had actually been filled with spaces of light, too. Alas, I cannot tell him of my revised thinking nor can we sign the peace pact between us. Surely this is a human tragedy — that realisations can sometimes come too late? But believing in the spirit as I do, I know that he and I have both been teachers to each other, and I know that he and I shall meet in the spirit world for our reconciliation. Perhaps by then, I would have released all of the mental and physical pain he had inflicted on me personally. What good does it serve to keep on harping about a past that we cannot change? I must try to focus on the pearl, not just the grit — and get on with my own journey. Perhaps then I shall be able to embrace him and thank him; for without him, my soul would not have found a body to inhabit. Perhaps it would be time, too, to tell him that despite everything, I do love him.

I have been back three weeks now, have struggled through a mountain of post, called up friends; in short, regain my footing in my adopted country. Crossing continents and cultures requires a period of adjustment, when the mind and tongue can let go of the last place and slip back into the customs and language of the present. It's like re-adjusting oneself to wearing woollen jumpers and warm clothes when all you've been wearing is light cotton clothes, T-shirts and shorts. It's like adjusting your mind to accept that when you wake up, the sun may not be shining and it's going to be dark and wet all day. Adjustments require an ability to control and manipulate the mind. My mother is beyond this, the controller having become the controlled. I used to call her weekly on a Monday so that she is conscious of a routine and awaits my call with anticipation. But it doesn't matter now what day I call her, her days and years sliding like mud into one another on the slippery slope of her mind. I feel sad for her when I think there can be no hope or anticipation for her because, for her, there is no visible future. If every moment exists only in this pin-prick of time, it is not possible to look forward. And this is what my mother's life has become. Through emails and telephone calls, I learn from Agatha and Bernadette about Mak's continuing condition.

"I guess she's over the hump," Agatha writes. "I can go on holiday now."

We have been given a short respite. In an Alzheimer's patient, you worry about the deterioration of the body as well as the mind. It's a dark race, no ribbon for the first to reach the tape. Only oblivion.

Some weeks later, Bernadette calls, "She doesn't know how to walk anymore."

Can it get worse? Our reference book says yes. Some patients go blind, some cannot speak. It all depends on which of the brain cells die. In the end, they can succumb to a simple cold, a chest infection, whatever. Their body is already weakened, too weary to fight any invasion of germs. Then the war will be over. So my family and I wait this agonising wait. We have to be vigilant about different things now, whether she is comfortable, how we can prevent bedsores. I send across some strong antibiotic cream. When I pick up the telephone to call her these days, I am not assured that I can actually get to speak to her. It is the price I have to pay for it was I who wrought the distance between us, choosing to go to a place where she cannot follow. Yet, I cannot be separated from Mak even though we are 10,000 miles apart. She and I share the same soul space. Sometimes when I call, she is too poorly and cannot be put into the wheelchair to get to the phone or she may not be in a frame of mind to talk into the mouthpiece. Even a simple thing like talking into a telephone is a task that is sometimes insurmountable, like climbing a flight of stairs is a monumental task for a disabled person. My mother is disabled in so many ways now. This is her lot, the frog under the coconut shell. But I can re-capture her the way she was, tall and slender in her *sarong kebaya*, her face a delicate shape, her full head of hair, the way she moved, fluid and elegant, everything about her so fine. As though I have the Beast's magic mirror, I can conjure up her face in every chosen moment to see the way she tilts her head or the way her lips form crescents of smiles. I can see her as a young teenager sitting on her paino stool in her father's bungalow by the sea, sitting upright, her slender fingers rippling along the piano keys, her long black hair lifted by the sea breeze, a soft smile on her face.

"Mak," I say, grateful that today she can come to the telephone. "It's Ah Phine."

"Cannot be, cannot be," she says vehemently. "You can't be Ah Phine. Ah Phine is right here with me now, feeding me my dinner."

Someone had said that Alzheimer's is like a long funeral. I never understood what that meant before. Now I take it to mean that it is a long grieving before the person is even dead. Despite her pretence at confidence, I can hear the confusion and agitation in her voice. So I don't correct her anymore. Perhaps it is better for her to think I am there with her. Her race is over. I am her hope and dreams, she has passed the baton for me to finish the race and now I must. It is what she would have wanted. It is a heartbreaking acknowledgment but I know that I have lost her whilst she is still alive.